ESCAPE FROM EVIL

ESCAPE FROM EVIL

CATHY WILSON
with JEFF HUDSON

PAN BOOKS

Dedicated to the memory of my beautiful,
talented but troubled mother Jennifer, for giving me life,
to my grandparents for the stability they gave me,
and my gorgeous son Daniel for breaking the cycle.

First published 2011 by Pan Books

This edition first published 2022 by Pan Books
an imprint of Pan Macmillan
The Smithson, 6 Briset Street, London EC1M 5NR
EU representative: Macmillan Publishers Ireland Ltd, 1st Floor,
The Liffey Trust Centre, 117–126 Sheriff Street Upper,
Dublin 1, D01 YC43
Associated companies throughout the world
www.panmacmillan.com

ISBN 978-1-5290-9387-2

1 3 5 7 9 8 6 4 2

A CIP catalogue record for this book is available from the British Library.

Printed and bound by CPI Group (UK) Ltd, Croydon CR0 4YY

This is Where it Ends

'Cathy, turn on the news – now!'

It was September 2006, a Saturday morning, and my aunt sounded anxious. I hung up the phone and flicked the flatscreen remote. A second later I screamed. Shock turned quickly to confusion.

It can't be him. It's not possible.

I don't know why my teenage son, Daniel, was up at nine o'clock on a weekend, but as he ran into the room, I was glad he was.

'Mum, what is it? What's wrong?'

But I couldn't speak – I just stared at the screen, shaking and pointing at the picture of the man they said was wanted for the murder of a young girl.

'You're scaring me, Mum,' Daniel said. 'Who's that man? Do you know him?'

Until then I'd been able to protect my son from the poison of his past. Now it was time for the truth. I took a deep breath.

'Daniel – that's your father.'

*

Part of me wishes I'd never set eyes on Peter Britton Tobin. Part of me wishes he had never taken a single breath. I'm sure I wouldn't have any trouble finding people who'd agree. Just ask the grieving families of Angelika Kluk, Vicky Hamilton and Dinah McNicol. If I were them I would definitely consider death too good for the man who took my daughter's life.

Just ask the two young girls he tortured, raped and left to die, the prostitutes who were hurt because of his excessive, brutal tastes or the countless others rumoured to have been his victims over a possible forty-year campaign of terror. Ask any of them and I'm sure they'd have nothing good to say.

But mine is a hideous, unique position. It's why I can only ever partly wish he'd never been born. Because, like it or not, the serial killer Peter Tobin is the father of my only child, my beautiful son. And as any parent will know, there is nothing you wouldn't do to protect your child. Unfortunately for me, Peter Tobin knew that.

With knowledge comes power and Peter knew without a shadow of a doubt that there is nothing stronger than the bond between mother and child. He played on that. That was how he controlled me during our marriage. One word out of place, one step out of line and he didn't have to threaten me. He just threatened Daniel.

Our poor, innocent baby boy, from the moment he was born, was just a tool with which I could be manipulated. I see that now. He was a bargaining chip. A means to an end.

I was a wild child when Peter Tobin, twice my age, fell for me. A free spirit, confident, loud and independent. I was the sixteen-year-old with the world at my stilettoed feet. That's how I felt and that's how everyone saw me. Everyone except Peter.

He alone saw the confused, scarred girl beneath the veneer. The hurting, abandoned teenager desperate for validation, hiding behind her image of the life and soul of the party. To Peter's expert eye, I wasn't a wild child in need of taming. I was vulnerable, fragile, damaged – ripe for falling under his control.

That's why he tricked me into getting pregnant. I don't think he ever wanted a child. He just wanted leverage.

The day I made my escape from him was the scariest day of my life. It had to be timed to perfection. One error, one delay, and he would catch me. And he would kill me.

I knew in my heart that he would have no choice. In Peter's eyes, I was no more than a possession, maybe even his most precious possession, but not a person with rights of her own. When I ran away, he didn't feel abandoned; he felt like he'd been robbed. And I knew he would exact his revenge.

Smuggling my son out of Scotland and fleeing the five hundred miles to the sanctuary of my family in Portsmouth was the longest night of my life. I was convinced Peter would be following, waiting for the coach to pull over, biding his time before storming on and reclaiming his property.

Every set of headlights that passed my window was his, I was convinced. Every time we slowed, it was because he had caused it.

I told my family and friends that I thought I would die that night if he found me. They all said the same thing: 'It can't be that bad.'

But they didn't know. I hadn't told anyone about the abuse, the beatings, the violence, the atmosphere of terror he'd forced me to live under for three years. They wouldn't believe me when I said he would have killed me to stop me escaping. But I knew.

Then, in September 2006, he was arrested for the murder of Angelika Kluk.

And then we all knew.

My son was so young when his life was in peril, but he has recovered. He has had his counselling, he has had his therapy and, more than a decade later, has emerged as a healthy, unscarred young man. I'm confident he's found his closure.

This book, I hope, will be mine. I have never told this story before. Not even my closest friends know what I suffered as the plaything of Peter Tobin and no one has ever heard how the parallels with my mother's short life led me into his clutches. I've gone to great lengths to rebuild my life, but I've wasted too much time running from the truth. Until I face my past, my escape from evil will always be incomplete. If I don't share my story, it will always be there to haunt me. And I don't want that anymore.

This is where it ends.

And this is where it began . . .

ONE

The Choices Mum Made

'Who's this, Grandpa?'

I was fourteen years old and sitting at the kitchen table in my grandparents' house. In front of me, spread out in neat little piles, were dozens of small, square photographs. One had caught my eye.

Grandpa pushed up his glasses and studied the picture I was holding.

'That's you,' he said, a warm smile lighting up his face.

I stared at the mop-topped little bundle in the duck-egg blue cardigan with navy trim. Was I ever so blonde and curly? And look at those chubby little legs!

Baby me, grinning towards the camera, looked so happy on the hip of the slim woman in the gorgeous, white, thigh-length A-line dress. If anything, she looked happier still. No prizes for guessing who that beaming lady was, but I checked anyway.

'And this is Mum?'

Grandpa nodded. 'Yes,' he said, a flicker of pride in his voice, 'that's your mother. Doesn't she look beautiful?'

He didn't have to ask *me* that. I'd never seen anyone look so stunning. With long blonde hair cascading over her shoulders and slim, tanned legs, Mum looked like a film star to me. At the very least, a model. And as for her amazing little white outfit . . .

'I love the dress,' I said. 'She looks so smart.'

I noticed the smile fade slightly from Grandpa's lips. 'She does, doesn't she?' he said quietly. 'But then people tend to make an effort on their wedding day.'

Wedding day? But I'm in the picture.

I don't remember if I couldn't work it out or I didn't want to. 'Grandpa, I don't understand.'

As he handed back the picture, I'm sure I saw his shoulders sag a little, then he took a breath and pulled himself up straight. 'I'm afraid, Cathy,' Grandpa said, a steely tone to his voice, 'there's no other way to put it: you are a bastard.'

There must have been a dozen different ways to break that news to me, but it was typical of Grandpa to use the correct term. I was technically a 'bastard' and that was the end of it. That was him all over: Mr Correct, Mr Proper. He liked things done and said the right way – however much it hurt other people. As far as Grandpa was concerned, he was the one who'd been hurt most.

Admitting his daughter had had a child out of wedlock was still as shameful to him fourteen years later as it had been back in 1969. From Grandpa's point of view, that wasn't the worst part. The wedding took place on 26 May 1970 – my mother's sixteenth birthday. I'd been born the previous November and that was the earliest she could legally marry.

Wow, I thought. *Born out of wedlock to an underage mum. Not exactly the start a girl hopes for.* Glancing at Grandpa, now furiously polishing his shoes, I realized it was definitely not the start he would have wanted for me.

Reginald Ralph Seaford Beavis was a proud man. He'd served as a major in the Royal Corps of Signals, the army's intelligence division, and years after his discharge still conducted himself with a strong military bearing. He worked as a salesman for the Wills cigarette company, who made brands like Strand, Embassy and Woodbine, and enjoyed some success and the recognition of his peers without ever really rising to great heights.

Reg had met his future wife, Daphne, while still serving in the army. Granny was a hairdresser at the time and had once styled the hair of the wonderful Peggy Ashcroft, as she never tired of reminding us. Granny only worked for two years, but till the day she died she refused to let anyone else perm, dye or set her hair. 'Why would I, when I'm a trained hairdresser?' And so, in all the years I knew her, Granny's hair never changed once. It was like she was stuck in a time warp.

My grandparents married in the late 1940s and moved from Bristol, where the Wills factory was based, to Peterborough. In 1950 they had their first daughter, Anne, and couldn't have been happier. They were the perfect family unit. Grandpa was the warden at the local church, while Granny used to do the flowers. She didn't work anymore, but his career was solid, if not amazing. They were both dependable, respectable people. Everything was just so. Everything, that is, except my mother.

Jennifer Mary Beavis was born in May 1954. By then Granny and Grandpa had settled into a nice routine with little four-year-old Anne. I'm sure they expected Mum to just fit into their schedule. From what I know of her, I doubt very much that happened. But for a while everything was fine. Church played a role in the family's life, there were nice holidays on a beach somewhere, days out to Stonehenge, everything as it should be. Neither daughter wanted for much.

Both girls settled well into school in Peterborough. In fact, when Grandpa's work moved the family to Saltdean, near Brighton, in 1960, he received a glowing report from Miss Franks, Mum's headmistress. In it she said, 'We shall be very sorry to lose Jennifer. She is one of our best scholars. Her reading is excellent. It is unusual for a child so young to be able to read so fluently.'

Reading the letter now is like reading about a stranger. Such potential . . .

Mum and Anne's new school was Telscombe Cliffs Primary, after which they both qualified for the girls' grammar school in Lewes, about a twenty-five-mile round trip every day. They'd catch the bus from Saltdean to Newhaven, then hop on a train to Lewes. Anne dutifully looked out for her little sister in the early years, but they were only together briefly before she left.

In short, each girl had a wonderful start to life. Most importantly, they had the *same* start. Same schools, same loving parents, same opportunities. So why did they take such different paths?

If Grandpa had plotted out the perfect blueprint for his daughters' lives, I don't think it would have been too dissimilar to the way Anne's turned out. As far as I can tell, she did everything correctly. From school straight to nursing college. Aged twenty, she met the man of her dreams, but sensibly waited a year before tying the knot. After three years they had kids – one of each, obviously. The children were educated at grammar schools from the age of eleven, they both got fantastic degrees, have wonderful jobs and are now starting their own families. After a few years abroad Anne and her husband, Geoff, stayed briefly with my grandparents before moving to Portsmouth. They now live in a beautiful house on Hayling Island, mortgage-free. They've even got a dog. It's the perfect family. Absolutely textbook.

And then there was Mum. It seems that when Anne turned right, young Jenny chose left. Again and again and again. We don't know when exactly and we don't know why. All we know is that eventually it cost Jenny her life.

It's such a puzzle. What made Mum take the path she did? She had the same options, the same support network, the same genes. But it wasn't enough. Nursing wasn't for her. Academia seemed to be a waste of her time as well, although she was, according to her early reports, very bright. By the age of fourteen she was no longer interested in what Lewes Grammar School for Girls could offer her. And they, it's fair to say, were running out of patience with her too.

I don't have many of my mother's possessions, but on my sixteenth birthday Granny and Grandpa gave me a box containing various letters and documents. For years I left that box unopened, too afraid of what I might discover. When curiosity did get the better of me, I felt sad that I hadn't had the courage before. Wonderful new clues to a fuller picture of my mother's life were hidden in letters, photographs and newspaper columns. It's emotional stuff. I just wish Mum came out of it better.

One letter was a note to Grandpa from the headmistress of Lewes Grammar, Miss Margaret Medcalf. She claimed she'd gone to the café in Newhaven and discovered Mum and a couple of friends. Mum had sworn she was there with Grandpa's blessing, but obviously she was playing hooky. In any case, the head wasn't fooled and wrote to Grandpa, who replied, by return, saying he would do everything 'to uphold the reputation of the school'. It all sounds wonderfully prim now, but at the time I'm sure it was mortifying for Grandpa. As a soldier, he'd been prepared to put his head above the parapet in the line of enemy fire. It was another matter in civilian life. All he wanted from his family was for them to keep their heads down. It wasn't much to ask, was it?

It was for my mother.

The truanting school letter was dated 16 May 1968 – a week before Mum's fourteenth birthday. I'm sure Grandpa hoped his intervention would be the end of it. Unfortunately, a few days later, things got worse.

A note from the school posted through my grandparents' front door explained the bare bones: 'Dear Mr Beavis, your daughter Jennifer was committed to the Victoria Hospital in Lewes today suffering from the effects of some pills she had taken. She is being kept overnight for some observation. I'm very worried indeed about the whole matter and I would be grateful if you could come and discuss it with me at your earliest convenience. I do hope Jennifer will recover soon.' It was again signed by the headmistress.

I can't imagine how Grandpa must have felt. Obviously he was worried that Mum had been taken to hospital, but at the same time ... the ignominy of it all! The knowledge that a daughter of his had taken some sort of overdose and ended up in hospital must have been so much for him to bear. The only saving grace was that, as far as he knew, only he and the headmistress's office were aware of the matter. Unfortunately, that wasn't to last.

The case made all the local papers. They were fascinated by the story of three middle-class girls bunking off school to take, as they reported, 'barbiturate tranquillizers known as Yellow Dollies'. Every report, while austere in its view, couldn't help slathering over the fact that one of the girls was kept at Victoria

Hospital for psychiatric tests. No prizes for guessing who that was.

Just when Grandpa thought things couldn't get any worse, they did. The story of the pill-popping teens went national. Most excruciating of all, it reached the offices, and the front page, of his paper of choice – the *Sunday Telegraph*. By coincidence, they ran their story on Mum's fourteenth birthday.

Part of me feels the shame my grandparents must have felt over what would be, in today's schools, pretty much ignored by anyone other than the head. But part of me is grateful for the national attention. Without the report from the *Telegraph*, for example, and without my Granny cutting it out and storing it so carefully, I would never have known about this phase of my mother's life. I would never have known that she and her friends were found in the school science laboratory, thought at first to be suffering the effects of 'intoxication'. I would never have known they were sent to hospital and given eight pints of water to flush out their systems. And I would never have known Grandpa immediately made plans for Mum to change schools.

All Granny ever told me was that Mum 'fell in with the wrong crowd' and I never knew any more until I opened this box of letters. Thanks to them, I know that she was examined by the hospital's consultant psychiatrist 'as is normal in cases of emotional trouble'. Neither of her friends was. Just her. For some reason, Mum was identified as the ringleader – and the one most in need of help. The clue is in the line 'as is normal in cases of emotional trouble'. What emotional trouble? What could she possibly have been going through that led her to nearly overdose on barbiturates?

I don't know how long her treatment, if any, continued. Not long, I suspect, because it seems to have been considered enough to move Mum to another school. I don't think everyone was satisfied with that. I might be reading too much into it, but there's a rather condemnatory edge, I feel, to the way the *Telegraph* made a point of announcing the incident was 'not reported to the police'. In their eyes, she'd got away with it – unless the police happened to read the country's bestselling broadsheet.

So, with Anne away and unable to help, Mum was transferred to the local comprehensive. I don't suppose she had a particularly easy time at home, having dragged the Beavis name through the mud.

I get the feeling the spotlight would have been on her. Not exactly like being frisked when you go through security at Heathrow, but not far off it either. If I know my grandparents, the constant interrogations would have been wearing enough. 'Where are you going? What's in your bag? Who were you with?'

In all likelihood, Mum avoided drugs for the rest of her school life. If her parents' wrath wasn't enough to keep her away from them, then the idea of being publicly humiliated in black and white again probably was. But if Granny and Grandpa thought that would be the end of her mischief, they were wrong. A girl like my mother will always find a way to fall into trouble. Longhill Secondary may not have given Jenny access to drugs, but it did present another distraction. Boys.

Putting a fourteen-year-old girl into a mixed school at a time when her hormones were just kicking into overdrive was always going to be explosive and I don't think Mum lost any time in getting to grips with the rules of dating. I'm not saying she would have done anything wrong, but when you come from a single-sex school, boys are going to seem like this exotic new thing. It would have been like a kid tasting sugar for the first time. I'm sure she learned the truth about them soon enough!

Most girls soon realize that boys their own age tend to be a bit on the immature side and Mum was no different. Unfortunately, at fourteen or fifteen, there wasn't anyone quite old enough still at school. Luckily, there were friends' older brothers, dance halls and parties. It was at one of these that she met an older boy who whisked her off to the 1968 Isle of Wight Festival on the back of his motorbike – an absolute nightmare for her parents, who had read all about these 'mods and rockers' in the *Telegraph*.

It was also at one of these parties that Jenny was introduced to my father, five years her senior and just about the most sophisticated person she'd ever met.

I'm sure Mum wasn't the only girl of her age fooling around with older boys at the time. But, whichever way you look at it, she was one of the unlucky ones. At some point shortly after her fifteenth birthday, she had to admit to herself that she was pregnant. I can't imagine how scared she must have been, but that was the easy part. Next she had to admit it to her parents.

Like so many of their time, all Granny and Grandpa wanted from life was respectability. Mum knew this better than anyone. She'd heard enough lectures. So, terrified at how her news would affect them, she did what so many young girls in her position do: absolutely nothing. It was only by chance, when Granny spotted a bikini-clad Jenny sunbathing during the summer of 1969 and said, 'Your tummy looks bigger than usual,' that the subject came up at all.

It's fair to say that Mr and Mrs Beavis weren't happy. The whole Yellow Dollies affair had been bad, but at least it had blown over. I'm sure plenty of people told them that today's headlines are tomorrow's fish wrappers and I'm sure they didn't believe it – I know because I hate it when people say it to me.

But it's true. Mum left hospital, switched schools and got on with her life. That feeling of everyone knowing your business, imagining strangers staring at you wherever you go, would have stayed with Granny and Grandpa for ages. But there came a point when even they had to admit the only people still talking about the scandal were themselves.

On the other hand, this new family catastrophe could not be so easily ignored. In a week or two people would start to notice Mum's size. Then, at the end of the year, there would be an actual baby. This was just not the way things were done in 1969. Not the way nice people did things, anyway.

I feel for my grandparents, I really do. They must have felt their world was crumbling when Mum presented this latest bombshell. But, unlike the newspaper headlines about the drugs, this was one family embarrassment that could not be swept under the carpet. Or so I thought.

Once I came to terms with the fact that I was actually present at my own sixteen-year-old mother's wedding, I assumed I knew the rest of the story. Okay, my parents had been a bit careless – I accept that I probably wasn't planned! – but they were in love, so of course marriage was something they were going to do anyway. My arrival had just sped up the natural course of things, that's all. How naïve.

When I sat down to write this book I forced myself to open the treasure chest of letters again. As soon as I'd read the first one I instantly remembered why I hadn't finished them all those years before. Just a couple of lines in, even skimming over the words, and I began to choke up. It wasn't a treasure chest. That little wooden container held my kryptonite. It was the only thing I still had from my parents' life – and it had so much power to hurt me.

Flicking through the contents was like opening Pandora's box. Every note, every scrap of paper inflicted another wound. I wanted to learn as much as possible about my mum's life. At least I thought I did. But when I came across the letter stamped with the adoption agency's address, I knew I'd seen too much.

Adoption agency?

Just two words, but enough to strike fear into anyone – whatever your age.

No, it's not possible. She wouldn't have done it!

She couldn't have, could she?

I've spent thirty years trying to come to terms with the idea that my mother abandoned me. Yes, I know she died. Yes, she would have done anything to stay with me – and often did. But grief isn't logical. She died and I was suddenly alone. Those were the facts. She'd gone and I was left behind. Alone and abandoned. That's how I felt.

At least I've always known it wasn't her choice. But adoption? That's a very different story. I had to prove it wasn't true.

Tears streaming down my face, I tore through the box, pulling out sheet after sheet of all that remained of my mother's life. Then I saw it. It wasn't much, but the first few words told me it contained what I needed to hear.

My hand was shaking as I clutched the letter. It was neatly typewritten and dated November 1969 – the month I was born. The text barely covered half a page, but in those few words my life had been decided.

According to the letter, Mum, Dad and both their sets of parents were strongly advised that the best course of action would be to have me adopted. But they'd refused. *Mum* had refused.

They'd stood up to officialdom and hung on to me. This silly

15

young schoolgirl and her older boyfriend, probably without a penny between them, had decided, 'No, you're not taking our baby!'

It's incredible how much power that tiny scrap of paper held over me. Now I knew the truth, I could relax. In the space of a few minutes I'd felt the bottom fall out of my world and then discovered it was all a mistake. A few minutes and two tiny pieces of correspondence from the past. No wonder I'd ignored that box for so long.

Gradually, I pieced together the true story. With a baby on the way and having pledged that they would be married as soon as legally possible, Mum and Dad moved in together. If they hadn't, then it wasn't just my future that was hanging in the balance. According to Grandpa's correspondence, there was talk of a criminal prosecution of my father because he'd had inter-course with a minor. Like a lot of cases today, though, the authorities took a view that Mum and Dad were in a relation-ship. Yes, at fifteen she was too young, but they loved each other. At that age you think you'll spend the rest of your life together.

Even though I'd discovered that Mum had fought to keep me, I still couldn't stem the tears. She must have felt so vulnerable. Granny and Grandpa were obviously not her biggest fans at that moment, her boyfriend had his own problems with the possible police action and here was some outside agency, some stranger, deciding whether Mum could keep her baby or not. Just think-ing of her going through all that on her own made me feel awful. Mum must have felt so alone. Unfortunately, not for the last time.

Her problems didn't end there. Another note revealed that I wasn't the only one the authorities had their eye on. Mum herself was considered as a potential victim in all this. I've actually read, in black and white, how some stranger had judged her poorly brought up by Granny and Grandpa, to the extent that they considered making her a ward of court. Only once I'd read further did the ramifications of this sink in. Becoming a ward of court essentially means handing over control of your life to the state. You become their responsibility, their child almost. If you can't make the right decisions yourself, they seem to be saying, we'll make them for you.

So not only was Mum fighting for me, she was fighting for her own freedom as well. Knowing that just made me feel even worse for judging her.

Even without the letters, I should have known the truth. At fourteen I knew, in my heart, that my mum would have done anything to keep me. In the short time we were together I saw some of the things she would do to shield me, the vile tortures she put herself through to keep me out of harm's way. This wasn't a woman who would give her child up.

How dare I even think it! I'm sorry, Mum, for doubting you.

The pressure on her must have been immense. Still, if there is one memory of my mother that I have above all others, it's that she was a fighter. She never gave in. No matter what the cost. Something I saw again and again and again . . .

TWO

Toast with Margarine

One of my earliest memories is of performing for the mayor of Brighton. I sang and I played and at the end he applauded loudly. Not bad, considering my start in life . . .

Unfortunately, it wasn't as grand as it sounds. Fisher-Price was launching a new range of musical goodies at the local toy fair and they ran a competition at my nursery school to find children to bash out a tune for the press. I was one of the lucky six chosen to pitch up at Brighton's Metropole Hotel and hammer out a few bars on a little wooden glockenspiel in front of an audience of the great and the good.

Half a dozen four-year-olds singing 'Baa Baa Black Sheep' while attempting a loose interpretation of the tune is not everyone's cup of tea, but the mayor, bless him, led the whooping and clapping like it was the Last Night of the Proms.

The fun didn't stop there. Of the six, I was then asked if I'd mind having my picture taken for the local rag down on the beach. 'Of course,' I replied, convinced my musical prowess had set me apart, and off we went. Sadly, there was no glockenspiel this time. Instead I was handed a chunky plastic airport, aimed at cashing in on the new craze of foreign holidays, and asked to play with it in the sand for a few minutes while photographers snapped away. Mum or Granny kept a clipping from the newspaper, which I found in my box of memories.

It's not bad as earliest reminiscences go, is it? Quite memorable, in fact. Pictures in the local press and hobnobbing with do-gooders and dignitaries. Unfortunately, that wasn't my daily routine. Away from the spotlight, life was very different.

I don't know if they were running away from their problems, following my father's work or just trying to prove that they didn't need anyone else, but shortly after their wedding my parents moved up to Stockport. Years later, I would let myself be persuaded to do something similar. For me, it was a disaster; for Mum, it wouldn't turn out well either. But right then, at the start, they had me and they had each other. I'm sure they thought they could take on the world. Then reality caught up with them.

At first it was the perfect set-up: Dad worked and Mum looked after me. As the weeks turned into months, however, being cut off from her friends and family began to take its toll. The new home that had been an escape from the nagging of their families now became a prison. The more she was left on her own, the more trapped Jenny felt.

As if it wasn't bad enough that Mum had had a baby at fifteen followed by a shotgun wedding, breaking it to my grandparents that she and my father were going to separate didn't exactly get the bunting hung in the streets. As far as they were concerned, things were going from bad to worse. At least Jenny being so far away spared them the initial public embarrassment.

Even so, I know that Mum only had to ask and they would

have welcomed her back to live with them. Even with a toddler in tow. But she was too proud to ask and Grandpa was too stubborn to suggest it. He wanted her to admit she'd made mistakes. Mum refused. What had happened, had happened. To confess to mistakes was to admit she was unhappy with the way her life had turned out. It would have been an insult to her beautiful baby. To me.

I'm sure, however, that if Mum had gone cap in hand to Grandpa he would have helped out financially. As disappointed and angry as he was, she was still his daughter. She was still the mother of his granddaughter. All Mum had to do was ask and he would have put his hand in his pocket. But that was the last thing she would have done. That would be like admitting defeat. During the adoption discussions, she had argued that she would be able to take care of her own baby. Now she had to prove it.

But talk about the blind leading the blind! Jenny Beavis was eighteen years old when her husband packed his bags. No one had told her how to be a mum. It wasn't that long ago that she was still playing with her own dolls. Yet there she was, alone in a flat in Stockport with a two-year-old, trying to put food on the table on a non-existent income and wondering when her luck was going to change.

And while she was confined to chasing a toddler around, her friends down south were out partying, working or going on to university. They were the ones with choices; Jenny didn't have that privilege. But she didn't mind. She was blessed in another way. She had her daughter.

It sounds a bit weird – a bit vain even – saying that, but from everything I can remember, everything I've read and everything other people have told me, my mother would have done anything for me. Yes, I'm sure she'd had the stuffing knocked out of her when she realized I was on my way, and yes, given the choice, she probably would have done things differently. But from the moment she discovered she was pregnant, that was it. She was going to be a mum. She really did think she was blessed. Her baby was a gift. Unfortunately, a child was all she had.

Even after relocating to Peacehaven, just along the coast from Brighton, Mum couldn't easily work with a child to look after, so we existed mainly on state benefits. It's possible my father also paid some support. A few pounds here and there doesn't go far, though. We really had nothing.

Home was a series of cheap apartments, each as sparsely furnished as the last. By the time I was eight I was telling people I'd lived in eighteen different places. A lot of my early memories are of us unpacking or packing and waking up somewhere new. Most of the properties were very similar. There were few home comforts to speak of, rarely a stick of furniture and no toys. We had a gorgeous tri-coloured cat called Mushka and a guitar. Apart from a suitcase of clothes, that was pretty much all we turned up with at each new flat.

Granny told me how hard Mum fought to make it work. How she devoted herself to looking after me and doing as much as she could on her limited budget, with trips to parks and zoos. Sometimes it was just a case of letting me play with friends. Because we were constantly moving, our different flats are blurred together in my memory. The earliest one I remember, as a four-year-old, was pretty indistinct inside. I just recall it had a wooden verandah – the only one on the street – which I thought was terribly exotic. Mum would let the other kids on the street come up and play there. Whole days would whizz by and we never tired of it. It was our little kingdom.

'She did her best,' Granny told me, absolutely no judgement

in her voice. You don't need money to be a good parent, she understood that. You just need to want to do your best – and we both knew Mum did.

Even so, staring at four walls all day couldn't have been easy for such a free spirit and she was happy when Granny offered to babysit. I've seen wonderful photos of me pottering around in Granny's garden or playing in their house. I obviously spent a fair bit of time there when I was young.

The only downside was having to conform to Granny's fashion sense. Two years of hairdressing hadn't just given her a hairstyle for life – if Granny had had her way I'd still have my hair the same today as she used to style it then, with a tuft of hair pulled through a little cotton toggle on the top of my head. Any other style and Granny thought I looked scruffy. At two I looked quite cute with a little curl looping down across the middle of my forehead. At four I still looked sweet, if unimaginative. By ten, though, I was thoroughly embarrassed about it. But that didn't matter. That's how little girls wore their hair, Granny said, and all the while she was teasing the strands into place she'd sing, 'There was a little girl who had a little curl, right in the middle of her forehead . . .' That was me, she said. I never really thought about it at the time, but did she really think I was horrid when I was bad?

For the first few years I lived in blissful ignorance of our impoverished state. I knew all the flats were cold, but I never realized it was because Mum was too poor to afford heating. I knew I moved house a lot more than other children, but I never appreciated it was because we hadn't paid the rent on the last place. Not even when Mum made me tiptoe down the stairs, our meagre belongings dragged behind us, did I question anything. Why would I? Children just get on with things. Their whole view of the world comes from their parents. As far as I was concerned, moonlight flits were normal. That's how everyone moved house.

The first inkling I got that all was not well came when I was four. A friend of Mum's had come round – this was rare – and she'd commented on how cold the flat was.

'It's the power cuts,' Mum said. 'They're playing havoc with the gas.'

The friend nodded sympathetically. This was 1973 and power cuts were the scourge of the western world, thanks to the oil crisis. Obviously I didn't know any of that – but I did know that whatever these 'power cuts' were, they had nothing to do with our heating. We hadn't had any for as long as I could remember.

Mum's not telling her friend the truth, I realized. *I wonder why?*

To her credit, Mum was always looking for enterprising ways of making money and I loved helping – even if it did sometimes mean getting up at the crack of dawn. We were going out to a park one Sunday morning and happened to walk past the local pub. I was yapping away when suddenly Mum darted over to the kerb. There in the gutter was a screwed-up pound note. Mum whooped as she put it into her purse and I remember thinking how nice it was to see her so happy. I certainly didn't think any more of it, but obviously Mum did. The following Sunday she had me up and dressed at six o'clock. I could hear rain on the windows.

'We'll get wet,' I moaned.

Mum was excited. 'Stop grumbling,' she said. 'It's perfect weather.'

I didn't have a clue what she was talking about or why she was so cheerful when we were obviously in for a soaking. But I followed her out without another word. I don't know where

I expected to end up, but it certainly wasn't outside the pub where we'd found the pound note the previous week.

'Why are we here?'

'To look for more of these,' Mum replied, then, right on cue, bent down to rescue another note from the road. It was soggy, but still in one piece. Mum had such a smile on her face, it almost made the early, wet start worthwhile.

When she explained her plan, I got excited too. We were there to find as many pound notes as possible.

'See if you can find more than me,' she suggested.

'I'm going to win!' I declared and ran off to hunt.

I have to admire Mum's logic. Saturday was the big drinking night and, back then, you could still down a skinful and be allowed to drive. It's incredible to think how lax the law was, but it helped us out at the time. When she discovered that first pound, Mum could just picture some old drunk staggering out of the boozer and bumbling around, all fingers and thumbs, for his car keys. He'd probably turned every pocket inside out looking for them and, in the process, not noticed he'd lost the odd note. And if one bloke could drop the odd note in his drunken state, so could a few others.

I don't know who found the most money that morning – which makes me think it was Mum, otherwise I would have remembered! – but I do recall taking a handful home and lovingly laying them out on the table. Then Mum strung a line in front of the fire, pegged them all up and we sat back and watched a week's spending money dry out before our eyes.

We did that every week for ages. Sometimes we were lucky, sometimes not. But rain, as Mum suspected, usually meant it was a good morning because the paper tended to stick where it was in the wet. On summer nights the notes would have blown everywhere.

Speaking of summer, I was a bit older when Mum had another money-spinning brainwave. It was a really hot day, which can totally transform a seaside town. But on this particular morning we weren't heading to the beach. The Bay City Rollers, the hottest young band of the time, were coming to do an open-air gig up in one of the hillside parks and Mum had decided that we would earn some money from the event. Her plan was quite simple: it was scorching weather and fans had to hike half a mile up a hill to reach the concert, so obviously they'd be desperate to buy some lovely, fresh melon from her! So there we were that morning, out buying as many melons as we could carry, then chopping them up, wrapping the slices in cling film and lugging them up the hill to sell to dehydrated music fans at 20p a go. It was a brilliant idea. We were a godsend to those people – and I got to hear the concert as well! The only downside was having to carrying the stuff up there in the first place – by the time I reached the park, I was ready for the melon myself. We made shedloads of money, but I think we could have made more if we hadn't needed to eat some of our profits ourselves.

Those two episodes are really happy memories for me. They might seem a bit weird now, but as a kid I loved doing crazy things like that. Life was never dull with Mum. Every day was a bit of an adventure, which I absolutely adored. She was obviously inventive and a hard worker. If only she could have channelled her ideas. She had so much to offer.

As soon as Mum had a bit of cash in her pocket she was desperate to spend it. Not on things for herself – usually it was treats for both of us. My favourite thing we did regularly was eat out together. With money being scarce, we're not talking about the Ritz. But whenever Mum had a pound or two in her pocket we'd walk to a café on the corner of Preston Park and I would be allowed to have toast with margarine on it. That's how I know how poor we were – because two bits of lovely, thick, white, toasted bread coated in marge was a real treat for me. I can't remember having much in the way of cooked food at home at all. I certainly don't recall Mum ever standing at a stove. Food just didn't seem to be a priority for her. We had occasional tinned food – cold – but mainly packets of biscuits, cakes, bread, anything convenient. Mushka had dry biscuits, but otherwise was left to forage. I remember Granny offering me a choice of cereals one day at her house. I was staggered. I'd never had cereal at home. Having these little sugar-coated parcels to start the day was like a naughty treat.

Mum's finances usually stretched to a round of toast once or twice a week. Very, very occasionally, I was allowed to look even further down the menu and have a sausage sandwich. That was an amazing meal for me. Two sausages cut in half and wrapped between slices of that same thick, white loaf was my idea of heaven. Being there with Mum, tucking into my 15p sarnie, I really couldn't have been happier.

It's only later, of course, that I associated it with the time we were at our poorest. As a child, I never made the link. I just thought it was a lovely way to spend time with my mother.

It was the same with the money-making scams. I never saw them as essential, so we could eat for the next few days. They just felt like an adventure to me, a bit of fun, with the added bonus of hopefully finding some cash. It was no wonder, then, that I hit upon my own wheeze to pick up a few pence here and there.

My favourite trick was to stand outside one of the big red

phone boxes we used to have then and try to look distressed. Then I'd say to passers-by, 'Can you help? I really need to phone my mother and I haven't got any money.'

A local call in those days was 2p. A few people would ignore me and some would tell me to clear off, but often they dipped their hands into their pockets and handed over a nice brown coin. Of course, there was no way I was going to use the money on a phone call. For a start, Mum didn't even have a phone. I couldn't have called her if I'd wanted to.

No, as soon as I had a coin in my possession, I would dart into a shop and buy sweets. You could get an awful lot of sugar for 2p, so I'd be straight out to find my friends to share my good fortune. It wasn't just this entrepreneurial spirit that I inherited from Mum: I also realized that there's no point in having money, however much or little, if you don't share it with your loved ones. Two wonderful lessons.

Being a kid, though, I didn't always care how I achieved those targets. I remember buying all the kids on our street an ice cream once. That's typical Mum generosity coming out there. The only problem was, I hadn't tricked passers-by into parting with their pennies or sold anything to baking music fans. I'd pinched the money out of Mum's purse.

I only did it the once, but I'd never felt so ashamed. The second the ice cream touched my tongue, I felt like gagging. There was no way I could enjoy that treat knowing where the money had come from. Luckily for them, my friends had no such principles.

Not appreciating our dire financial straits was one thing, but, looking back at the photos, I realized something else had passed me by: just how beautiful Mum was. Of course, I'd always thought she was, but she was my mother and we all think that about our mums when we're small, don't we? But she was so pretty, so slim and, I keep forgetting, so damned young; a total head-turner for sure. I can't find a bad picture of her from that time. Real knockout stuff.

Unfortunately, looking after me full-time didn't give her much time to go out with friends her own age. Even when Granny looked after me, our lack of income meant Mum couldn't afford to do much anyway. That was why her parents were so delighted for her when she came to pick me up from theirs one day and announced, 'I've got a job!'

I was the only one not so thrilled. Money didn't mean anything to me, but I wasn't the one struggling to make ends meet each week. No, the only result I could see from Mum's news was that she would be away from me for the entire day. I'd been with her virtually every day since I was born. Apart from the odd day or weekend with Granny and Grandpa, we'd been cooped up like battery hens in a succession of tiny flats.

In short then, while Granny was cheering loudly enough to be heard in Eastbourne, I couldn't see any good at all coming from this news. As far as I was concerned, I had a wonderful life. Mum getting a job was going to ruin everything.

Within a year, I would be proved right. But not in the way I expected.

THREE

The Eye of the Storm

With more than 3,000 employees, American Express is Brighton's largest employer. It was just as dominant in the 1970s as well, which I suppose explains how Mum was able to get a job there with no qualifications. Every day she'd pull on a suit, walk or catch a bus down to Edward Street and disappear inside the modernistic, white, angled building that had been built for the company a decade earlier. She was a clerk, basically shuffling paper all day, but it was work. It was something that paid a wage. And it got her out of the house.

As a four-year-old you don't want to consider that perhaps Mum would rather spend some of her time with other grown-ups. You think, *I've got you, you've got me – brilliant!*

I didn't really know what a job was. She may as well have said, 'I'm going to the moon.' I had no idea what it would entail. But I soon found out: in a nutshell, it meant we would be separated.

In order to make the job work, Mum had to sort out child-care for me. That's how I came to be enrolled in the Rainbow Nursery, where I was when Fisher-Price came to town. Looking back, I don't know if she needed the salary before she could afford to get me in or whether it was a state-run thing. At the time, all I knew was that I was dumped there because Mum wanted to be somewhere else.

Obviously, that's not what was happening. Things were desperate. We needed money. We were chasing pound notes around rainy car parks, for God's sake! But I liked those things. I never appreciated how much stress the financial situation placed on Mum's young shoulders. So for a while I resented being at Rainbow. It was fun to play with other kids, but every day Mum dropped me off and every day I thought, *I wish I was staying with her.*

It's probably the only time in my life when I entertained ill thoughts about her. It really felt that she was choosing other people over me. I hated it. But then the door would close, the nursery teacher would wave a paintbrush at me and I'd be lost in the wonderful cacophony of thirty children enjoying themselves.

As a mum myself now, I know it can't have been any easier for her to leave me than it was to be left. It's a mother's role to feel guilty about every single choice you make. And, let's face it, Mum had had four years of suffering guilt about the life she had given me so far. As much as she hated seeing my tearful face at the nursery window in those early days, she knew it was for the best. She was the only parent in my life. She'd been mother and play pal for four years. Now she needed to be the breadwinner too.

'It will be worth it,' she kept promising, 'you'll see.'

'I don't know how. I hate it at nursery.'

Actually it wasn't so bad. And then a funny thing happened. Things began to get better. In fact, I have to admit, it very nearly was 'worth it'.

Once I settled into the routine of going to Rainbow, of course I loved it. I'd gone from having no toys to being surrounded by all manner of plastic, clockwork and metal treats. It was like being in Aladdin's cave. There literally weren't enough hours in the day for me to play with everything. I even loved story time, when our teachers read from some of their wonderful books. We didn't have books at home. I suppose I thought that was natural – that all the other children hadn't seen a book until they came to nursery as well. In truth, I didn't think twice about it then. I just remember loving the exciting mysteries and adventures that these fantastic heroes were having.

And then there was the other advantage of Mum's work – the very thing she'd taken the job for in the first place. *Money.*

I didn't see it at the time, and she never discussed it, but her starting to wear a suit coincided with little treats cropping up in my life. The village hall near our flat used to put on film shows every Saturday which a lot of my little friends went to. It was only 10p, but Mum had never been able to spare it before. Now things were different. She would buy two tickets and we would sit back while the film of the week was projected onto a big screen at the front. We didn't have a television then – and even Granny and Grandpa only had a black-and-white set – so it was amazing to see these incredible colours dancing around in front of my very eyes.

Trips to the café for my sausage sandwich became more regular as well. The only problem was cramming it all into a weekend. There was only so much we could do during the week, with Mum working an eight-hour day, so Saturdays and Sundays became sacrosanct. They were 'our times'. That was when we'd go down to the seafront or the Brighton Lanes to shop. I remember winning a giant stuffed panda at an amusement arcade. I couldn't have been happier as Mum and I lugged it back home. After a month or so, I had to admit that life was great.

The longer Mum worked, the more she was able to straighten herself out financially – I imagine there were various debts to be repaid, probably to Granny. At some point, though, my treats got better. King of them all came on the day she said, 'Would you like your own bike?'

My own bike? I couldn't believe it. All the kids on our street had started to ride and I'd had a go on their bikes, first with stabilizers and then – don't ask me how! – riding solo on two wheels. I'd never really questioned why I didn't have my own. That was normal. I didn't have anything. But Mum must have seen me riding someone else's and had the idea. The next weekend she had a surprise for me.

'Close your eyes,' she said, barely able to contain her own excitement.

I did as I was told and Mum led me into the bedroom we shared. I didn't have a clue what was going on, but Mum's voice told me I was going to like it!

'Okay,' she said as we stopped. 'Open your eyes now!'

I did. There before me, leaning against the bed, was a spangly new red bicycle. I gasped. It was amazing. So shiny, so new – and so mine!

Then I noticed the wheels. Kids are funny about details; they get things into their heads. For some reason this bike had a black tyre at the back and a white tyre at the front. I hated it. Looking back, I suppose the bike was second-hand and that's how it had come. At the time I just thought, *This is not right*. Mum saw me falter.

'Is everything okay?'

I was old enough to know she would be hurt if I told her the truth.

'It's beautiful,' I said. 'Just what I've always wanted.'

I don't know if she ever knew how mortified I was by the mismatching tyres. I remember moaning about it to Grandpa though. His response was typically logical.

'Cathy,' he said, with that familiar air of knowing everything, 'third-class riding is better than first-class walking. Be grateful.'

But I wasn't. I was selfish – a normal selfish little girl. Everywhere I went I imagined people laughing. I was embarrassed, to be honest. But of course he was right. If I was that bothered I could have not ridden it at all. But that wouldn't have done. I loved having a bike. I didn't realize it, but a life-long love of all things two-wheeled began right there.

For a while, then, things were good. From Mum's point of view, they were probably the best of times, really – certainly since splitting from her husband. She had a small but regular income, her daughter seemed to have settled into nursery and finally she had a bit of freedom. I could never have guessed it at the time, but it was that freedom, I'm sure, that signalled the beginning of the end.

It started with Mum having the odd Saturday night out with friends. She'd drop me off in Saltdean and go skipping down the road to catch a bus into town. I didn't mind. I liked staying with my grandparents. I could take my bike and bomb up and down their garden or play with other kids in the woodland or the park at the back of their house. Sometimes I'd go with Granny to walk her dogs along the promenade between Saltdean and Rottingdean, or if the weather was bad she'd read me stories or teach me some new craft, like knitting, sewing, crocheting, drawing, flower-arranging or doll-making – you name it, she wanted me to learn it. Grandpa was more of a distant figure, but it didn't matter. My time there was always great fun. The only downside was knowing Mum was out during our weekend time.

Gradually, our sacrosanct mother-and-daughter time was being eaten into. I don't think Mum intended it to happen; it just did. First it was occasional Saturdays, then every week. Then she added a Friday or two as well. I can't blame her. She was barely twenty and she deserved to have some fun. I just wished she could do it on a weeknight.

Missing her on a Saturday night was okay because even if I'd been at home with her, I would have been in bed. The real kicker was not seeing her Sunday morning. As the months went by, Mum's pick-up time for me got later and later. Granny didn't mind – she just scooped me into the car and took me to church with them. I was there so often I became the flower girl, handing out posies on special occasions. It was fun – I enjoyed being centre of attention, even in a church. But really I just wanted to be with Mum.

Some Sundays Granny would give up waiting and just take me straight home after the service. If we were lucky, Mum would be up and running around, getting some lunch ready. Then there were the other days. Once, I remember getting to the building and knocking on the communal door. There was no answer so Granny rang the bell. Someone else who lived in the block recognized me and let us in and we went straight over to the door of our flat and knocked again.

'I don't think she's in,' I said.

Granny wasn't having any of it. 'She's in, all right. But what state she's in is anybody's guess.'

I didn't know what that phrase meant. Even when a zombie-looking Mum opened the door five minutes later, hanging onto the latch like she would fall without it, it didn't register. I was just so glad to be home I gave Mum an enormous squeeze and skipped into the flat. Granny wasn't so abundant in her cheeriness.

'You need to get yourself cleaned up, my girl,' she scolded. Again, the words meant little to me. I thought Mum looked lovely the way she was. I always did.

I thought nothing of it at the time. The following week the same thing happened and still I didn't notice anything was wrong. As the weeks wore on, it became another weekend ritual: wake Mum up, say bye to Granny, snuggle up with Mum if she went back to bed, or potter round the flat with her if she stayed up. I really didn't mind. Anything to be with her.

It was only years later that I questioned what she was doing. That was with the benefit of hindsight. When you're in the eye of the storm, however, you're not aware of half the chaos going on around you. As it turned out, I wasn't aware of any of it.

By the time Mum had been at AmEx a year, we'd settled into a routine. Or rather, we'd settled into several mini-routines. She worked hard all week, picked me up from nursery and we'd either play or she'd drop me at Granny's and head out for the evening. Then, sometime after my fifth birthday, I stopped going to nursery. Mum said I was too old now and I accepted it. Once again, why wouldn't I? I knew it was nothing to do with money. After all, lots of my friends had also stopped going. They were too old as well. What I didn't know, though, was that they all stopped nursery because they had somewhere else to go. School.

You don't miss what you've never had. That was the story of my life. It could have applied to a dad (I don't remember him as a child at all), to toys, to heating – anything. You name it, I probably didn't have it. But it's not in my nature to want what I can't get. Consequently, even if I heard friends talking about school, it never entered my head that I was missing out. I wasn't envious. Possibly I was a little curious about where they disappeared to in the days, but not enough to ask Mum if I could go too. And it certainly never once occurred to me that I should be attending.

Because I didn't go to school, I still needed day care. Granny stepped in for at least a couple of days a week and Mum would drop me off on her way to work. For the rest of the time, she found another solution.

I suddenly found myself being taken to a neighbour's flat, that of a man who lived alone. He was older than Mum, but was probably only about thirty, certainly no older than forty. Kids are really bad at ages. Everyone looks old to them. I don't recall ever meeting him before and we certainly weren't introduced first. It was just up, dressed, shooed out the door as usual – and across the hall into the neighbour's flat. I really didn't want to go in. Mum was in a rush though.

'Be a good girl. I'll see you later. Love you.' And she was off.

So there I was, just a few feet from my own home, but it felt like a million miles away.

The man was all right. He made me breakfast and lunch and, best of all, let me watch telly. That was the deal-maker as far as I was concerned. Without that, I wouldn't have wanted to spend a minute there. Unfortunately, without the telly, I also wouldn't have been subjected to what he put me through.

Once I got to know our neighbour – let's call him Paul – I really grew to like him. During the months he looked after me, he was never less than lovely and caring, always trying to make me laugh. He really knew how to make a day fly by. For a five-year-old, that's half the battle of childcare.

When it came to watching telly, I'd snuggle up to Paul on the sofa. Then, one day, he suggested I move nearer.

'Come and sit on my lap, Cathy.'

So I did, just as I would have done if it had been Mum, Granny or Grandpa suggesting it.

There was nothing like CBeebies or Milkshake on telly in those days. People were still getting used to having a third channel and BBC2 only really got going in the afternoon. Earlier in the day they would show that famous 'test card' of the little girl playing noughts and crosses with her clown doll. Whatever was broadcast was still better than nothing, though, and I lapped it up. Even when I didn't understand what was being said. And even when I felt Paul's hands moving over my legs.

I didn't know how long he'd been doing it. I was just suddenly aware of his hands sliding up my bare legs and underneath my skirt.

'What are you doing?' I asked, but he just giggled.

'You mind your own business and watch the telly,' he ordered.

Okay, I thought. *It's not like you're hurting me.*

Children just assume adults have their best interests at heart, don't they? Granny and Grandpa had caused me a lot more pain than that by telling me off, so I just got comfortable and ignored him.

I feel sick looking back and more than a bit apprehensive about even mentioning it. My life had been one round of surprises followed by another. Mum was always finding new ways of pulling the rug out from underneath me. So, if you like, I was conditioned to accept weird things as normal. Even when a man

I barely knew flicked my little pants aside and pushed his fingers inside me.

I didn't cry, I didn't scream. I don't even remember fighting him off. I'm ashamed to admit that I just sat there, watching television and trying not to pay him any attention.

As young as I was, I knew I wasn't being hurt. He was gentle with me, like he'd always been when we messed around. He never shouted or hurt me or really told me off. In every other way, as far as I was concerned, he was looking out for me. Yes, I thought what he was doing to me was odd, but, as I say, my life so far had been a series of odd events lined up next to each other.

When the programme finished, or when it was time to go, I jumped off his lap and that was it. No awkward words, no silences, no recriminations. In fact, when I returned the next day, he did exactly the same thing. And the next day, and the next, and the next. Every time I saw him, in fact, Paul would do that.

Another sign that I thought it was 'normal' is that I never told Mum. It wasn't like I was too scared to or I didn't think she'd care. It was just something that happened during my day, as regular as afternoon naps and cleaning my teeth after lunch. By the time I was at home with her, it didn't even register as an event.

By normalizing it, like Paul did, I wasn't even aware a crime was being committed. And that, I suppose, is how people get away with it for so long.

I wonder if Mum should have picked up on any change in my personality at that time. Apparently an abused child will give off signals, if you know where to look. I doubt Mum noticed anything untoward. For a start, as I said, I wasn't even aware I was being violated. And, more importantly, looking back, I'm amazed she even remembered my name sometimes.

The longer Mum worked at AmEx, the less active she seemed to get at home. When she wasn't out, she would spend a lot of time in bed. Once I asked her if she was going out as usual on Saturday. Imagine how my heart leapt when she replied, 'No, not this time.'

I had visions of us skipping through the park, paddling along the seafront or visiting our favourite café – maybe even all three. In the end we did exactly none of them.

Mum was as good as her word. She didn't go out Saturday night. But she didn't go out Saturday morning or afternoon either. In fact, I don't recall her getting out of bed except to visit the loo or have a cigarette.

Of course I was disappointed, but mainly I was worried. For Mum to stay in bed all day, she was obviously ill. I think I learnt how to make coffee that day – too young, I realize now, to be handling boiling water. And I was in charge of lunch as well. I managed to rustle up a sandwich.

By the time Monday morning came round Mum was right as rain again and it was back to our weekly routine. Or so I thought. By the middle of the week she was starting to slow down again. After a night out on Friday she once more retired to her bed. Saturday came and went. Sunday too. The only difference this time was that she didn't get up on Monday – not early enough for work, anyway.

I don't know if it was related, but Mum's job with AmEx ended soon after that. Granny was really disappointed, but Mum took it quite well.

'What will you do now?' Granny asked her.

Mum just shrugged.

'Find something else.'

But she never did.

Hearing that Mum wasn't working anymore was like going to bed on Christmas Eve. I was too excited to sleep, knowing all the fun we were going to have the next day. Yet again, it didn't quite pan out the way I envisaged.

Mum spent her first day off work in bed. This time, though, I knew she wasn't ill. When I asked, she just said, 'I'm tired.'

Fair enough, I thought. After a day of mooching around the flat she'd be raring to go tomorrow. We could have our fun together then.

Wrong.

Tuesday was another bed day. Once again, the only things that could entice Mum up were tea breaks, loo stops and the lure of another cigarette. Food seemed to pass her by. It would have passed me by as well if it had been up to her. I managed to open a tin of baked beans and heated those. Obviously I offered Mum the same.

'No thanks, darling,' she smiled, lighting another cigarette. 'I'm all right here.' Mum had always smoked. Now, though, her cigarettes smelled very sweet, like herbs.

Quite a lot of our time together ended up with me playing nurse and waitress to Mum, although she never actually asked me for anything. Not a drink or medicine or even to pass her matches. That didn't stop me offering, though. I was desperate to do something for her. But she always waved my offers away with a smile. Then I'd climb onto the bed with her and she'd fall asleep. I'd never had a doll of my own to look after, but I imagined this was what it must be like.

Writing this down, it sounds like a pretty horrendous life, but I can't tell you how happy I was. I didn't care that Mum wanted to mope around the flat in a fug of smoke. If I'd had my way, I would have sat on her desk at American Express. Just being with her was all I ever wanted. It's what I still want today.

So anything she did, I didn't judge. Anything she said, anywhere she went, anyone she spoke to – it was all fine by me. Me and Mum, the old team, were back together. I really couldn't have been happier.

Having Mum around during the week meant I didn't mind so much when she went out in the evenings. Without work the next day, however, she wasn't just limited to Fridays and Saturdays. It might be a Wednesday one week, or Monday, Thursday – you name it. There was no pattern that I could see. She would just announce she was going out, then Granny or Grandpa would arrive to pick me up or we'd catch a bus to their bungalow in Tremola Avenue. I didn't know who Mum went out with or where to, but I do know it always ended the same way: Granny would take me home the following morning and tut-tut as a bleary-eyed Mum let us in, while I would give her the biggest hug I could muster and skip happily indoors, calling out, 'Bye, Granny, see you later' as I disappeared into the small lounge.

I was aware of Granny's attitude towards Mum's partying, but not affected by it. She certainly never criticized her daughter in front of me. All my life Granny had been stern, if loving, so her attitude didn't particularly stand out, just as any change in Mum's behaviour didn't really register on my radar. To me, she was just Mum being Mum. Whatever she did was 'normal' for us. There was no need for explanation. That was who she was, that was how she was. I didn't care. I loved her every which way. I was every inch the doting daughter. I completely trusted her judgements – as hard as it sometimes was.

41

I don't remember what day it was or whether it was morning, noon or night. But I do remember Mum was smoking as usual and I was teasing the cat with a ball of string. I was blissfully happy, actually. Nothing could spoil my day. The voices at the front door soon put a stop to that.

Suddenly there was a ferocious knocking and a deep, loud voice called out, 'Police. Open up!'

I'd never seen Mum move so fast! She came flying out of her chair and dived into the small bathroom. A few seconds later she emerged, no longer smoking. Then she grabbed something from her pocket and thrust it into my hands. It was some sort of plastic package.

'Put it in the panda!' she hissed through gritted teeth. Her eyes were wide. She was obviously terrified about something.

I was too stunned to move. Realizing Mum was scared was like a kick in the stomach.

That's not how it's meant to be.

'Put it in the panda!' she said again, and this time shoved me towards the bedroom, where my stuffed arcade toy was lying on my bed. At the same time she darted to a window and, grabbing a copy of the free newspaper, started waving fresh air into the room.

All of this took place in the space of ten seconds. At eleven seconds there was another crashing knock.

'Open up or we'll open it for you.'

Regaining her composure, Mum patted down her clothes, did a quick fiddle with her hair and called out, 'I'm coming, I'm coming.'

That cheered me up. It couldn't be so bad if she was worrying about her appearance.

Checking that I was back in the lounge, Mum flicked the bolt and opened the door. Standing there were four of the biggest men I'd ever seen. Framed by the doorway, they were giants in police uniforms. To my young eyes, I'd never seen anything more scary.

'Jennifer Wilson?' one of the policemen asked.

Mum nodded. 'What can I do for you?' she asked quietly. I think that sudden burst of activity had taken it out of her.

The policeman stared over her shoulder at me and the room. 'Do you mind if we take a look around?' he asked.

'Do I have a choice?' Mum said.

'None at all,' he said, and showed her a piece of paper. 'We have a warrant to search your premises for narcotic substances.'

I saw Mum's shoulders sag and instinctively ran over to wrap my arms around her waist. I hadn't understood half the things the constable had said, but I could feel Mum shaking. Whatever he'd said had rocked her, that much was obvious.

Resigned to whatever it said on that piece of paper, Mum stood back and watched as the four of them marched into our tiny flat. While three of them hung around the doorway, a fourth powered straight into the bedroom. He emerged a few seconds later clutching my stuffed panda!

I couldn't help gasping. I had no idea what I'd tucked inside him, but it was enough to know Mum wanted it hidden. I had a crushing sense of failing her. Panic washed over me. *I must have done something wrong.* There was no other explanation.

I stared, open-mouthed, as the policeman unzipped the back of the bear and stuffed his hand inside. Moments later, a smile broke out on his face.

'What do we have here then?' he said theatrically, and pulled out the little plastic pouch.

I genuinely had no idea what it was, but it was obviously what the lead officer had been expecting to find. He took one look at the package, had a quick sniff, then said to Mum, 'Jennifer Wilson, you are under arrest.'

It all happened so fast. One minute I'd been tormenting the cat, the next four burly policemen were terrorizing Mum. And then, within the blink of an eye, it seemed, we were all sitting in the back of a police car. Me, Mum and Mr Panda. With the sirens wailing above our heads, for all I knew, this was the end of my freedom forever. Would I ever see our home, our cat, our family again? I looked at Mum. Her face was blank, staring ahead. No answers there.

Oh, Mum, I thought. *What have you done?*

It felt like the end of the world. Little did I realize this was the lull before the storm. Compared to who would be knocking on our door soon, the police's visit seemed like a beautiful dream.

FOUR

Mother Knows Best

A lot of children dream of riding in a speeding police car, blue lights illuminating the night sky, sirens clearing other traffic out of its path. I was never one of those kids. Policemen always looked so intimidating and scary. The last place I ever wanted to be was cooped up inside a cop car with two of them. Normally I would have been happy anywhere, as long as Mum was with me. Not this time. I'd never seen her look so down, so shattered. So out of it.

I suppose we were taken to Brighton police station. I didn't recognize the building, for obvious reasons, but I remember that everything inside was pale grey or blue and so shiny. The desks, walls and floors all had that nasty, hard gloss finish. They took Mum one way and me another – and Mr Panda somewhere else entirely. A policewoman came over and showed me into a small office with a desk and two chairs. As soon as Mum was out of sight, the floodgates opened. Mum had been so scared at the flat and I was desperate to see her again, to give her a hug. That would make everything all right.

The policewoman was lovely though. She put her arm around

me, said she'd find me a nice cup of juice and told me everything would be all right. I had no reason to doubt her.

'Where's Mum?' I asked.

'She's helping my colleagues.' The WPC's smile was warm. 'Nothing to worry about.'

'Helping them do what?'

'Oh, they're just asking your mother a few questions, that's all.'

'Can I ask *you* a question?'

My police babysitter couldn't have looked more pleased.

'Fire away,' she said.

'How did you know to look in the panda?'

The policewoman chuckled. 'Oh, it wasn't any magic, if that's what you're wondering,' she said. 'One of the officers was peering through the letterbox and saw everything.'

'Oh,' I said. What else was there to say?

We sat there in silence for a couple of minutes. Every time I tried to say something, the policewoman looked over from the other side of the desk, then away again as no words came out. Finally, I said, 'I've got another question.'

'Okay.'

'Will we be allowed to leave soon?'

'Yes, very soon.'

'You won't lock Mum up?'

'Not today, no.'

That was all I'd wanted to hear.

'Good.'

The policewoman smiled again. I could almost see a thought forming in her mind.

'How would you like to have your fingerprints taken?'

Fingerprints? Like a criminal? I'd heard about that. That was how the police caught robbers and baddies.

'Yes please!'

'Come on then,' she said, and led me out of the room.

It had been terrifying being driven through town to the police station. Partly because I didn't know what we'd done wrong. Mainly, though, because I was worried about what would happen to Mum. On the way home it was a different matter. I couldn't wait to tell Mum all about my fingerprints and she was lapping it up. When I showed her the black smudges on my thumb, she held her own hand up.

'Snap!'

I hadn't seen Mum laugh like that in ages. She didn't seem tired for once, or distracted. I didn't know what the police had said, but it was good to have her back.

The mood soon altered when we got home. Mum had called Granny and Grandpa from the station and they were waiting in their car as we pulled up. From the looks on their faces, they weren't happy. As soon as we stepped through the front door Grandpa wanted to know the full story. They were whispering on the other side of the lounge, but I could tell they were talking about the package and the panda. I think Mum tried to deny everything at first because her dad raised his voice.

'So the police came all the way round here for that tiny little packet?' Grandpa said.

Mum nodded.

'They sent four officers for that?'

Another nod.

'Well, it seems a bit heavy-handed to me,' he concluded. 'Are you sure you're telling me the full story?'

Mum was adamant, but you could tell from Grandpa's face that he didn't believe her.

'It's like using a sledgehammer to crack a nut,' I heard him tell Granny as they left.

Like so many things, it was only years later that I appreciated how deeply this latest episode must have upset Mum's parents. After three or so years of relative quiet they'd dared to hope she was going to settle down and, if she couldn't win Daughter of the Year, at least be a responsible adult at last. Apparently not. But what was she doing getting involved with the police? Hadn't she brought enough shame on the family? And why did it have to be drugs?

This was all kept from me. I knew nothing of the marijuana Mum had been smoking openly around the house for months. I knew nothing of her history with Yellow Dollies, or of how she'd sworn to Grandpa years ago that drugs would never be a problem again. All I saw were the angry exchanges between them, and that just made me sad.

The fallout from the police's visit didn't end at the *froideur* between Mum and her parents. A short while later, maybe a couple of days, there was another knock on the door. I swear my heart stopped.

The police have come to take Mum again!

Then I noticed Mum wasn't surprised. I didn't know if she was expecting the call or whether she just had nothing to hide this time. There was no panic, no rushing around trying to flush things down the toilet. Just a resigned sigh as she made her way over to the door.

The relief I felt when she flung it open and I saw a man and a woman in suits waiting for her. *They don't look like police.* But I wasn't sure. I'd seen people in normal clothes when I was at the station.

The visitors came in. They said hello to me and Mum explained they'd come to talk about me. Specifically, why I wasn't going to school.

It was all pretty good-natured. Mum made them tea and nodded a lot while they spoke to her. I didn't follow most of it. When they finally left, everyone was smiling. The second the door closed, however, Mum's face changed.

'Pack your things,' she said. 'We're leaving.'

Looking back, I can't decide if I was spectacularly dim or just a normal kid. I think it was the latter. We're all brought up to think that Mother knows best, aren't we? Whatever happened, that's genuinely what I thought. She was the one constant in my life. Of course I was going to believe what she said and support what she did. Even when it was obviously so ridiculous ...

We didn't have much, but when you have to cart it all onto a bus, it can seem like a hell of a lot. We must have made two trips to our new home in May Road. All I really remember is that by the time we'd finished, I was standing in a new hallway in a new block in a new part of town. The landlady had just left and Mum smiled as she put her latest front-door key down on the little kitchen table.

'Home sweet home, Cathy.'

She never explained why we'd run away so suddenly, but I guessed it had something to do with our smart-looking visitors. What had they said to her that made her so scared? And why did they say I had to go to school? That was up to Mum, wasn't it? She was in charge.

That's genuinely what I thought. It just didn't enter my mind that Mum would be flouting the law. To this day, I still don't know why she was so against me going. Was it laziness? Or had her own experiences scarred her so much she didn't want to put me through it? All I can really surmise is that by disappearing from our old address, she hoped the social workers – as I learnt they were called – wouldn't be able to find us. But, God, I wish I knew what she was thinking.

Please tell me there was a plan!

Our new place was a split-level basement bedsit, although jargon like that meant nothing to me at the time, of course. All I knew was it had stairs and passages and doors – three great ingredients for adventures! You stepped inside the front door straight into the lounge, where a large open fire offered the flat's only means of heating. There were a couple of chairs already there and a sofa which turned into a bed. That was where Mum slept. I had my own space – under the stairs.

It sounds awful when I tell people now, but I was so thrilled at the time. I had armchair cushions as a mattress and plenty of room for me, my reclaimed panda and Mushka to cuddle up together. I've always hated sleeping in the dark, so Mum unscrewed – or maybe just snapped off – the angled door of the cupboard and hung a curtain instead, which I could have open or shut depending on my mood. I was so happy in there. It felt like I was in a tent.

The adventures didn't stop there. Rising from the lounge were a few stairs and suddenly you were up by the toilet and kitchen. Best of all was a back door leading out into a garden full of beautiful red poppies. That was my secret passageway.

The garden being in full bloom makes me think we moved in warm weather. Coastal summer nights can still be chilly though. Unfortunately, Mum couldn't afford to buy coal for the fire. Ever resourceful, she got hold of all the junk mail that shared blocks of flats accumulate by the front door and set light to those. When that died down I could sense her eyes scanning the lounge, looking for something else. Luckily I didn't own anything suitable, otherwise I got the feeling it would have been sacrificed. Drawing a blank, Mum said, 'Come on, we're going out.'

It was pitch black outside. I probably should have been in bed long ago.

'Where are we going?'

Mum smiled and her whole face lit up.

'We're going hunting!'

That was all the encouragement I needed. Our prey, however, didn't quite live up to its billing. For the next half an hour we traipsed up and down the local roads, looking in bins, going through gardens, scrabbling around for anything that looked like it might burn. Finally, laden with boxes and branches and bundles of newspaper, we struggled back home and, a few minutes later, cuddled up together in front of a lovely roaring fire.

That became another of our little rituals. I liked it. We got to spend time together and always had a hug at the end. Even when Mum was too ill or tired to come out scavenging, I would happily do it on my own, trawling the night-time streets without a care in the world, knowing we would be all toasty together soon enough.

Just writing these words makes me feel terrible. No one in their right mind would allow a six-year-old out at night to scrabble for sticks in dark parks and poorly lit streets. And that's the tragedy of it all. Mum obviously wasn't in her right mind. I just didn't realize.

You can only live with what you're given and kids are supremely adaptable. I honestly never noticed anything wrong with the way we carried on. We did what we did. There was nothing for me to compare it to. As far as I knew, every house in the country got by the same way. There must have been hundreds of us up and down the length and breadth of Great Britain, collecting kindling at night. I honestly thought that, if I thought about it at all. I never once suspected it was anything other than normal.

Staring at the fire was pretty much the only entertainment we had. We didn't have a TV or radio, although at some point Mum did take delivery of her old record player and boxes of LPs from Granny's house. I was really excited about it, but Mum wouldn't let me play it while Granny was there. So, as soon as she'd gone, I grabbed the plug and shoved it into the wall. A large button marked 'on' seemed the obvious place to start, so I pressed that and—

Nothing.

Confused, I looked at Mum, who was just staring. Her eyes looked sad.

'Sorry, love, there's no electricity.'

So that's why she wouldn't let me touch it in front of Granny.

I was really disappointed, but not for long. Feeling sorry for myself is not in my nature. I hadn't had a record player that morning and, to all intents and purposes, I didn't have one now either. I was no worse off.

Evenings, then, were spent staring at the red flames burning whatever trash I'd managed to reclaim. Mum would read or doze or smoke her sweet cigarettes, staring into space, just thinking. Sometimes I would sew or knit or crochet, drawing on those life skills Granny had insisted on teaching me. There was nothing I liked more than adding another few feet to my latest *Doctor Who*-style scarf or weaving a few woolly pom-poms for the cat to play with. A few months after moving in, our flat was full of the things.

I also began to play cards. Typical of what I recall as their suburban Jerry and Margo from *The Good Life* aspirations, Granny and Grandpa had regular whist or bridge nights at their home, attended by Grandpa's boss, colleagues and friends. The more I stayed at their house, the more card games I picked up. Granny was the real enthusiast and was happy to give me my own deck and a couple of 'teach yourself' books.

Mum was never interested, so it was just as well that Granny had shown me half a dozen different versions of solitaire. I didn't mind. I enjoyed playing against myself. I loved mastering any new skill. Then, once the fire had died, the light went with it, so that was bedtime. Life was pretty simple.

Without paying the electricity or gas bills, there wasn't much in the kitchen that worked. This didn't seem to bother Mum, though. As I've said, she never really had an interest in food. Apart from our treats at the café in Preston Park, I don't really remember her eating at all. She was much more comfortable with a cigarette in her hand. It's only now that I think: *but why didn't she feed me?*

Mum must have thought she was being clever by not letting Granny discover our lack of power supply when she brought the record player over. It turned out that Granny wasn't fooled for a minute. The next day there was a knock on the door and, before I could panic, I heard her voice. When I opened the door she was holding two foil parcels.

'I've brought your lunch, dear.'

Wow!

I didn't realize how hungry I was until I smelled the warm pie cooked that morning in Saltdean and transported so lovingly the six miles to our house. Mum thanked her, but she didn't eat hers, despite Granny's best efforts.

'Well, I'll wrap it up and you can have it later,' she said.

In the end, I think I had it for tea.

Granny popping round with meals wrapped in foil or cling film became a regular occurrence. She never stayed long, just dropped them off and vanished. It was really lovely of her, especially going to such an effort to keep the food as warm as possible. I couldn't even remember eating a hot meal at home before that. Not that it bothered me. It was just another one of those things.

Granny didn't come every day. I think Mum told her not to. She'd say she could cope. She couldn't though. If Granny didn't appear I'd go out on my bike and see what I could forage or scrounge from the other kids. When that didn't work I turned my attention to the sweet shops. It's amazing how many sweets you can stuff in your pockets while the shopkeeper's turned the other way. It was totally wrong, I knew that. But if I didn't have those sweets I wouldn't be eating that day.

Soon the local shops became wise to my tricks. As is so often the case, it was getting greedy that proved my downfall. I remember at Easter really craving these little chicks made out of pipe cleaners at the sweet shop. Even though it was the chocolate I really needed to fill my rumbling tummy, I couldn't leave without making a grab for one of the wire toys – which is when the shopkeeper's hand landed on mine.

He shouted at me, but I'd seen him do it a dozen times to other kids. I wasn't the only one with sticky fingers, although I might have been the only one who needed to steal to eat.

I was never banned from any of the shops that caught me – I think they expected all children to have a go at shoplifting – but I quickly realized I needed to think of something else. So, with Granny's help, I went shopping for groceries.

'Mum's going to make a roast,' I told her.

That made Granny so happy I didn't dare tell her the truth:

that there would be a roast – but I would be the one cooking it.

That afternoon, while Mum slept, I disappeared into the tiny kitchen and began peeling vegetables, the way I'd seen Granny do it. I took out this large piece of pork and laid it all neatly on a baking tray. I covered it with some grimy oil that looked like it hadn't been touched for years, then shoved it all in the oven. I didn't know what number to turn the dial to, so I span it all the way round. Granny's roasts normally took a couple of hours, so I decided to come back and check then.

I really thought it was that simple. I didn't have a clue what I was doing really. I didn't know if the vegetables needed the same time as the meat or if they went together or even how long the meat required in the first place. It was all guesswork, based on meals Granny had cooked for me down the years – so it was obviously never going to end well.

My biggest mistake, I realized some time later, was not appreciating that the cooker ran on electricity. It didn't matter what number I set the temperature to; with no power, that oven wasn't going to do anything. But I didn't know that. I'd never seen Mum use it, so I didn't know lights should have come on. It didn't even occur to me that it should have been getting hot.

Two hours after I'd put it in, I called Mum to the little table and proudly served her uncooked meat and raw carrots. It was disgusting. Bless Mum, though, she ate a few of the veg. But I was mortified. All that effort and I couldn't get it right. I'd only wanted to feed Mum and I'd failed.

Not every flat we lived in had an indoor toilet, but May Road did, which was lucky because Mum spent a lot of time in there being sick. Sometimes her illnesses came out of the blue. On other occasions they followed a night out. Either way, I would stand next to her with a cold flannel or just hugging her or sometimes crying to see her in distress. I didn't like it.

Mum's nights out weren't as regular as they had been when she was working, but they were a lot more random. They went on for longer too. I watched her dabbing some perfume on one night and studying her face in the mirror, and guessed something was going on. I caught her eye in the mirror.

'Am I going to Granny's?' I asked.

Bending down, she gave me a squeeze. 'You're a big girl now. You'll be all right.'

Yes, I thought proudly, *I will.*

I wasn't scared, I wasn't disappointed. I certainly didn't feel abandoned or anything like that. As much as I loved staying at Granny's bungalow, with all its home comforts, nothing beat the thrill of just being at home. Everything I had – and it wasn't much – was here. Most importantly, though, I wanted to be there when Mum came home. Just in case she needed my help.

So Mum went out and I collected kindling and lit the fire as normal. I promised myself I'd stay awake until she got in, but of course I fell asleep. When I woke, at about five in the morning, she still hadn't returned.

I hope she's all right.

Then I rolled over and didn't wake again till noon.

Sometimes Mum stayed out all night, sometimes she didn't come home for a day or two. I wasn't unduly bothered. It just meant more opportunities to play with friends during the day and more time spent cleaning the flat, crocheting pom-poms or beating myself at solitaire at night. And there was always Mushka to play with in my little cupboard room.

Mum never apologized when she came in, but then I never expected her to. She was the boss. If she popped out for five minutes or five days, that was up to her. It was my job to be there when she returned, to have the place looking as welcoming as I could muster. And besides, she was often so poorly when she came home that no one would have had the heart to be cross with her. I'd just help her undress, whatever time of day or night it was, guide her to her little sofa bed and tuck her in. Then I'd kiss her forehead, wish her sweet dreams and get on with my day. Perfectly fine. And perfectly normal.

Mum never told me not to mention her comings and goings to Granny, but instinctively I didn't. If she called round with food and Mum wasn't in I'd say she'd nipped to the shops. If Granny wanted to hang around I'd say I wanted to play with friends so we'd both leave together. It's not that I thought Mum was doing anything wrong; I just sensed that Granny had her way of thinking and Mum had hers.

One of the things I really loved about Mum, I now realize, was that she treated me like a grown-up. I wasn't, of course. I was six. But every kid thinks they know it all, even the ones who can't tie their own shoelaces. They all dream of killing dragons, flying to the moon and bossing large numbers of people. I was no different. So when Mum let me clean the kitchen, I was delirious. When she allowed me to tidy the hearth and the toilet, it was an honour. Anything I wanted to do, she'd just look at me, smile and say, 'Go ahead.'

Sometimes there were problems even I couldn't fix. Every so often, thanks to Granny's generosity, Mum had enough money to put coins in the meter for a month or two. We didn't have central heating, but suddenly we were able to turn the oven on for a bit of warmth or, best of all, actually play music on Mum's record player. I'd never seen her happier than when she was listening to her music. On nights when she didn't come home, as long as we had power, I'd just play records till I fell asleep. I loved Mum's Bay City Rollers and David Soul albums and I even had my own Brotherhood of Man single and an *Adventures in Toytown* children's LP. I could recite every word of that early talking book – which was useful when, one day, the player just stopped working. I presumed the money had run out, but the lounge light was still glowing.

'Must be the fuse,' Mum said.

'What's a fuse?'

She explained about the plug and said she'd get Grandpa or a friend to fix it. A couple of days later, however, I was at Grandpa's house and I asked him if he had any spare fuses.

'Don't tell me your mother's going to fix something?' he said. 'Wonders will never cease.'

He gave me a couple of fuses and two screwdrivers – one a flat-tip and one a Phillips head. 'Bring back whichever one you don't need.'

Not long after that I was back at home and Mum was out. Nothing out of the ordinary there. Then I remembered the new fuses.

It can't be that hard to fix, I thought.

I got the hang of the screwdriver pretty quickly, then saw where the old fuse was housed. I levered it out with my little tools and popped the new fuse in its place. Then I screwed the backing in place and plugged it into the socket. Hey presto – music!

Not long after, I remember wiring a plug. Nobody told me how to do it; I just looked at another plug and copied what I saw. Can you imagine letting a child play with electricity like that today? Doesn't bear thinking about. But the most dangerous chore I ever attempted was still to come.

*

I don't want it to appear that I was in any way some sort of a slave. I have to stress, I didn't do anything I didn't want to. It just so happened that the thing I liked doing the most was helping Mum. If I could have gone out to work instead of her, I'm sure I would have.

It wasn't so long after the plug change that Mum and I were having an afternoon nap and I was woken by sounds of laughing outside. Mum eventually came round and went to the door. When she opened it, two men just waltzed straight into the lounge.

'Hey, Jenny, how's it going?'

Mum didn't try to stop them, but she didn't look too pleased either.

They must be her friends, I thought, *otherwise how else would they know where we live?*

One of the men put his arm around Mum for a cuddle. Then he noticed me.

'Hello, who's this?'

'It's Cathy,' Mum said. 'My daughter.'

'Hi, Cathy.' The man smiled, but he looked about as pleased to see me as I was to see him.

Then the other man spoke. 'I've got a job for you, Cathy. Do you want to help me?'

Mum looked shocked.

'No, she doesn't!' For a second I could see she was scared. That made me scared too. Just as quickly, she laughed it off and said carefully, 'What do you want her to do?'

'Just a bit of rolling,' the man replied.

Mum relaxed at that. Whatever it was, it wasn't as bad as she'd expected. I, on the other hand, didn't have a clue what anyone was talking about. In the kitchen the man – I'll call him

Mark – pulled out a pouch of tobacco and a packet of Rizla cigarette papers. I'd seen Mum with both, so no surprises there.

'Now,' he said, 'what we're going to do is roll a nice cigarette for everyone and add a bit of this.'

When he pulled out a small, clear bag I actually gasped. It looked exactly the same as the one I'd been told to secrete in the panda.

'What if the police find that?' I said.

Mark laughed. I don't think he imagined a six-year-old would have any idea what he was showing them. It certainly never occurred to him that I'd know it was illegal. Of course, I didn't. All I knew is that the police had come looking for that stuff and taken us to the police station because of it. The last thing I wanted was them calling again.

Mark assured me everything was all right and then he very carefully showed me what he wanted me to do. Illegal or not, I loved a challenge. Watching him sprinkle some tobacco and then a pinch of this other stuff into a flat Rizla, licking and rolling it, then adding a little white filter, was hypnotic. When he'd finished he said, 'Think you can do that?'

'Easy.'

'Show me then.'

So I did.

My first go wasn't the best and he made me do it again. But second and third time lucky, Mark was really impressed.

'Not bad,' he said. 'Now, when I come here again, that's your job, okay?'

I nodded. It had been fun. He seemed nice.

The next time I saw Mark he was with two different guys. Once again he dispatched me to the kitchen with his little bag of herbs. This time, though, he had something else for me.

It looked like something from one of the Saturday morning science-fiction films I'd seen.

'What's that?'

'It's a bong,' he said.

'What's it for?'

'It's for smoking. This is going to be another of your jobs.'

Rolling a cigarette that doesn't look too much like a trumpet is one thing. Getting your head around this glass contraption, with its arms and tubes, was something else. But Mark showed me what needed to be done and off I went. Once again, I had a puzzle and I was determined to solve it.

Mark and his friends came round quite a lot, probably about once or twice a week. I couldn't put my finger on who they were because Mum never looked overjoyed to see them, but she never made any attempt to get rid of them either. So one or two guys would arrive, followed by another pair and another couple, and before you knew it the lounge was chockablock with men – and us.

I was kept busy rolling cigarettes – or 'joints' as they called them – and keeping the bong operational. I liked it. Anything to make Mum's friends happy. But if I'm honest, I seemed to enjoy it more than Mum did. Every time I looked at her she would be smoking and smiling, occasionally inhaling from the glass tubes. But she never looked me in the eye. Her mind always seemed to be someplace else.

Usually everyone just sat around in a huge cloud of smoke, talking and laughing. If I wasn't in the kitchen, I would try to squeeze up close to Mum, but the sweet-smelling fog made me cough. Mark or one of the others would sometimes suggest I go out to play. If Mum agreed, then I would. And Mum always agreed.

*

When Mark and his mates weren't clogging up the flat, and when Mum was awake, we still had a lot of fun together. In the past every day with her had been an adventure. Those days were fewer and further between now, but when Mum was in the mood it was the best feeling in the world.

Sometimes, after the men had been, Mum had a bit more money than usual. Whenever there was a pound or two in her pocket she liked to go out to a café. So, after one impromptu party that had ended in the early evening, off we went. Mum was in a giggly mood all night, which of course was contagious. On the way home we were like a couple of young friends, not mother and daughter. Whatever the other said seemed to be the funniest joke in the world. It was a brilliant night. Then, about five minutes from our house, the night got even better.

'Look at that!' Mum said, stopping suddenly outside a beautiful terraced house.

I followed her gaze to the front door, outside of which stood a terracotta pot containing a sumptuous, colourful trailing plant. I had no idea what it was, but I knew it was stunning. Mum did too. But whereas I was about to consign it to memory and move on, she a better idea.

'Come on,' she whispered, desperately trying not to laugh. 'Let's get it.'

So that's what we did. The pot was heavy and it took the pair of us to lift it. Then we staggered home like a pair of drunken sailors, weaving all over the pavement until we reached the flat. Once inside, Mum put it next to the fireplace, then collapsed on the bed, exhausted.

What a night, I thought, still smiling. *Brilliant.*

Unfortunately, it was about to take a turn for the worse. We'd been in about twenty minutes, maybe half an hour. I'd managed to get the fire going and our new acquisition looked stunning in the flickering light. I was thinking of joining Mum and going to sleep when there was a knock at the door.

Not those men again. They've only just left.

Mum was sound asleep, so I opened the door. But it wasn't Mark and co. It was the police.

'Hello, miss,' the officer said. 'Is there a grown-up at home?'

I must have instinctively looked towards Mum because the policeman followed my glance.

'Is that your mum?'

I nodded.

'Would you wake her up for me, please?'

That was easier said than done, but a few minutes later a bleary-eyed Mum was upright – and ready for an argument.

'We have reason to believe you have stolen a flower pot from a house near here.'

'No I bloody haven't!' Mum said, as indignantly as she could muster. 'How dare you come round here suggesting that.'

The policeman was not fazed by Mum's fury. All the while she was speaking, he was staring at the flowerpot by the fire.

'Can you explain where you got that from?' he asked.

'I bought it.'

'Okay,' he sighed. 'Be like that if you want.'

Great, I thought. *He's giving up.*

'But,' he continued, 'can you explain where this has come from?'

My heart sank when I saw where he was pointing. Just by his feet, at the front door, was a little pile of mud. On closer inspection, it went across the hall and out the door of the building as well.

'In fact, we followed the trail all the way from the house

you stole it from,' the policeman said. 'So you may as well admit it.'

It's laughable really, isn't it? We were so incompetent we'd left a muddy line all the way to our front door. Mum didn't have a leg to stand on, but she was still denying it when the policeman picked up the pot and, chortling to himself, took it back outside. When he closed the door she was still swearing about the liberty he had taken accusing her of stealing.

'But we did steal it,' I said, confused.

'Oh yes,' Mum said, 'we did, didn't we?' and broke out into a huge laugh. I had to join in; it was contagious. 'Did you see the look on his face?' she squealed. 'Why didn't you spot that mud?' But she wasn't angry. She was relieved, I think, that they hadn't put us in the patrol car again.

'What are we like, eh?' she said, and I shrugged.

We were what we were. A team. Which is exactly how I wanted it to stay.

Even though Mum wasn't arrested this time, there was another consequence. If I'd thought about it long enough, I would have remembered that it was the same consequence that had happened after the panda episode. By being naughty, by getting herself noticed by the police, Mum had flagged us up to all the authorities. Sure enough, a few days later, there was yet another knock at the door. Once more I was met by the familiar smartly dressed couple from social services.

'Would you like to come in?' I asked, out of habit.

'That would be lovely,' the woman said. 'Now, is your mother here?'

Then they saw her, waking up from her afternoon nap.

'Mrs Wilson?' the man said firmly.

Mum squinted at the guests.

'Oh, it's you. What do you want?'

'We're from social services,' the man said. 'We have a warrant from the courts . . .' He paused and looked at his colleague.

'And we have come to take Cathy into care.'

FIVE

When Can I Go Home?

It had come out of nowhere.

What had we done wrong? We'd given the plant back. We were so happy, ask anyone. All these thoughts, and more, rushed through my head. But it didn't matter. No one was listening.

The adults started talking. I couldn't follow everything, just a few phrases. They said Mum hadn't replied to letters. They said she had failed to turn up to meetings. They even accused her of not caring enough about keeping her daughter by refusing to talk to them.

That made her angry. I hadn't heard her swear much before, but I did then. It sounded like she'd picked up a few phrases from Mark and his pals.

The upshot was that Mum told them to go to hell and they said that, in fact, she was the one lucky not to be going anywhere because of the way she'd been bringing me up. She was offended, but I was just confused. 'Neglect', 'unruly behaviour', 'a disorderly house', 'enabling truancy'. There were too many words I couldn't comprehend, but the overall meaning was clear: they weren't happy. And, whether I liked it or not, I needed to get ready to leave.

More than thirty years later, I can't believe the actual process of getting me out of the house wasn't more protracted than that, unless Mum really had been seriously slack and had forgotten she'd arranged the meeting. But that confrontation was the only one I remember – just them arriving and me packing a bag and leaving. Alone.

I cried as I left the house and climbed into their waiting car. Normally I would be brave in front of Mum, but she wasn't there. And the realization that she wasn't there made me sob even harder. Wave after wave of questions flooded my head. What had I done wrong? Where was I going? And why?

The two grown-ups in the car with me had the answers. They had briefcases and a file about me and everything. As much as I hated them, I could tell they thought they were doing the right thing. But how wrong they were. They were taking me away from the home where I felt so safe, from the person I loved more than anyone in the world, and replacing it with what? I soon found out.

Whatever the social workers thought I was exposed to at home, they were about to subject me to something far, far worse.

They kept saying it was Mum's fault, but that's not how it felt. If they had such a problem with her behaviour why was I the one going to prison?

No, I decided, *they want to punish me for some reason.* And, boy, did they succeed.

We pulled up outside a large detached house and one of the social workers asked me what I thought of it. I just shrugged. I wasn't going to make this any easier for them.

Actually the house looked nice enough. It stood on the corner of the street and had a garden stretching all the way round. The turf was looking a bit worse for wear during the scorching August of 1976, but the space was large enough for some decent games. There was even a park across the road. In theory, then, it had everything to suggest a very welcoming home.

One step inside, though, and I knew something was wrong. On the way over the social workers had gone to great lengths to explain how special you have to be to be a foster parent. It takes a special person to step in and care for a stranger. It sounded like I was going to meet Jesus himself. In fact, the couple who owned the place were both fat and grubby-looking. I was probably seeking anything to complain about, but for some reason their appearance really offended me.

They look worse than Mum ever has. Why are they allowed to have kids?

There was something about the way they spoke over my head to the social workers that told me it wasn't going to be the most loving of homes. I didn't know how long I was meant to be there, but I already knew that every minute with this pair would feel like an hour.

Of course, they said all the right things to the social workers and even told me how much they'd been looking forward to meeting me. At least, that's what their mouths were saying. Their eyes, on the other hand, looked like they already wished I was out of their sight.

Then I got the tour. I'd almost believed the spiel about foster parents being a special breed, but as soon as I saw the bedrooms I changed my mind. In fact, they weren't so much bedrooms as dormitories, with two sets of bunk beds squeezed into each. It wasn't a haven for the disadvantaged; it was a conveyor belt, one big sausage machine, with children going in one end and money from the local authority churning out the other. There's no way these people were doing anything for the love of it. You could see it in their eyes.

Proof of how little they cared about any of us came when I was shown my bunk. I was sharing a room with another girl and two boys. It didn't bother me – I was too young to be worried about undressing in front of the opposite sex – but I did think it was odd. Then one of our hosts explained everything to me.

'Different ages in different rooms.' Didn't matter if you were a boy or a girl, that was the system.

That wasn't all. Not only did age denote your dorm, it also dictated your bedtime. Seven-year-olds at seven, eight-year-olds at eight, etc. I think there was a cut-off at ten, but either way, what a weirdly regimented set-up.

Coming from an environment where almost anything went, being confronted by all these rules was an unpleasant eye-opener. I'd never had a bedtime with Mum. Granny used to try to get me to sleep at certain times, but usually I could string her out for a few extra minutes. This was different and I hated it. Even with about ten or eleven other kids running around, I don't think I'd ever felt so alone.

As a six-year-old, my bedtime was rounded up to seven. On the one hand, I was glad to get a moment to myself. On the other hand, the second that light went out I just burst into tears. The other kids in my room, the boys in particular, weren't too impressed.

'Oi, shut up!' came one unsympathetic response.

'Yeah, be quiet, baby!' came another.

That made the rest of them laugh. I felt so small and so very alone. But the more I tried to stop crying, the harder it was and the harsher the insults.

'Not scared of the dark, are you, baby?'

Yes, I was – I always had been.

'Maybe she misses her mummy.'

Yes, I do! Didn't they miss theirs? If they did, no one showed it.

'Has poor little baby lost her mummy?'

Laughter.

'Has your mummy dumped you here and run away?'

'No!' I cried. 'That's not true.'

That was the worst thing I could have done. It only gave them fresh ammunition. I was still denying it when I eventually fell asleep, still sobbing.

In hindsight, those kids had their own troubles and they were working through them as best they knew how. It wasn't personal. I was just the latest target. For all I knew, they'd all been through the same tough initiation. Unfortunately, my tears weren't the only expression of my unhappiness.

Waking up in your own urine is a horrible way to start the day. There's that confused moment when you first come round and you try to work out what the odd sensation is. Are you awake or is it still part of a dream? And then you realize. And then you scream.

Suddenly it wasn't just the boys in my room who were shouting at me to put a sock in it. There were bangs on the walls either side. A minute later the door crashed open and my foster dad stormed in.

'What's this bloody racket?'

I was so mortified I could barely find the words. 'I've wet the bed,' I said eventually.

'Have you now?' he grunted. 'Well, sheets are changed once

a week, so you've got a while yet. My advice is, don't do it again.'

And that was it. He just walked out, leaving me to lie in my own wee. I'd been there less than twelve hours and already I hated him.

I must have managed to curl around the damp area, but by the morning it wasn't so much the wetness that was the problem as the smell. I realized then that that was what the whole house stank of: soiled laundry that this pair of so-called caring citizens couldn't be bothered to clean.

In my first week I think I wet the bed three times. You can imagine the stench of my pyjamas and the quality of sleep I must have been having as a result. The worse it got, the harder it was to get back to sleep. And the less I slept, the more scared I became.

Every house has its own voice, those noises you hear in the dead of night when things seem to be clicking and creaking. Some of the other kids loved to pretend there were monsters creeping along the landing and the younger ones always fell for it. That never bothered me. It was the dark that I hated. Even in my little cupboard under the stairs at May Road, I'd always had a bit of light at night, even if it was coming from the moon and stars outside the window. In fact, even though I'd already lived in more places than I could remember, none of them scared me like here because I'd always been with Mum.

Just remembering her set the tears off once more. Yet again I found myself demanding why I was being held captive here. It was horrible and scary and I felt so lonely.

I just want to go home!

Not being allowed visits from my grandparents or mother seemed so cruel. I made an effort to play with some of the other children, but my heart wasn't in it. It didn't matter what the game was, at some point I found my mind wandering back to Mum. I would wonder what she was doing, where she was. More often than not, I worried about whether she was all right. Was she eating? And were those men still coming round all the time?

I hadn't thought about Mark and his cronies for ages before then. Now, with a bit of distance between us, I realized there was a cloud over my head whenever I thought of them. I couldn't put my finger on it. Mark had always been nice enough with me and Mum had always seemed happy enough to see them. She'd certainly never thrown them out. So what was it? What was causing this feeling that something about them wasn't quite right?

The foster dad at this house evoked similar unexplainable fears as Mum's male friends. He was easier to dislike. I didn't like the filthy way he dressed and he was always breathing heavily and wheezing unattractively because of his weight. I'd never make that snap judgement now, but kids live by such random prejudices. He just looked a wrong'un to me. On this occasion I was right.

I don't know how long I'd been there when he first touched me. I was in my bedroom, alone, when he came in. At first I thought he was going to do the laundry early to help me out. But he didn't. He just closed the door behind him and stared at me while I was getting dressed. Then he called me over and made me sit on his lap for a cuddle. I felt like cornered prey. I had no choice. I walked over to him and he crouched down, his back against the door, and then I sat on his knee.

I don't remember what he did exactly, but I knew it wasn't right. The closed door told me that. The fact that he'd never had a good word to say about me told me that. Everything about our cuddle was wrong.

And all the while I could hear that disgusting breathing, like an animal, each new foul exhalation making me have to fight the urge to puke.

It was only after that encounter that I remembered Paul, my old babysitting neighbour, who used to ask me to sit on his lap as well. He was nice. But hadn't he done the same things to me that this man had just done? For the first time, I realized Paul hadn't been so nice after all.

Even though I now suspected the truth about what our neighbour had done to me, I still promised myself I would never tell Mum. She had enough on her plate. It would break her heart to know she'd sent me into the arms of a bad man. That is, it would if I ever saw her again.

The worst thing about my stay at that foster home was not knowing when it would end. Just about the only question I asked in my first few days there was 'When can I go home?'

'That's for us to know and you to find out.'

Something else to hate you for . . .

Then, after about three weeks of hell, my luck changed. For all my claims that it was a prison, we were quite free to come and go, as long as we didn't miss meal times. The foster couple were contractually bound to provide three square meals a day – and that is what they were going to do. No more, no less. Ironically, I probably enjoyed it more than the others. However basic, it was, after all, still cooked food.

I was playing on the climbing frame in the park opposite the house when I heard a voice.

'Hello, my angel.'

I nearly fell off the frame.

73

'Mum!'

I didn't know how she'd found me, but I couldn't get down quickly enough. Before I reached her, Mum started backing away like I'd done something wrong.

'Not so loud,' she said quietly. 'If anyone discovers who I am you'll be moved somewhere else.'

I couldn't believe it. I couldn't even give my own mother a hug in case one of the fat fosters was peering out of their window and saw us.

Reason number three to hate them.

But they couldn't stop us talking. As long as I carried on playing on the swings and roundabouts, I could chat away. No one would suspect we were having anything other than a casual conversation.

The truth is, I would have been happy with that. I would have been happy with anything. I was just so delighted to hear Mum's voice, she could have been talking in her sleep and it would have sounded like music to my ears.

I don't remember much of what was said. Just Mum promising that she would get me out and telling me she was so sorry I was there at all. She would have said more, but I began to well up and she had to stop. There was no way she could not cuddle me if I was crying! Then our cover would be blown.

After what seemed like no time at all, Mum said, 'I'll come here every day at this time. Can you get out?'

'I think so.'

'Wonderful. I love you, Cathy.'

'I love you, Mum.'

And then she was gone.

Going back to my open prison that night was a lot easier,

knowing I had something to look forward to the next day. And I didn't wet the bed.

Straight after lunch, I bounded across the road like a puppy off the leash for the first time. A couple of other kids from the home were there as well and they wanted me to play with them. I tried to join in, but my heart wasn't in it. I couldn't help scanning the park, searching for that familiar figure. But she never came.

The exhilaration I'd felt the previous day was replaced by gloom as I slumped back home. How could she do this to me? How could she just not turn up like that?

The worst thing was, I couldn't tell anyone about it, so I had to endure endless comments about how I needed to cheer up. By the time I went to bed I was still furious. Only in the darkness, with the house beginning its nocturnal symphony, did that slowly change to fear.

What if she tried to come but couldn't? What if she's hurt?

It took no time at all to go from hating her for oversleeping to worrying she was dead under a bus. The dark does that to people, especially kids.

The next day I had two choices: go to the park or not. If I didn't, I would never know if she was all right. But if I did and Mum didn't appear, could I really take that pain?

Of course I went. I'd just about given up hope when I saw her.

'Where were you?'

'Oh,' Mum looked confused, 'you know ...'

I didn't, but I let it pass. She didn't look well. I wasn't going to ruin today by worrying about yesterday.

And so we continued. September turned into October and

that, in turn, quickly became November. By now the weather wasn't exactly park-friendly, but every day I still went out, which had the added advantage of reducing my foster father's opportunities to corner me alone. Some days I'd be home early, dry but disappointed. Other days, successful days, it wouldn't have mattered if I'd been drenched head to foot. I'd seen Mum and that was all that mattered.

There was only one blip. I got used to Mum not showing up more than four or five times a week, but I really pinned my hopes on her being there on one particular day – 15 November. My birthday. And she didn't show up.

I don't think anyone else knew that was the day I turned seven. If they did, they certainly didn't celebrate it with me. But Mum must have known. So why didn't she come?

I couldn't answer that. When I went to bed I reflected on the most miserable birthday ever. No cake, no presents. Not even a single burst of 'Happy Birthday'.

I was so furious I couldn't get to sleep. I'm glad now. If I had nodded off, maybe I wouldn't have heard the sound of pebbles cascading against my bedroom window.

What on earth's going on?

I pulled myself out of my lower bunk and peered through the glass.

No way!

Hiding behind one of the bushes was the unmistakeable figure of my mother. Suddenly I was terrified that she might be seen – but Mum had already thought of that. She was waving and pointing somewhere. I couldn't see from my window, but I could guess where she was directing me to.

A few minutes later, clutching my clothes under my arm, I tiptoed down to the little ground-floor toilet. Throwing trousers and a jumper on, I looked up at the open window. That was what Mum had seen. That was how she expected us to be reunited again.

One foot on the cistern, one on the seat, somehow I managed to pull myself high enough to scramble over the metal window ledge and drop down outside. Luckily, Mum was there to help me down.

I couldn't get over how delirious I was to see her silly, grinning face. For a second we just stared at each other. Then I thought, *I don't care who sees*, and gave her the most massive hug.

'Come on,' Mum said, and we ran over the road, holding hands. I didn't know where we were going, but that didn't matter. I'd have followed that woman anywhere.

About ten minutes later we arrived outside a familiar door. Our own flat. I'd been so close for so long and never suspected. In a way that made me feel even worse.

I couldn't wait to get inside. I'd been away for nearly three months. I just wanted to be home again. I didn't care what the social workers said; this is where I wanted to be. As freezing cold as it was, this is where I felt safest.

We went into the lounge and kept our coats on till Mum got the fire going. Then she lit a cigarette from the flames – one of the special herbal ones I used to roll for Mark – and we both fell back onto the sofa. Suddenly, though, Mum leapt up.

'I nearly forgot, I've got some things for you!'

'Happy birthday, Cathy,' she said, and pulled two presents out of her bag. For that second, I was so happy I thought I was going to burst.

'You remembered!'

'Of course I remembered.'

As I tore off the wrapping, I didn't care what was inside

77

– which was just as well. The longer, more interesting-looking gift was a blue, plastic baseball bat.

Okay, fine. Thanks.

The other one was a jumbo colouring book. On the face of it a much better present, except I didn't have a single colouring pen to my name. I never had.

'Thanks, Mum, they're wonderful,' I said, and flung my arms round her neck. That's when I saw the cat prowling behind us. Without hesitating, I screwed the wrapping into a ball and threw it for the cat to play with.

She loved it. I'm sure she thought it was a mouse, the way she was leaping all over it. Cats have such a way of waiting and then pouncing, leaping up in the air like they've had 4,000 volts through them. Mum and I were soon in hysterics at her antics. You don't need a television when you have a cat pawing paper all over the floor. But then she took a massive swipe and knocked it into the fire.

That wasn't the problem. As soon as it fell into the flames, the paper began to open slowly in the heat and a second later it floated out of the fire and onto the carpet.

I hadn't seen Mum move so quickly since the police had appeared at the door. She leapt up and grabbed the first thing she could reach to put out the smouldering paper. It just happened to be my baseball bat. She smacked the wrapping paper again and again, then, when she was sure it was out, she whacked it back into the fire, prodding it into the heart of the flames for good measure. All of which had a terrible effect on the bat.

In her desperation to extinguish the fire, Mum hadn't noticed the bat getting hotter and hotter until the end actually began to melt. By the time she'd finished, it was completely unrecognizable.

I had to laugh. I'd only ever received two birthday presents from Mum that I could remember in my whole life – and she had just destroyed one of them. As for the other one – a colouring book with no means to colour in – well, she may as well have that for fire food.

But I didn't care. Just seeing her would have been enough. Actually being together in our flat was more than I could ever have dreamed. I genuinely believed I was the luckiest girl in the world.

For the first time in months I slept through the night and woke with a smile on my face. It didn't stay there long. Standing over me was a man in dark clothing. As my eyes began to focus, I realized it was a police uniform. And next to him, there was Mum. The policeman spoke.

'If you'd just like to get up and ready, miss,' he said, 'I'd be happy to drive you back to your home.'

I could have screamed.

Don't you understand? This is my home! I don't want to go back.

'You can't make me go,' I shouted. 'I won't go.'

But, Mum explained reluctantly, they could make me go – and they did.

79

SIX

Don't Touch Me

I don't know whether someone decided to give Mum another chance or whether the warrant was only due to run for a certain period. Maybe my foster parents got sick of me. Whatever the reason, release day came and Mum and I were reunited. A fresh start and, yet again, a fresh home.

Our new place was back in the Preston Park area. A one-bedroom flat this time, a bit tattier than the last one, but quite high up in the block, with a lovely view of St Peter's Church in the town centre. Everyone in Brighton called it 'the cathedral'. I remember staring out at the four gothic spires rising from the top of that majestic building, thinking how beautiful they were, reaching up to the sky. Little did I know they would soon become the source of my worst nightmares.

Seven years old and back with my mum – I couldn't have been happier. Three months is a long time in a child's life and part of me fretted that Mum would have forgotten me somehow. I needn't have worried. We soon slotted back into our old routines. I couldn't do enough for her. Our meals wouldn't win any awards, but I did my best. The flat was a bit grubby, with tattered lino on the kitchen floor, and we didn't have much in the way of cleaning equipment, but I scrubbed and brushed as much as I could. Sometimes Mum would chat to me while I did it. Sometimes she'd say, 'Leave that and come and sit down,' but I needed to do it. On some level, I worried that if the home didn't look nice, the police would take me away again.

I'm not going to let that happen.

For a while Mum and I were inseparable. Then she went out one night and I didn't see her for two days.

Was I worried? Of course I was. But only about her. The only thoughts going through my head were *Who is cooking for her? Where is she sleeping? Who is looking after her?*

It never occurred to me to be worried about myself. I had my own bed, I had our few possessions around me, I could cook any groceries I could slip into my pocket in the shop and play records whenever I liked. The only thing that would have made it better was having Mum to talk to. I was content enough on my own, though.

Mum's nights out weren't the only familiar thing. We were home one afternoon when there was a knock on the door. Before I could get up, it swung open.

Apart from the times Granny came to visit, no good ever came of that door opening. I couldn't hear a knock without fearing the police had come to take me away. On this occasion it wasn't the boys in blue or social workers. It was Mark and another man.

I said hello and went back to sit with Mum. I hadn't quite reached the seat when Mark said, 'And where do you think you're going?' His voice was firm.

'Leave her alone,' Mum said. That's when I realized he was talking to me.

'She knows her job,' he said, walking over. 'Don't you, Cathy?'

I did. How could I have forgotten? I started to head to the kitchen, ready to begin rolling. As I stepped out of the lounge, I glanced back at Mum. She wasn't smiling.

She doesn't want them here.

It was the first time I'd ever noticed.

Mark's friend gave me the stuff to make the cigarettes. He wasn't as nice as Mark, but he was all right. He didn't raise his voice. In fact, he just stared silently. I don't think he trusted me to do a good job. Feeling someone's eyes burning into you is enough to make anyone all fingers and thumbs.

An hour or so later, there were about six men in the tiny flat. By then someone had brought the bong, so I was kept busy preparing that. Mark watched me this time. It was the first time he'd been in the kitchen of our new flat.

'Christ, this place is a tip,' he said, kicking the loose flaps of the well-worn lino. 'We're going to have to do something about this.'

'Yeah,' I replied, not really knowing what he was referring to, and carried on getting the bong ready.

Just then, another man came in. I'll call him Brian.

'We going to get started, or what?'

Mark looked at me, then back at Brian.

What else do they want me to make?

It turned out they didn't want me to do anything.

'I've got something for you,' Mark said, and he fished a small packet out his pocket. It looked like a little paper bag.

'What is it?' I asked nervously.

'It's a sweet.'

I wasn't convinced.

'I'll ask my mum.'

As I went to leave the kitchen, the one called Brian blocked my way. Without thinking, I dived to my knees and scampered through his legs.

'Mum! Mum! Mark wants me to take something!'

Mum's face was suddenly alert – and terrified.

'Leave her alone!' she shouted, pulling me over to hold. 'Don't even touch her.'

The four other men immediately looked to Mark for instruction. He, in turn, looked calmly at Mum.

'We need to have a party, Jenny. I suggest Cathy takes one of these pills.'

I felt shivers run up my spine. The way Mum gripped me, I knew she felt it too.

Pills? What pills? What will they make me do?

Mum was standing now. 'She's not taking anything.'

I held Mum's hand tight. Mark moved to within an inch of her face.

'You know what will happen if she doesn't take them, don't you?'

I couldn't believe what I was hearing. That was a threat. An actual threat. Mum was shaking, I could feel it. What did he mean, 'You know what will happen?' *What will happen? What will he do to her?*

Then a thought struck. *Or is he talking about me?*

I didn't have time to decide. Mum was looking at me.

'I'm sorry,' she said, desperately trying to fight back the tears. 'Come with me.'

Mark stood back and let us pass into the bedroom.

'You'd better do as he says.' Mum sighed. 'They're just sleeping tablets. They won't hurt.'

'But I don't want to sleep.'

'Just do it!' Mum shouted.

Shocked, I slumped backwards onto the bed. *Why is she shouting at me? What have I done wrong?*

Then I realized. She was scared. Scared of what would happen if I didn't take the pill. Scared because she knew exactly what would happen because she'd seen it before.

I had no choice. I was crying now, like Mum, but I held out my hand, took the pill and popped it into my mouth. Mum handed me a glass of water from my bedside cabinet and I swallowed it. Then she helped me lie on the bed and stroked my forehead and told me, 'I'm sorry. I love you.'

And that was the last thing I remember.

The next time I saw a clock it was already after noon. I'd slept for about fourteen hours straight – although, from the cloudiness in my head, it felt more like ten minutes. Looking back, a pill designed to knock out an adult was obviously going to have a severe effect on me, but I couldn't understand why I felt so groggy after such a huge amount of sleep. Gradually the fog cleared, however, and I got on with my business of cleaning the flat and making sure Mum was okay.

The next time I saw Mark and Brian they were carrying a huge, thick tube. Large as it was, I still assumed it must have something to do with smoking.

I suppose they'll want me to do something with that.

They did – but not in the way I imagined.

Mark went straight into the kitchen and called me through. In the past I'd been happy to make his joints for him. It was one of my chores, something for Mum to enjoy as well. Since the last time, though, since I'd seen him speak to Mum in that threatening way, things had changed. I was seeing him with fresh eyes now, like he was a completely different person – one I didn't like one bit. This new man was uglier, he looked older, his teeth were yellower and he stank, mainly of smoke, but after-shave as well. His clothes were stained in places and his breathing was heavy. All things I hadn't noticed before, things I hadn't picked up on when I thought he was a friend. Now I knew the truth. He definitely was no friend of ours.

'You'll be needing this,' Mark said, and he handed me a chunky knife with a short, savage-looking blade.

'What's this?' I asked.

'It's a Stanley knife.'

'What do you do with it?'

He laughed. 'Lots of things. But in this instance, you lay lino with it.'

The penny dropped. The long thing they'd brought in was floor covering. But what was I meant to do with it? 'Just pull up this old crap,' Mark said, kicking the current linoleum sheet, 'and put this down.' He showed me how to hold the knife. 'Think you can manage that?' He was smiling, but there was a tone to his voice I didn't like.

I shrugged. He took that as a yes and left.

I stared at this roll of vinyl, then at the knife, then at the kitchen floor. It was about five foot square. It never occurred to me to say no. The only question in my head was *Where do you start?*

All the while I was working – on my knees, cutting and pushing and trying to inch the stuff into place – I could smell the sweetness of the joints and hear the sound of the bubbling water in the bong, as well as the rowdiness of half a dozen or more men. Some of them were familiar faces, others were new to me. Everyone was laughing. Everyone, that is, except Mum.

I kept straining to hear, trying to make out her voice, but the noise was too great. What if they'd hurt her? What if they'd given her one of those pills?

Every fibre of my body wanted to rush out and check, but I didn't dare. Mark was being nice today, but I'd seen his true colours. If I went out to check on Mum, who knew what he would do to her? It was clear now: he was that sort of man.

It seemed to take forever, but eventually I got the lino down. Absolutely shattered, I stood back and admired my work. As much as I'd hated doing it and I'd hated Mark for making me, I felt really proud of myself. I didn't know why he'd bothered enough to get it done, but there was a part of me that couldn't wait to show him my handiwork.

I stepped cautiously into the lounge. One of the men noticed me.

'Here she is.'

Mark span round. 'I hope this means you've finished,' he said coldly.

I realized I'd been stupid to hope to impress him.

'Yes, finished.'

His face broke into a large smile. 'I've got to see this.' He marched into the kitchen and let out a little whistle. 'Not bad, not bad at all.'

That feeling of pride rose again in my chest. It swelled even larger when Mark said, 'I've got a reward for you.'

A reward? Wonder what it is?

His hand reached into a pocket and I couldn't wait to see what he pulled out. When I did, my heart sank.

'Swallow this and make yourself scarce, there's a good girl.'

I took the pill and, with just a hopeful glance at Mum, made my way to bed. She went to get up, but a strong hand pushed her back down. I closed the bedroom door, forced down the tablet, then buried my head under the pillow. Whatever the men wanted me out of the way for, I didn't want to hear.

I didn't know what business our kitchen floor was of this unpleasant man and nor did I care. The end result was impressive, even if I say so myself. It gave the kitchen a clean feeling. It would be a lot easier for me to keep tidy.

The only thing I cared about was the party everyone had when I wasn't there. I wasn't envious. I knew adults did things that children weren't invited to. But what was it?

My seven-year-old mind couldn't really work it out. Looking back, I obviously did things and saw things that no child should ever do or see, but it was normal for me. Even the Stanley knife was within the bounds of what I was expected to do. It was no different to wiring a plug or cooking a roast. I wasn't aware anything was out of the ordinary. Apart from the sleeping pill.

What were they doing? They could have been going out to a party, but why did I need to be forced to sleep? Mum was often disappearing for a night or two. She didn't have a problem leaving me. Why didn't she just tell Mark and his friends that I was old enough to look after myself?

So I decided the party had to be taking place at the flat. For them to want me out of the way made me think that I would have heard things they didn't want me to. Otherwise they would just have told me to stay in my room. Looking back, I have to imagine drugs featured heavily, but at the time I wasn't aware of what drugs were – the joints to me were just cigarettes. Marijuana was such a regular feature of home life that if it hadn't been for the episode with the police and the panda, I would never have suspected there was anything illicit about it at all. It was as commonplace at the Wilson home as tea or eggs. More commonplace, actually.

The one thing I do know is that Mum always fought it. She was always resistant to the pills. Sometimes she stood right in Mark's or Brian's or whoever's face – they all seemed to carry these tablets – and screamed that she wasn't going to let them do it to me. That made me more proud than any workmanship in the kitchen. But she never won. Usually the men just raised their voices. Then, one day, they raised their hands.

I thought I was going to be sick on the spot. I was on my way to the bedroom anyway, resigned to the usual routine. Mum needn't have got herself into trouble, but she was in a spirited mood. She paid for it with a crack across her face.

Stunned, her legs gave way and she collapsed. Before I could move towards her, a man put his arm in my way.

'Bed or she'll get another one.'

I didn't need to be told twice.

After that, I never hesitated again when they sent me away. I didn't want them to touch a single hair on Mum's head and I knew that was the only way to stop them. I wish Mum had realized it too. If she did, then she never showed it. Time after time, she stood up for me and got a hard swipe across the cheek for her trouble. It seemed to be every time now. Something had escalated. The relationship between her and the men, whatever it was, had somehow got worse.

I never lost the sense that I needed to look after Mum. Whether it was cleaning or cooking or worrying that she'd remembered her coat on a cold night, I always looked out for her. Knowing that if she didn't let them drug me she would be hurt drove me mad. I found myself almost sprinting into the bedroom.

If I'm quick, Mum won't have time to argue – and she won't get hit.

Sometimes it worked. Other times I'd hear the smacks through the thin walls. Seeing her be hit was horrific. Hearing the attack – because that's what it was – and wondering what had happened to her was somehow even worse. I didn't dare cry out in case it made things worse for Mum. But anyone listening at my door would have heard me crying as quietly as I dared, cowering under my blankets, imagining horror after horror.

Mum, though, didn't give in. One day I was in the kitchen rolling joints when I was told it was pill time, so I had to make sure everything was neat before I could leave. That gave Mum plenty of time to object. Too much time. Even though we were in different rooms, I could hear every word of the argument. I realized I was tensing, just waiting for the moment someone's hand struck her face. This time, however, Mark went further.

'If you don't shut up,' I heard him say, slowly and calmly, 'I'm gonna do to Cathy what I'm about to do to you.'

That was it. Silence. I didn't hear another peep out of Mum, not even when I emerged from the kitchen and traipsed over to the bedroom. Just before I closed the door I dared a glimpse in Mum's direction and shuddered. Her face had a new level of terror etched all over it.

Why?

Mulling it over in the bedroom, I realized Mark hadn't hit her because that never seemed to work. So he'd threatened to hurt me instead. I didn't know how. Something about doing to me what he was going to do to Mum. It sounded ominous but unclear. Whatever it was, Mum knew exactly what it meant. And that was enough to keep her quiet. I cried as I realized she was sacrificing herself for me.

Over the course of I don't know how long, things worsened. The men were still only coming round about twice a week, but their manner changed. They used to be friendly. Mark, in particular, would go out of his way to keep me onside. I thought he might have been trying to impress Mum, like a boyfriend, by making me like him. I couldn't think of another reason. And she'd seemed to like them all in the early days. At least, she'd appeared to. Was there ever much more than indifference in her eyes when they'd arrived those first few times? Every time I thought about it, the memory was just too far out of reach.

Now, though, with the pills and parties and the threats against me, the atmosphere in the flat whenever the men were there was hideous. I literally felt sick whenever the door opened and there they were. I prayed each time that it wouldn't be them, but more often than not it was. We had no friends, so who else would come round? I wasn't the only one devastated by their arrival. Mum began making less of an effort to pretend she was happy to see them. Some days it was as though she barely registered they were there until the threats started. Then she'd look at me, like she was trying to focus on my face, and say, 'Leave her out of it.'

Mostly the men did leave me out of it. Mostly.

As I went to close the bedroom door one night, I felt the handle lift back up. Someone was trying to come in.

'Mum!'

But it wasn't. It was one of the men. Brian.

'What do you want?' I asked him. 'I've got my tablet.'

I held it up to prove it. In fact, eager for him to go away, I swallowed it down, no water.

'I'm not here for that. I just wanted to make sure you were comfortable.'

This isn't good.

I closed my eyes and willed the sleeping tablet to do its work, but my senses were on red alert. I couldn't switch off. I was so intent on listening that I didn't even dare breathe. Then I felt the mattress sag with the weight of someone sitting down next to me on the edge of the bed.

My last thought as I passed out a few minutes later was *Why is Brian touching me there?*

It was my old foster parent's behaviour all over again. Outside, I heard my mother scream.

Violence was slowly becoming a way of life – no longer was there just the threat of it. And the worst was still to come.

I didn't know what I'd done to offend them, or what Mum had done, but there was a distinct change in attitude. Some of the men had virtually ignored me at first. Now they seemed to go out of their way to throw insults in my direction. One or two occasionally held me in ways I didn't like.

'Come on, Cathy, sit over here. Keep me company.'

I knew that if I did I'd be fighting off wandering hands, but, as much as I hated it, I always thought, *If they're hurting me, they won't be hurting Mum.* But it didn't always work like that.

Sometimes the men weren't interested in parties and making me sleep. Not immediately. Sometimes they wanted food. Mum never cooked for the two of us, but Mark or Brian insisted that she fix them something. I offered to do it instead.

91

'Jenny's all right, aren't you?' Mark laughed unpleasantly.

'I'm fine,' Mum said.

They made me leave the kitchen, but as soon as I heard raised voices I was back. I don't know what had been asked of her, but Mum was adamant she wasn't going to do it.

'You will,' Mark was saying.

'No, I will not!' Mum virtually spat the words into his face and ran towards the door. She was quick – but Mark was quicker. He grabbed her long blonde hair, the hair she was so proud of, the hair I loved to sit and brush for her, and tugged it hard, stopping Mum in her tracks. It must have hurt because she screamed the place down. Instinctively I screamed too. My reaction was fear. Hers was pain. Mum was on her knees, but he was still holding her hair.

Why hasn't he let her go?

Stupidly, she went to move again, but he jerked her head back, like he was yanking on a dog's lead. Mum swore at him and he did it again, but this time dragging her backwards across the floor.

I couldn't stand it anymore. I flew over to Mark and started beating his chest with my angry little fists. I wanted to hurt him, but mainly I just wanted him to let Mum go. He didn't want either of those things.

Still holding Mum's hair so tightly that her head was tipped right back, he waved his other hand in my direction and knocked me clean to the floor. My ear was buzzing where he'd caught me. I went to get up again, but he started swearing at me, so I sat still, crying, and begged him to let Mum go.

If only Mum had begged as well. She might have stood a chance. But she wasn't having a bit of it. I didn't understand half the words that were pouring from her mouth, but I knew they weren't complimentary. What happened next will stay with me forever.

Reaching over to the cooker, Mark flicked one of the gas hobs on. Still Mum kept screaming at him, and still he kept swearing at her to shut up and behave. I honestly had no clue what he was doing with the hob – until he gave Mum's hair a massive tug and dragged her backwards towards the oven.

The next few seconds passed in slow motion. Somehow Mark got Mum's head right next to the flame and, just as I thought he was going to put her face in it, he twisted her round so her hair trailed across the fire. It went up in an instant.

I'd thought I was all screamed out, but I found a new voice. So did Mum. We were both wailing and I was convinced she was on fire. But suddenly she slumped to the floor and I could see she wasn't. For a moment I thought Mark had let her go. Then I saw that he was still clutching about a foot of Mum's beautiful, beautiful hair. The second the flame had burned its way through her tresses, she'd fallen forward. As she knelt sobbing on the floor, I studied the back of her head. She looked terrible. But at least she was alive.

Three days good, one day bad, two days good, one day bad. That was an average week – except there were no averages. We couldn't predict when Mark and co would arrive. If we could have, maybe we wouldn't have been there.

I'd really like to think that Mum would have been strong enough to avoid them. Yet even as a child I was aware that there was something that made her keep seeing them. Something that stopped her from going to the police after the hair-burning incident. Something that they had and she wanted.

Just reliving the hair episode now has had me in floods of

tears. I wish I could forget the memory, but it just won't fade, the sight of my mother, dragged around like a rag doll, then terrorized near that naked flame. I can still hear her screams. They're always with me. Sometimes I wake up at night, shaking, with her fear searing through me as though it had happened yesterday. And every time I remember, I hate myself for not being able to stop it. She was my mum. Why couldn't I save her? And why did she let them come back?

That whole period is full of pain I've tried hard to forget, but two other incidents have stayed with me.

Looking back, realizing what these men were capable of, I question why Mum or I ever dared to argue with them. I guess the answer is, we had to. If you give in blindly, the game is over. I didn't understand the rules as a seven-year-old, but that's definitely how it was. If we hadn't fought with them, then maybe they would never have left. It might have been seven days on, no days off.

Fighting back every so often is what kept us alive inside, I'm sure of that. I hated myself at the time for not being able to stop the vicious bullying, but at least I tried. Time after time, I tried. Even when they held a knife to my face.

One of the men had asked Mum to do something. I didn't hear what, or at least I don't remember – maybe this is my brain being kind to me. What I do recall is shouting out 'No!' and rushing to her side. One of them pulled me back by the arm, so I tried to bite him. I didn't make any impression through his leather coat, but he was annoyed. He wrapped his arm around my neck and whispered in my ear, 'If you don't behave, you're going to suffer.'

I was so intent on breaking free from his grip that I didn't notice what his other hand was doing. Then I saw a glint of light out of the corner of my eye. A second later, I felt something cold on my cheek.

A knife!

It was the Stanley knife I'd cut the kitchen vinyl with. This blade had sliced effortlessly through tough plastic. I knew exactly what it could do to me.

Instinctively, I pushed back into the man's body, twisting my head, trying to put a few millimetres between my face and the knife. I felt his grip tighten, but at least he pulled the knife back.

That's when Mum saw what he was doing. The look on her face told me how much danger I was in. This wasn't a game.

'Put it down,' she said calmly. 'I'll do anything you want.'

'You hear that?' the man said to me. 'Your mum's going to behave. The question is: are you?'

'She'll behave,' Mum answered for me. 'Won't you?'

I nodded as best I could.

'Good,' my captor grunted. 'Because I don't want to have to remind you what will happen if you don't.'

Then he let me go and my knees buckled. I wanted to run to Mum, but I couldn't. She came over to me instead and led me to the bedroom. As we went inside, I heard the man talking to the others about football or something. They were laughing. It was as if the last few minutes had meant absolutely nothing to him at all.

The sensation of the knife pressing into my skin and seeing the light reflecting off the sharp steel blade had been awful. It was a wake-up call, I suppose. After what had been done to Mum in the kitchen, I knew he wouldn't have been afraid to use it. He was prepared to back up his threats with action – which just made the threats themselves all the more potent.

I don't know if the men sensed I was more scared than ever, or whether they enjoyed the power, but even though I tried to behave, they never stopped the ultimatums. 'If you don't do this, I'm going to do that.' Everything was a threat now. It became their currency. Consequently, a lot of the time, the intimidation barely registered. I was programmed to behave anyway. It didn't matter what the specific details were. In a sense, accepting that gave me a little bit of power. I was the one deciding to obey them. I had control. All their menacing strong-arm tactics were water off a duck's back. I remember thinking, *There's nothing you can say to hurt me now.* But I was wrong.

Mark came up to me in the kitchen. I was rolling joints like a good girl. In the past he'd leave me to it or even chat to me while I beavered away. That time was long gone. The relationship had changed. He seemed to take pleasure in reminding me that I was doing it for him.

He was looking out the window when a thought seemed to strike him.

'Cathy, you know what I'll do if you or your mother don't behave today, don't you?'

'No,' I said, not interested. We were going to behave, so it wasn't an issue. I didn't need to hear the gruesome details.

'See the cathedral?' he continued.

I looked up briefly. Of course I could see it. It was my favourite view. When I was alone I loved staring out at that amazing structure.

'See the spires?'

I nodded. I didn't have to look. I could picture the four shards tapering towards the sky with my eyes closed. They were my favourite part. But Mark wasn't interested in what I liked or didn't like.

'If you give me any trouble today,' he said smiling, 'I'm going to drag you up to the top of that tower and I'm going to hang you by your neck from one of those spires. Do you understand me?'

I tried to nod again, but my head felt so heavy. The idea of being tied by my throat to the spire weighed on me more than anything else he'd ever threatened. I could see the spires, just like I could see the knife when that was brandished. These weren't idle threats.

He'll do it. I know he'll do it.

In one fell swoop that vile man in our kitchen had quashed every romantic dream I'd ever had staring out of that window. Gazing across to the church and imagining its marvellous past had always filled me with a sense of wonder, a feeling of hope. The majesty and the magic of the building sometimes made my head feel like it might explode. But all that was over now. He'd killed it. The spires were no longer things of beauty. They were threats. Weapons that taunted me.

For days afterwards I couldn't look out of the window without crying in genuine fear for my life. Irrational, but real at the same time. How would he have managed to drag me up there? If I'd thought about it, I would have realized it didn't make sense. But you don't analyse when you're too afraid to breathe. To this day, I can't see St Peter's without the pit of my stomach churning.

After that I was a changed person. More compliant than ever, meeker. I tried to be strong for Mum, but it was hard. Mark seemed to notice that he'd struck gold with this threat. He only had to gesture towards the window and I'd shrink, hide, do whatever he wanted. He'd won. My one sanctuary in the whole mess had been desecrated.

The thing about bullies is, they only succeed if you let them. That's what I've always been told. They're just cowards, the theory goes. They look for a sign of weakness then work away on it, concentrating all their efforts there.

Well, by accident or design, Mark had found my weakness. Being hanged from a steeple, it turned out, really was my worst nightmare. But I also knew he'd discovered Mum's weakness a long, long time ago. Her Achilles' heel was much closer to home. Me.

I hadn't picked up on it at first, not in the early days, when the men had tried to appear nice in front of me. I'd see Mum arguing and then she'd suddenly go quiet. Often one of the men would have mentioned my name. I hadn't put two and two together at the time, but now the sums all added up. Whenever she wouldn't stay in line, they'd make a suggestion about me. That was the only thing she couldn't fight. I was the stick they were using to beat her with.

That dawning realization almost sent me crazy. My initial reaction was: *I have to get away. Things would be easier for Mum if I weren't here. I could go to Granny's. She'd let me stay. Then the men would stop hurting Mum.*

But what if they didn't? That was even worse. At least in the same flat I could monitor what was going on. *I can protect her if I'm here.* I don't know what exactly I thought a seven-year-old could do to help, but in my mind it seemed things had to be better in the long run if we stayed together.

Looking back, these same thoughts must have been running through Mum's mind as well. I thought I was so in control, but she was the one protecting me. I didn't know what she did when I was made to sleep, but I know now that it was for my benefit.

Realizing that the men were using Mum's love for me to

manipulate her had a weird effect on me. Partly, I felt ashamed, as though I were somehow on the men's side. Partly, though, I felt such a swell of pride. To think Mum would put herself through so much pain for me. Her sacrifice still brings a lump to my throat all these years later.

It was a very emotional time. One thing was clear, however. I swore that I would never, *ever* let myself be blackmailed like this by anyone. Even as a child that was obvious.

Don't give anyone the opportunity to control you, like they control Mum.

If only I'd listened to my own advice . . .

After the spires threat, everything seems to have become jumbled in my memory. Lots of things happened at once, all as horrific as each other in their own way.

One day Brian appeared more attentive than usual. He also seemed very drunk. I know now it was the effects of marijuana, but in those days I didn't really associate any strange behaviour with the joints I was rolling. I didn't see, either, that this explained Mum's up-and-down behaviour – sleepy, mellow or hyper-hyper. It's obvious to me now that her moods were drug-related.

'Get your coat,' Brian said, the words more slurred than I'd ever heard. 'We're going for a walk.'

I looked at Mum and she looked back. We both knew what would happen if I resisted. So, weird as it was, I got ready and out we went.

'Where are we going?'

'To the park. You like parks, don't you?'

Of course I did. I had such happy memories of illicit meetings with Mum at one. But why did this unpleasant man want to go to one with me? More strangely, why did he want to go for a walk when he was struggling to stay upright?

Preston Park itself is pretty huge, so I didn't know if we would go to the playground part of it. Eventually we found ourselves at the rockery, apparently the largest rock garden in the country, even then. It's really beautiful and you can get lost in the wonderful scenery, but as I splashed my way through the puddles there was only one thought in my mind.

Why has he brought me here?

Deep down, I knew the answer, or at least a variation of it. He was going to touch me again, like he did in my bedroom sometimes. For some reason, though, he didn't want to be near his mates.

The more I thought about it, the more terrified I became. I couldn't imagine what his intentions were, but if he wanted privacy from his equally disgusting friends then, I convinced myself, it had to be really bad. Before I knew it, I was shaking in fear.

I was so petrified, in fact, that when I saw Brian lose his footing and fall headfirst into a pool of shallow water, I didn't move. I didn't help him when I saw he was face down and not moving. I didn't even ask if he was all right. I just stood there, watching. And then, after about five minutes, I walked back home.

Every day after my walk with Brian I waited for him to come back through our door. I waited for him to hurt me in the privacy of my bedroom. To grab me by the hair and throw me onto one of the spires at St Peter's. He would exact his revenge, I knew that.

Then I thought, *What if he doesn't come for me? What if he never woke up?*

That thought was even more terrifying. Then I really would be killed. Mark and his friends would see to that. They would have to prove I was under control.

A feeling of dread settled in my stomach as the days passed. At times I struggled to breathe. Each footstep I heard in the communal hall sent me running for my room. Every creak of the old house at night had me convinced Brian was coming back for his retribution. But it didn't happen. And the next time there was a knock at the door it wasn't the men at all.

It was a social worker and two policemen. And, yes, they'd come to take me away again.

SEVEN

Did You Miss Me?

At my lowest points at Preston Park I admit to occasionally thinking, *I would be better off in care.*

I never meant it, though. It just seemed a way out, once I realized that Mum's men friends were using me as a bargaining chip in their game of wills. But I'd felt a lot more uncomfortable under the unyielding regime of the smelly foster parent with the wandering hands than I'd ever felt at home. Because at home I had Mum. We were a team. As far as I was concerned, as long as we were together, the world was all right.

Then I found myself taken into care for the second time. I couldn't believe how sudden these things were, but Alice, the social worker, claimed Mum had ignored all their correspondence. I didn't know what to believe. Alice looked honest enough and certainly opening letters wasn't Mum's favourite pastime, judging by the bundles by the front door. I did wonder why it had happened now, though.

'There were a number of factors,' Alice explained.

'Like what?'

Alice took a deep breath. 'Where do I start?' She then reeled off a list of what she called evidence. For a start, without me knowing, Mum had been picked up by the police a few times recently and taken to the station to cool down. It was usually for shoplifting, Alice said, which had escalated into an argument or fight when she'd been caught. Ever the dutiful child, of course, I denied it was possible – even though I'd seen Mum shoplift plenty of times. But who didn't do that?

Then there was the fact that council records showed I was still not enrolled at school, which was a serious offence. Finally, the last time Mum had been spotted by the police, they'd noticed her hair. Mum had made up some story, but policemen aren't stupid. They know the signs of domestic abuse when they see it. And that was when they'd reported it and I'd been removed for my own protection.

When she put it like that, Mum's life sounded horrible. Mine too, I supposed. And that was without mentioning the men. Even so, I still didn't want to be taken away. And I certainly didn't agree with her when she said I'd been 'rescued'.

I lost track of how long we drove for. Even though I stared glumly out of the car window, I wasn't taking anything in.

Eventually we stopped outside an ordinary-looking block of flats on a non-descript Brighton street. It could have been anywhere. I would be moving into a flat on the third floor. At first glance it didn't look anything like as nice as my last foster home – but that place had been hellish the second you stepped through the front door. This one was less imposing on every level. But would it, I wondered, be any better?

The answer, if I'm honest, is yes. I hated being there, of course, but then I would have hated being anywhere. I felt like I'd abandoned Mum, thrown her to the wolves, and the guilt made me feel nauseous. But my new temporary family genuinely did their best to help me take my mind off it.

For a start, it didn't seem like we were all part of a foster-care production line. There were two parents, two of their own children and then two of us fosters. I shared a room with the family kids, rather than the other foster girl, and went to bed when the others did. There were no weird rules, no special treatment for the actual family kids. So when the family sat down to eat breakfast, we all had the same thing – porridge. The problem was, everyone else seemed to love it. I thought it was revolting, but we were allowed to stir in one teaspoon of malt syrup to make it taste nicer. The big game was to try to sneak another spoonful in when the mother wasn't looking. That made breakfast a little more fun.

It took me a while to realize that, however tasteless I found the porridge, it was actually a treat to have someone cooking for me. Not only that, but my washing was done and although we all chipped in with a few chores, the flat was spotless. It was nice to have a break from doing all that myself.

I shouldn't have to mention it, but, considering my past experiences, I was also aware that no one tried to touch me inappropriately. It's terrible that that counts as a plus.

The other girl and I were so welcome as part of this couple's family that at the end of the week, when their own children were given a couple of pennies as pocket money, so were we. I'd never got pocket money from Mum before – this was a new experience for me. The only proviso, the mother said, was 'You have to buy liquorice with it. I'm not having you all getting rotten teeth, not while you're under my roof.'

She was paranoid about tooth decay and so we were only allowed to shop at one particular sweet shop, where she knew the owner and would be told if we bought anything other than liquorice. I wasn't a huge fan of the aniseed flavour, but just going to the shop on a Friday was a treat for another reason.

The first time we set off for the little sweet shop I didn't pay attention to the streets. The other kids knew where we were going – that was good enough for me. But when we arrived I thought, *I know where I am!* I may have lost track of directions in the car, but, unless I was very much mistaken, we were only ten minutes from home! As soon as the other three kids came piling out of the shop, I said, 'I'm just going for a walk – I'll see you later,' and I ran off down the street.

The look on Mum's face was a picture. Once she'd got over the shock of it being me and not the police or those men, she couldn't stop smiling.

We had a lovely time, but after about half an hour Mum packed me back out the door before I was noticed as being missing. She didn't want more trouble with the law.

'I'll come back next Friday!' I promised.

'You'd better!'

And I did. I think I was at my new home for twenty-eight days, so that was three or four clandestine visits back to Mum. I didn't care whether she was tired, slurring or full of beans. I just cuddled her tightly and listened as she said, over and over, that she was sorry.

'I'm going to sort everything out, Cathy,' she said. 'I'm going to make everything all right.'

And I truly believed she meant it.

In 1977 my grandfather had the option of taking early retirement from work. If he did he was entitled to a lump sum of £4,000 plus a reduced pension for the rest of his life. Grandpa was a busy person; he loved having something to do. He really wanted to stay on at Wills Tobacco, but more than that, he really needed the money. Because Grandpa had a plan.

After I'd been taken into care again, Mum had reached a watershed moment. She'd confided things to Granny, who in turn had told Grandpa. I don't think she could have told him everything. Grandpa never even knew about the meals Granny used to bring us every other day. As a former army man, he acted swiftly. He said, 'We have to put some distance between you and these men.'

So, with the £4,000 early-retirement cash, he bought Mum a lovely attic flat in a four-storey townhouse in Telscombe Cliffs, about twelve miles from Preston Park.

'You should be safe here.'

That was the plan. And that was where I was taken when I emerged from my month in care. It's possible Mum had to agree to move house and try to sort herself out before I would be allowed out. I don't know. All I can say is that she really made an effort. For a month or two everything was just about perfect.

The flat had one large bedroom, a little kitchen, a bathroom and a nice lounge in the eaves, with criss-crossing support beams. I was eight years old by now and Mushka the cat was probably older, but we both loved running in and out of the rafters. Granny gave me a ball on a piece of string and the cat and I would hare around, with her trying everything to catch that ball. Looking back, it's staggering to think of the bounce-backability of children. After everything I'd been through, every horror I'd witnessed, it took no effort at all to revert to a normal child, happy to waste hours on the most innocent of games.

Just when I thought I'd exhausted the possibilities of the flat, I discovered the cupboards leading out into the thinnest points of the roof. They were so dark and so deep – and so full of treasure! The previous tenants hadn't cleared everything out, so I spent a day dragging what they'd left behind out and sorting through it. Most of it was rubbish, but in amongst it all was the prize I'd been hoping for. A toy.

It was a car and about four feet of plastic track. I worked out that if you assembled it all properly, the car would whizz down the track and loop the loop like Evel Knievel. What a fantastic game – and something else the cat tried to play with!

I couldn't remember a time when I'd been any happier. For a while it really felt like we were living inside a bubble, free from the outside pressures of the world. When I wasn't exploring every inch of our flat, I'd be out in the cold, playing on my odd-wheeled bike. With the saddle and handlebars extended, it was still the right size for me. We found another hall that sometimes showed Saturday morning films, like in the old days. I even enrolled for the Brownies, which I really liked, and I joined the church choir with Granny. Most staggering of all, one day I found myself dressed in a little blue jumper, grey skirt, white blouse, knee-high socks and round-toed shoes and was introduced to a tall, thin woman.

'Hello, Cathy, I'm going to be your teacher.'

After eight years I was at school. I admit, it was hard. I liked being around all the other children, but keeping quiet was a strain. I wasn't used to sitting still much either. Most of my days had been spent keeping busy, busy, busy, cooking, playing, cleaning and looking after Mum. The shift in gear was incredibly difficult to get used to. From the teacher's point of view, she'd been handed a girl who'd been in and out of care, had seen things no child should ever be subjected to and had become almost totally self-sufficient. Finding a way to connect with me was as taxing for her as the whole experience was for me.

And then there were the actual lessons themselves. Apart from a few happy months at the Rainbow Nursery, I'd never had anything close to a day's schooling in my life. Suddenly I was being confronted by books and exercise pads and pens and blackboards. Until that day, it had never occurred to me that I couldn't read or write. All the other kids could recognize their own names and write them, as well as other words. For the first time, I got a genuine sense that my life might not have been as normal as I'd assumed.

Like so many children, I enjoyed my first day at school, but this was mainly because of the novelty value. When Mum said I had to go back the following day, I tried to fight her. It just wouldn't sink in that I should be attending every day. In the end, the only argument that persuaded me was coated in threat.

'If you don't go to school the social worker will take you away again. It's up to you.'

As arguments go, that was pretty persuasive.

As much as I resented being made to go to primary school every day, I soon began to enjoy the order of the day. First thing, I'd make breakfast and take Mum hers. Then off to school. It didn't take long to find some other local kids to walk with and the journeys passed in no time. I was having so much fun one morning that I was nearly run over by a Mini. I tripped crossing the road and, when I saw this car hurtle towards me, I really thought that was the end. There was a squeal of brakes, just like in films, and a smell of rubber. In the end, it skidded to a halt inches from my body. My legs were like jelly for the rest of the day.

Then, after school, it was home again to cook some tea for me and, if she was there, Mum. But as soon as I started school I noticed Mum began to be around less and less during the day.

And, as was so often the case with her, an afternoon would quickly turn into an evening, and perhaps longer.

On the days when Mum wasn't in, I just turned back round again and went out to play. It didn't bother me. How many other kids had that choice? Even though I was new to the area, I always found someone to mess around with. That was never a problem. Of course, you didn't always know what they were really like. One day a couple of us climbed a wall. It was about double my height, so probably around six foot. I was sitting up there, like the king of the castle, when I got shoved in the ribs and suddenly I was plummeting towards the ground. I put my arms out, but my nose got a taste of the pavement. I remember being in agony. It was the most pain I'd ever experienced. I was sure it was broken. I started running back home, but the pain was so bad I could barely see. Blood was streaming down my hands as I tried to stem the flow. Worst of all, in all the chaos, I clean forgot I was returning to an empty flat.

We had no first aid kit, no TCP, not even plasters. All I could do was stuff toilet paper up my nose and curl up on the sofa to cry until the pain subsided. Then I got up and dared to look in the mirror. Nothing looked out of place, nothing was broken. It was over.

I wished Mum had been there, but not because of any medical need. She wouldn't have known what to do any more than I did. I was comfortable with that. Something else that was normal. A hug would have been nice though.

Not having a parent around to look after me was so second nature that I never questioned it. I didn't even query why Mum was spending so much time away from our lovely flat. She'd always come and gone as she pleased. That was how I expected her to behave. While she was away I'd cook, sometimes even attempt to bake a treat for her. Then I'd sit in the lounge or in the bedroom, staying awake as long as possible after a hard day at school, playing with Mushka or just singing along to records. I'd found the David Soul album that included 'Don't Give Up On Us' in Mum's collection and that was on repeat for as long as I was alone in the flat. Again, how many kids had that freedom?

When Mum came home, it was action stations. Not from her – whether it was morning or night, she usually returned looking completely vacant. She always reminded me of Brian staggering and stumbling up the hill to the rockery. The only difference was that she was lovely, so very lovely, and he really wasn't.

There would follow a day of recuperation. Sometimes sleep would be enough, sometimes she'd eat. If I presented her with a cake she always made an effort to eat it. Often, though, she was too ill. I hated seeing Mum too sick to make it to the toilet in time. At least I could clear up after her, make her as comfortable as possible. As long as I could be useful, I was content.

Looking back, it was all upside-down, wasn't it? For a moment, when I'd fallen off that wall, I'd been a normal eight-year-old girl in search of parental aid. When I hadn't found it, I'd reverted back to my default position – of looking after my own dependant instead. Mum was the child, I was the adult. It was all wrong.

Mum didn't seem in the best of shapes. She was often so lethargic that days would disappear before she even emerged from her bed. And yet she still looked so tired. I began to notice dark rings under her eyes. When I asked her, she said she was fine. Everything was fine. That was good enough for me.

When she wasn't ill or absent, we had really good times

together. Our Telscombe Cliffs flat had such a lovely, light atmosphere, just being there made us smile. Compared to the Preston Park place, it was heaven itself. I couldn't think of those small rooms without my blood going cold. It had become synonymous in my memory with the evil goings-on of those vile men.

But that chapter was behind us now. Thanks to Grandpa, we had a chance at a new life and I, for one, had taken it with both hands. Mum, in her own way, was relishing the freedom as well. We spoke about how nice it was not to be worried about the next knock on the door. Social workers couldn't complain because I was attending school. The police had no reason to bother us, Mum assured me, because she had nothing illegal in the house. And the men who'd come close to ruining our lives had no idea where we were. Everything was rosy.

And then, one afternoon, I came home from school, pushed open our front door and heard a familiar voice.

'Hello, Cathy. Did you miss me?'

About a week earlier, Granny had taken me aside. She was behaving weirdly, I thought, a bit cryptic.

'Cathy, I think you might need to phone me this week,' she'd said, and pressed a couple of five pence pieces into my hand. 'This money is only to be used for the phone, do you understand? Don't go spending it on sweets. Save it. I think you'll need it.'

I had no idea what she was talking about, and she wouldn't tell me.

'I hope you don't need to call me,' she went on. 'But if something happens that you don't like, anything at all, then you tell me straightaway.'

I learnt later that Mum had confided to Granny her fear that the men had tracked her down. She didn't explain how it had happened, although Granny felt that if Mum insisted on still going out to her regular haunts at night, then she wouldn't have been that hard to trace. Granny had said she would help. She was sorry she hadn't known what was going on before. And that is why she'd given me the money for the phone box. She knew the men were coming back.

They were there en masse. About fourteen blokes, more than I'd ever seen at one time, were squeezed into our little flat. I could barely see for the fog of joints they'd obviously rolled themselves, but I recognized most of the faces. They'd all been to our various homes at one point or another. They'd all contributed to our unhappiness, even if they had usually done it in pairs or small groups. This crowded approach was very unusual. And very, very scary.

Before I was even out of my uniform, I was rolling Rizla papers as usual. There was no point fighting it. As I entered the kitchen, where the stuff was already laid out next to the huge bong, I froze.

Brian!

Was he here? I tried not to appear worried, but on the pretence of saying hello to Mum, I stuck my head in the lounge. I needed to know, for my own peace of mind, whether I could expect my bedroom door to be opened later by Brian out for revenge. But I couldn't see him anywhere. In fact, I would never see him again.

Making roll-ups for so many people took a while. By the time I'd finished and I could hear the bong bubbling away in the lounge, I just stood in the kitchen, chin on my chest, waiting for the moment when I'd be sent to my room. When I'd be drugged. When the men would 'party' with Mum. I was sick with the anticipation. And then I remembered the coins.

This is what Granny was talking about! She knew the men were coming back.

So why hadn't she told me? I suppose she didn't want to ruin the time I had before it happened. There was always a chance they might never have come, after all.

I put my hand in my jacket pocket and felt the coins she'd given me. This is what they were there for. Now, though, I had to use them.

The noise from the lounge was louder than anything I'd ever heard. *Would they notice if I popped out?*

I had to try.

There was a big red phone box on our street, so I dashed in there and rang Granny. As soon as she heard the pips, she knew why I was phoning.

'Are those men back?'

'Yes. There are loads of them.'

'I'm coming over.'

I ran back to the flat and headed straight for the kitchen. If anyone had noticed my disappearance, they didn't mention it. Then I waited, heart in mouth, for the cavalry to arrive.

Looking back, I don't know what Mum had told Granny about these men. I can only imagine it was a watered-down version of the truth. She'd probably confessed that they had something to do with drugs. But I bet she'd kept quiet about the levels of physical abuse they were happy to mete out, not only to her, but to me as well, if she couldn't stop them. How else do you explain why a little old lady would walk into that snake pit alone and think she could possibly do anything to stop them?

I remember Granny bursting in. She wasn't a retiring sort of person and she tore straight into the lounge and shouted at everyone to get out. Nobody moved.

She started screaming, 'Get out or I'll call the police!'

Still no one budged an inch.

Gingerly, I peeped round the edge of the door. The men were just staring at Granny like she was some TV documentary they didn't really understand. Then one of them – it had to be Mark – spoke. He didn't raise his voice, but then he didn't need to.

'Let me tell you how it is, old lady,' he said slowly, puffing on his cigarette between words. 'We're all just having a nice little party with Jenny here, so unless you want to join us I suggest you make yourself scarce.'

Granny shouted some more, but she'd lost the fight and she knew it. I couldn't believe her plan was just to come round on her own. Why hadn't she brought the police? (Later she admitted to being worried that Mum would have been in trouble as well.) She hadn't even brought Grandpa (she hadn't even told him, I learnt).

She has no idea what these men are capable of.

So, tail between her legs, she left. On the way out she gave me a hug and said I should come with her. I refused.

'I'm not leaving Mum.'

The second she closed the door everyone seemed to move at once. Whatever calmness Mark had shown when he was intimidating Granny, he was livid now. He came flying into the kitchen and grabbed my neck.

'You called her, you bitch, didn't you?'

I denied it, but it was obvious I was lying.

'Right, in the bedroom. Now!'

I thought I was just going to be given tablets and told to shut up. I was wrong. That wouldn't do, not this time. I needed to be punished.

'Don't hurt me.' I was surprised to hear my voice, small and weak. 'I won't do it again. I promise.'

Mark just stood there. In my imagination he was weighing up how to hurt me most. I felt my entire body tense.

What's he going to do to me?

I heard screaming and suddenly Mum was shoved into the room as well. Then it dawned on me. Mark probably wouldn't lay a finger on me. Why would he, when he could hurt me in a different way instead?

I could have kicked myself for going along with Granny's plan. This was all her fault. She didn't know about the threats, the hanging from the spire, the knife in my face. She didn't know that the way these men operated was to not hurt the ones they were angry with but their loved ones instead.

I'm sorry, Mum.

I was forced to look on as two men ripped the clothes from her body. Then she was bent over the dressing table and one of the men forced himself inside her. I know now he was having sex with her – raping her, actually. Back then, I just knew that he was hurting her and she hated it. She was screaming and screaming and I was crying my heart out, begging them to stop, but the men were just laughing. This was fun for them. They took it in turns to do things to her.

And I was made to watch it all. That was my punishment for phoning Granny. My poor, poor Mum. She didn't deserve this. No one did. They were animals. They treated her like meat and they took pleasure from it.

In one evening, two months of bliss had been totally destroyed. And all because of me.

EIGHT

This is Normal

I can't remember if I was fed a sleeping pill or just fell asleep naturally, but the next thing I knew it was morning – and I'd missed registration at school.

That was the difference now: I had places to be. It took me ages to clean up after a visit from the men normally, even when it was only a handful of them. After so many of them, it seemed to go on forever. And then there was Mum to think of. Looking at her, with her silly grin and deep, dark, sunken eyes, just made me never want to leave her side. *School?* I thought. *I can't go to school. I've got too much to take care of here.*

But Mum made me go. Sluggish and seemingly out of it as she was, Mum knew I had to go. She didn't want to talk about the previous night and I was trying desperately to pretend it was all a bad dream, so we had a silent understanding to move on. I hated leaving her, but she always promised she'd be okay. Nine times out of ten she was. Half the time I'd leave her at death's door and by the time I'd returned she'd disappeared for the night. She obviously had a good recovery system.

I knew Mum was right about going to school. Things were

116

different now. I had a life outside our home. The teachers and my classmates would notice if I weren't there or I arrived late or dishevelled or showing any of the other side effects of my regular home life. It was a problem. But I knew I had to keep up appearances otherwise I'd be put straight into care again. And that wouldn't help anyone.

Kids are pretty resilient. That's what I've learnt in forty-odd years. I guess I must have been the same. I'd had an almost euphoric few weeks with just Mum in our wonderful flat – that she owned, not rented – but now we were back in our old routine and I just accepted it. It was as if my brain thought, *Okay, that was then, this is now – let's deal with it.*

Mum must have been the same. Again and again I've looked back and thought, *Why did you stay? Why didn't you just admit defeat and move in with Granny and Grandpa for a while?* But she was too stubborn. Too proud, just like her dad. And, I would later realize, just like me.

Mark and friends were regular visitors again, usually in fours or fives, and I was chief joint roller. No one mentioned the phone call to Granny. No one laid a finger on me, actually. It was as if that nightmare experience had never happened. I made joints, set up the bong, took my pills and disappeared. Mum did whatever she did with them and was either there or not in the morning when I woke up. I'd tidy up and go to school. It really was business as usual for a month or two. Horrible, but bearable. Unpleasant, but normal.

And then, one day, I came home from school and Mum wasn't there. Nothing out of the ordinary there. I hadn't seen her the previous day either, but two days was normally her limit, so I got changed and decided to make her a chocolate cake. Granny had helped me buy the ingredients ages ago and I vaguely remembered how to mix it all together. That was going to be my little gift to Mum whenever she came back.

She'll probably be feeling ill again. This will cheer her up.

An hour or so later I heard footsteps climbing the stairs.

No, it's too soon! The cake's not ready yet! Even so, I was ecstatic Mum was back. *She's probably not hungry anyway . . .*

When the door opened and Grandpa was standing there, I was taken aback. Apart from visiting shortly after we'd moved in, he hadn't been round. I wasn't looking forward to explaining that Mum was out. I knew he didn't like it when she left me alone and now he could see for himself that she wasn't at home.

Before I could say anything, though, Grandpa said, 'Your mother's quite ill. She's been taken to hospital.'

Ill? That wasn't news. She was always ill. I wondered why Grandpa looked so concerned. *If she came home I would look after her. Like I always do.*

'Grab your coat, Cathy, and I'll drive you to visit her.'

Was he serious?

'I can't go now,' I replied. 'The cake's in the oven. Mum will need her cake when she's better.'

Grandpa sighed. 'I'm sure it will be fine if you finish it later.'

'I can't finish it later! That's not how baking works.'

'For goodness' sake, Cathy, just leave it.'

But I refused. In my head, Mum would need something to eat when she came home and it was my job to make sure she got it. And if she was as ill as Grandpa reckoned, that just made it twice as important to get it right. So we stayed. Grandpa couldn't relax and conversation was stilted. Eventually I announced that the sponge had risen and it was time to take it out.

'At last!' Grandpa exclaimed theatrically. 'Can we go now?'

'Of course not. I've got to ice it first.'

I can't believe now that I put him through this torment. It was my mother in hospital, but she was also his daughter. He was desperate to get back there – that's obvious now – but the last thing he wanted to do was alert me to the severity of Mum's condition. He was only thinking of me, but it was tearing him apart.

Before you can ice a cake, you must let it cool, so that used up another twenty minutes or so. Finally, with icing sugar everywhere and cocoa powder all over my clothes, I was ready to leave.

'Better bring your school things,' Grandpa warned. 'I think you'll be staying with us tonight.'

That's nice, I thought. It never occurred to Grandpa that I was used to spending nights alone. Nor did it occur to me that Mum wouldn't be joining us. I insisted that we go to Salt-dean to drop off the cake before, eventually, setting off for the hospital.

On the drive there Grandpa didn't say much, although he did mention something about Mum catching a bug while she was out late at night. He sounded confused. 'Why would she be out so late?' he asked, talking to himself more than me.

That, in turn, confused *me*. Mum always went out late. She stayed out overnight and I had no idea where. But it wasn't a problem. She'd done that all my life or for at least as long as I could remember. It was normal. But obviously Grandpa had no idea.

I don't know if I was in denial about the gravity of the situation, but I remember feeling surprised by everyone rushing around, worried about Mum. I genuinely couldn't escape the sense that they were overreacting. Of course I craved for Mum to be cured

119

of whatever it was that ailed her, and if the hospital could do that then, great, let them. But really, even as we parked the car, walked through reception and caught the lift up to Mum's ward, I just wanted to shout out, 'This is normal! She'll be fine! Let me look after her!'

Seeing your mother hunched over a toilet bowl or, occasionally, failing to wake up before she vomited was one thing. Witnessing her strapped to a high hospital bed with tubes and pipes coming out of her nose and arms and myriad machines lining the wall was an experience I just wasn't prepared for. I don't know what I'd expected to see, but it wasn't Mum lying there unconscious. Even then I tried to justify it.

'She's tired,' I told Granny who was sitting at Mum's side, holding her hand. 'She'll wake up soon.'

Granny smiled. She didn't seem convinced.

We sat there for ages, it seemed, and then a doctor came in and asked Mum something. Out of nowhere, she managed this slurred, quiet 'Yes'.

'See?' I told Granny. 'She's waking up!'

But that was about as much as we heard. She squeezed out a few more yes/no answers and in between gurgled and burbled like a baby talking in its sleep. Still, though, I wasn't concerned. My biggest priority, in fact, was the cake.

If we don't get home soon it will be too dry to eat.

Grandpa drove the three of us back to theirs, where I spent the night in the spare room as usual. The next morning he took me to school and then picked me up at the end of the day, announcing, 'Let's see if there's been any change in your mother.'

Hand on heart, I wasn't very happy at being dragged back to the hospital. I just thought, *Here we go again, another evening wasted waiting for Mum to wake up.* Because I absolutely believed with all my heart that she would wake up. No matter how rough she looked or sounded, Mum always woke up.

But I went in and I sat next to her and I tried to enjoy the magazine that Granny, who was already there, had bought me. It wasn't easy. I was bored. I couldn't help it. No one was talking, Mum hadn't budged since last night and Granny looked like she would burst into tears if you asked her the time.

Why was everyone making such a fuss? Why didn't they listen? *She does this every week!*

The next day Mum was still in hospital. I admit that surprised me. *She's normally up by now.* Even so, when Grandpa suggested going back to see her after school, I asked not to. Eventually he relented and I stayed and played at their house. It was the same the next day, and the next. In fact, probably a week passed before I returned. Even then, it was against my better judgement. Yes, it had been longer than usual, but nothing was set in stone with Mum. I'd learnt that years ago.

So back I went and tried to talk to her, but she barely reacted to anything.

Fine. I'll talk to you when you wake up.

I thought I deserved a medal for lasting as long as I had. Eventually though, patience absolutely exhausted, I said, 'Can we go yet?'

Granny sighed and spoke quietly to Grandpa. Then he said, 'Come on, Cathy, it's probably time to eat anyway.'

'What about Granny?' I asked, ever the practical little girl I'd been forced to become. 'We've only got one car.'

'Don't worry about me,' Granny replied. 'I'll make my own way home.'

I wasn't happy, but I accepted it. A second later I was

skipping out of the hospital entrance, relieved to have escaped that dreary place. I really, really hoped I wouldn't have to go back there the following day.

When I got up for breakfast Granny and Grandpa were waiting for me.

'I've got some terrible news,' Granny said, her eyes filled with tears. 'Your mother ...' she paused. 'Your mother died last night.'

As soon as the words left her lips, she slumped back as though she'd been building up to say them all morning. I took all of this in before the message hit home.

Died.

'She's dead?' I couldn't believe it. 'Dead?' The word sounded wrong even as I was saying it.

'Yes, dear,' Granny said and came over to hug me. I didn't exactly push her away. I was just too shocked. Immobile through disbelief.

'But there was nothing wrong with her,' I spluttered.

Grandpa looked surprised. 'She was very ill.'

'No, she wasn't,' I insisted. 'That was normal. She's like that, then she gets up. Normal, see?'

But they didn't see. They both shook their heads and Granny started crying. The more I protested, the more upset they both became. Whatever they'd planned for this moment, I don't think it was working out.

'She can't be dead. It must be a mistake.'

'There's no mistake, dear,' Granny said. 'I was there when she left us.' She wiped her eyes. 'She's gone. Really gone.'

Part of me wanted to rush down to the hospital and check for myself. Another part wanted to hare round the garden screaming. But yet another part wanted to gather up my satchel and set off for school. That was how my life worked: you got upset and you moved on. Things to do. Always things to do.

But I did none of those things. Looking back, Granny and Grandpa must have thought I had a heart of stone. But there was a reason I didn't cry. It wasn't because I hadn't loved Mum. It was because I refused to accept she'd gone. It was all a big mistake, I was sure of it. Mum needed me to remain vigilant, to work out how to get her back. Crying wouldn't help her or me.

In any case, the Beavises were not a crying family. I don't know if Grandpa ever cried in his whole life; I certainly never saw him shed a tear over Mum. Even Granny would usually remove herself to her room when she became emotional.

Tears or not, there was a horribly subdued atmosphere at Tremola Avenue that morning. I spent most of it in my room, while Granny and Grandpa had visitors or spoke on the telephone. There was a lot to talk about. People had a lot of questions. But I just had one.

How can she be dead? I've seen her like that a hundred times.

That was what I couldn't get over.

Time is a great healer, they say. That may be true, but time doesn't explain anything. I had so many regrets about Mum's death. More than thirty years later, they're still with me, every minute of the day.

The thing is, no one ever told me my mother was dying. I've thought about this many, many times over the years and I can't find it in me to blame my grandparents. They were doing what they thought was best. I was a child. Any responsible adult would have done the same thing. They were trying to protect me from the horrors of death. They could never have known

123

that I'd been living with the spectre of mortality for years. In a way, the horrors of life had been far, far worse.

Whenever I think of the time I spent at the side of her hospital bed, I cringe. I'd seen Mum comatose so many times it wasn't an event anymore. I'd lost count of the times she'd been unable to answer simple questions. On those days I just went out and played and returned when she'd perked up. Because she always perked up eventually. Not this time.

I felt almost embarrassed for not realizing what was going on. I'd looked at Mum's limp and bloated body, grunting occasional utterances, and thought she was getting over a night out. In fact, her body was going through the final shutdown. One by one, her faculties were switching off. And I didn't notice.

As the news of her passing began to sink in, I couldn't believe how bored I'd been. If I'd known they were her last moments, what would I have done differently? I don't know. But I would have felt different. I wouldn't have been desperate to escape. I would have stayed, like Granny, holding her hand until the very end.

As it was, I never got to say goodbye. That was the hardest blow of all. When I'd skipped out of the ward, I hadn't looked back. I just assumed she'd be there the next day. I couldn't even remember my last words to her. I'd probably said them when we were still together at home. I was probably on my way to school or looking for my shoes, something mundane like that. Had I told her recently how much I loved her? I couldn't remember. I should have done. I should have told her every day. I loved her so much, and maybe she never knew.

I didn't even get the chance to say goodbye at her funeral either. Again, as was customary at the time, because of my age, I wasn't allowed to go to church for the cremation service, although, as an adult, I have never missed visiting her memorial on the anniversary of her death. My last memory of Mum is her lying there, bloated and incoherent in that hospital bed. I wish I had closure, I truly do. I wish I remembered her in better times. But that was it. That's the image that stayed with me for so long afterwards.

Three times I went to see her in hospital. *Three times*, and for a grand total of maybe a couple of hours. That was all the time I could spare. And she never did eat that bloody cake! That was something else that made me angry, illogically so. But it's something I can smile about now. I can't say that about many things from those days.

I was so stunned by Mum dying that it was a day or two before I asked how. I don't think children contemplate causes of death that much. You're either alive or you're not. Knowing what killed someone doesn't make their death any easier to bear. It's a healthy way to think, actually. I wish adults could hold on to that simplicity of thought for longer.

Granny told me Mum had died from the cold. She'd been out, poorly dressed for the chilly spring night, and was found shivering and ill. She'd been taken to hospital and that's when my grandparents had been called. She'd lasted two weeks.

I couldn't work it out. I'd seen Mum cold many times. We'd both sat, freezing, in various flats and bedsits. I'd seen her breath come out of her mouth and her nails turn blue in our lounge. I'd never known that cold could kill people. Now I knew differently. Or so I thought.

I was eight years old when my mother died on 30 April 1978.

My father had left when I was two and I didn't have a single memory of him. I didn't know his name and I couldn't have told you what he looked like. If he'd passed me in the street, I would have been none the wiser. To all intents and purposes, I was an orphan.

On the plus side, even at eight, I was mature enough to reason that at least I'd reached rock bottom. *Life can never be this bad again.* How wrong I was.

NINE

Trying to be Brave

I'd become so accustomed to Mum disappearing for days and then suddenly popping up that for weeks after her death it just seemed like another one of those periods. I'd go a couple of days, getting on with life, having fun, and then it would hit me like a kick in the stomach.

She's not coming back. She's never coming back.

Granny and Grandpa were more pragmatic than me and certainly more efficient than Mum had ever been. Within a few days of her death, I'd been enrolled in a local Saltdean school. I'd been staying with them in their Tremola Avenue bungalow and it seemed logical to start rebuilding my life from there. That was fine by me. Settling into a new school was a chore, but tolerable. It was the order I hated, being told what to do and where to be at a specific time, although I never had a problem with the people in authority.

Ever adaptable, I just slotted into life with my grandparents. Then they dropped the bombshell: I might have to move out.

In a way, I was taking life a day at a time. On the other hand, I'd assumed I'd be living with my grandparents now. I probably would have preferred to live on my own in Telscombe Cliffs, but that was obviously not an option, despite the fact that I'd been doing virtually that since we'd moved in. As far as the authorities were concerned, I needed proper grown-up care and as Granny and Grandpa were my closest relatives, I'd naturally stay with them. Or so I thought. Technically, though, there was someone else who was biologically closer to me. Someone I had no recollection of ever existing. My father.

Granny broke the news. There was going to be a court hearing. Lawyers and magistrates would decide what was to be done with me.

I knew she was talking about something important, but the words didn't mean much to me. As far as I was concerned, it was adult business. In any case, I'd already moved around so many times that choosing where to live seemed less of a permanent decision than it actually was.

'Can't I stay with you?' I asked.

'Of course you can,' she replied. 'But it's not up to me.'

If it's not up to you, then who is it up to?

It turned out to be me.

Courtrooms are intimidating at the best of times. Whether you're a witness or a member of the jury, you somehow feel that you're the one on trial. There's an aura about them that really puts you off guard. That's what I feel as an adult who has seen the very worst of them. Imagine how it felt as an eight-year-old?

As I remember it, I had to tell the magistrate where I wanted to live. There were two choices on the table. Legally, my father had the strongest claim. Then there were my grandparents, whom I'd stayed with so often and with whom I was living now. Did I want to live with them?

My father didn't appear in court. Or if he did, I can't remember. I sat with Granny and Grandpa and then, when the magistrate called me forward, I went and stood near a lawyer. He asked me: 'Who would you like to live with as your official guardian or guardians?'

It was a lot of pressure on an eight-year-old who'd just lost her mother. The law doesn't seem to worry about things like feelings though – as I would discover again and again many years later.

I didn't hesitate. If there was anything of the romantic in me, I would have chosen my dad. But there wasn't. I was an impossibly practical child; I'd had to be. The fact that he hadn't even shown up confirmed my instincts: 'I want to live with Granny and Grandpa.'

I don't know what the court knew about my domestic circumstances, but it was as if that was the last thing they'd expected to hear. A child choosing her grandparents over her own father? Incredible! There was a hubbub of conversation between the three magistrates and the various legal advisers – lots of whispering and gobbledygook to my ears. I couldn't follow any of it. Then the lead JP came back.

'We have decided to accede to your wish.'

Which in English means what?

'You are now the legal responsibility of Mr and Mrs Beavis.'

Yes!

I'd won the day. But, as we drove home, neither I nor my grandparents really knew what we were letting ourselves in for. All we knew was that our lives would never be the same again.

Before the court case I'd been staying at Tremola Avenue. Now I was *living* there.

They tried to make me feel comfortable. I was given the room I'd always stayed in with Mum and they brought in her old wardrobe from the flat and her record player and albums. Even though Granny was a dog lover really, she let me put a cardboard box on the floor-mounted boiler, which we lined with a small crocheted blanket and pillow for Mushka. She loved it there. As a treat, they also got hold of a black-and-white portable television, complete with bendy wire aerial. It was great. Just one bed, rather than two. No sharing, no worrying about strange men following me in. My own little sanctuary.

Mushka didn't seem to mind the change of scenery, but then she had other things to worry about. Barely a fortnight after Mum's death, I was woken by a wet sensation in my bed. My first instinct was to cry out, ashamed and embarrassed that I'd wet the bed again after so many months of dry nights. Then my eyes adjusted in the half-light. Mushka was on my lap – and she wasn't alone. Two tiny bundles were mewing and wriggling next to her!

I called Granny and together we sat on my bed for the next few hours, sharing a bar of Dairy Milk, while Mushka had two more adorable little kittens. It was a wonderful night. I'd never felt so close to my grandmother and I had my mum's old cat to thank for it. Maybe life at Tremola Avenue wouldn't be so bad after all.

Of course I was happy that I wasn't sharing a room any more. Then I'd remember why. *Mum.* That happened so often it began to scare me. I could do so much and then her memory would crash down on me without warning. I loved her and I missed her, but I wished I had greater control over her memory.

It was a sombre household at first. I'd lost my mother and Granny and Grandpa had lost their daughter. I had to keep reminding myself of that. I would bound into the kitchen, eager to get the day off to a good start, and I couldn't understand why they'd be moping around. I really hope they didn't find me disrespectful.

I don't think I ever appreciated the magnitude of my decision that day in court. The clerk had told me what I had to do: 'Go up there and elect where you want to live.' That was pretty much it. But I'd moved around so often, I don't think it really seemed real. In the back of my mind was the idea that, if things didn't work out, I'd just move on again. Not necessarily to my father's, just away from Tremola Avenue.

A good while later Granny told me that I'd made the right decision. My father, she'd heard from a solicitor, had intended to put me into care had I chosen to go with him. He didn't know me, I wasn't part of his life and I was very young. He was terrified at the prospect of coping. When I met him later he swore this wasn't true, but those were the facts according to Granny.

I should have been offended, but I wasn't. I'd already been into care twice. I'd been abused in one residence and looked after well in the other. And on Mum's watch, as I could never forget, I was subjected to the worst degradation I could imagine. If I'd been put into care with my father in control, then so be it. I would have coped. I always coped.

I guess I took after Grandpa in that respect. Looking back, his reaction to Mum's death was quiet and personal and very straightforward. He stopped believing in God.

He still went to church, still remained a warden, but the candle of his faith had gone out. Non-religious people won't understand what a big deal this is for a believer. For church-goers, faith is everything. He was a middle-aged man who was being forced to question things he'd always taken for granted. It was very sad.

131

Granny, on the other hand, had her own way of getting through such a difficult time. Whenever the subject of my father came up, she couldn't help but be scathing about him. At first I thought it was because he hadn't taken a role in my upbringing. Then I realized her anger went deeper. He was the one, in her eyes, who had got her daughter pregnant and then abandoned mother and child. He was the one who'd walked away and let her fall into the clutches of those wicked men. By not being there, he'd let her die.

In her eyes, he was to blame for everything.

I never dared ask about my dad for that reason. Not that I cared anyway. He was just a name to me. Other kids had dads – I didn't. That's how it was. One more thing that was normal to me. I never gave it a moment's thought.

Reviewing my relationship with my mother today, it's obvious that our roles had been reversed. For so much of the time I was the carer and she the dependant. I was the one worrying about laundry, about getting food on the table. I never questioned it. That's just how we lived. Moving in with my grandparents obviously flipped the adult/child dynamic back to normal – but not entirely. While they provided for me far better than Mum had ever managed, emotionally they seemed to need pepping up. They were the ones moping about Mum's death, long after I'd stopped. They were the ones who couldn't get through a meal without one of them mentioning it and Granny breaking down and Grandpa sitting there in silence, tears not far from his eyes. Of course I missed her more than anything and I would spend hours dwelling on how she'd died from cold, wondering what I could have done to save her. But I suppose I adapted to the new situation faster than my grandparents did.

Going back to school probably helped. When you have a

routine, it's easier to stop your mind wandering back to dark thoughts. The trouble was, when I left the house Granny and Grandpa had nothing to do all day except dwell on everything that had happened. They'd still be doing it when I came home. I thought I was coping so well. It seemed a point of pride that I just had to get on with things. That's what I'd always done, whatever life had thrown at me.

I'm a coper. I'm in control.

Then, one day at school, I realized I wasn't in control of anything.

Everyone else in my class could read and write whereas, after a few months, I could still barely scribble my own name. I'd just never been taught how. But I'd picked up some basic reading skills at Telscombe Cliffs. I could sound out short words and names and I was getting better every day. It wasn't a thirst for knowledge that drove me on, though. I just hated the idea that everyone else in the class could do something better than me. I'd been Miss Independent for so long that being at the back of the queue for anything cut me deeply. So, not only was I a coper and in control, I was a winner too.

In those early days at my new school in Saltdean, I would stare at anything that looked like it had words on and try to decipher the strange hieroglyphics. Initially I didn't get very far, but I persevered. Add 'fighter' to the list.

I'd been there a month or two when the teacher said we were going to do art. I knew the drill, so when everyone else went to a cupboard and got out old newspapers to cover the tables with, I did the same. Unlike everyone else, though, I was more interested in trying to work out what the headlines said than what I was meant to be painting. Most of it was impenetrable to me, but there were also a lot of words written in really large type that I could translate. Even some of the smaller print was manageable. And two words in particular virtually leapt out.

'Jennifer Wilson'.

I checked and double-checked the spelling. That's definitely what it said.

Mum? Why was she in a newspaper? Suddenly my painting was over. I stared at those two words. *What are they saying about Mum?* My brain was fizzing, so confused, which only made trying to decipher the rest of the story more difficult than ever. But I kept going and going and going. And then I screamed the place down.

I can only imagine what my classmates must have thought. I wasn't aware of them or the teacher. All I could see were the words: 'Jennifer Wilson', 'dead' and 'drugs'. They filled my mind. That's what the story was saying, it had to be. Mum had died because of drugs.

I was out of control, I admit it. My composure at home had been an act, a brave front. It had to have been. How else can I explain how quickly and explosively I crumbled? In the space of a couple of seconds I went from a poor little girl doing her best to get over her mother's death to a howling, wild child screaming, 'It's not true! It's not true!'

The next thing I remember is Granny arriving. I don't know how long it took for her to get there or how hard they'd tried to console me before calling her. All I know is that as soon as I saw her I shouted, 'They're liars!' and fell into her arms.

Back at Tremola Avenue, the truth came tumbling out.

'Your mother did die of cold,' Granny – left by Grandpa to handle what he saw as women's work – explained. 'But that's not the end of it.'

She paused to catch her breath. It must have been hard for her to dredge up the painful memories, but I was desperate to hear them.

'What happened?' I urged.

'As the police explained it to me, she had taken so many drugs that she collapsed in an alley.'

'Didn't anyone help her?'

Granny shook her head. 'It was the middle of the night and it was freezing cold. No one was around. She was there for ages. By the time someone found her and called an ambulance, she had contracted pneumonia.'

So Mum had died of cold, that much was true, but only because she was out of her head on drugs. She'd overdosed, collapsed in an alley on a really frosty night and been too wasted to move. Those were the facts, but even as I made Granny go over and over the details, they wouldn't sink in.

So much of it just didn't make sense to me. It seems stupid now, but I never had any perception that joints or bongs were drugs. We might as well have got out a packet of biscuits. I had no idea at all.

'Drugs' was a word I'd heard about and I knew they were bad. When the police had taken that pouch hidden in my panda, they'd mentioned drugs then. But Mum had assured me they'd got it wrong. And of course I'd believed her. The fact that they'd released us so quickly backed up her story in my mind.

In other words, I knew early on that drugs were bad. People who took drugs were bad. So what did that make my mother?

But it turned out that Mum hadn't died from marijuana. She'd been addicted to heroin, Granny said, for years. Even though I didn't know what 'heroin' meant, I got the sense that it was as bad as you could get. 'The police and the doctors said it's the worst drug there is,' Granny explained, as innocent as me in such matters.

'So the newspaper was right?'

She nodded. In fact she went to a drawer and pulled out a different clipping from another paper. I've still got it today.

'Do you want to hear what it says?' she asked. When I said yes, she began to read.

'*A grim warning about the dangers of drug abuse was given at the Brighton inquest of a 23-year-old girl. Jennifer Wilson, a drug addict since she was just seventeen, died on April 30 from septicaemia and bronchial pneumonia brought about by a barbiturate overdose. Said coroner Dr Donald Gooding, "This is an oft repeated story of a young person who starts on marijuana, which is supposed to be harmless. It is not. It is dangerous and invariably leads to the situation where a person progresses from one dangerous drug to one even more dangerous."*'

'"Drug addict since she was seventeen"?' I repeated the words over and over, but they still wouldn't sink in.

How had she kept it a secret? Why hadn't I noticed?

Obviously she hadn't kept it a secret at all. Any adult who'd observed her behaviour for more than a day would have put two and two together. And if they'd turned up while the bong was being passed around, it would have taken all of a second to work it out. But how was I to know any of this? Even now, I keep reading that heroin is supposed to make you skinny. But Mum was bloated when she died. The pictures I have of her are of a woman with a lovely figure, nice and shapely, until the point when she'd put on weight, while we were at Telscombe Cliffs. If she'd lost weight maybe I would have noticed. But she hadn't.

But if she'd seemed to hold it together physically, the clues were certainly there in her behaviour. The days she went missing, her lethargy, her constant sickness, her mood swings, her dependence on me – all those things I put down as 'normal' were actually classic signs of heroin abuse.

There was a lot more in the newspaper article that Granny didn't read to me. I discovered that when I was fourteen, when I was finally brave enough to go back to it myself. It was gruesome reading.

Consultant pathologist Dr David Melchett said Jennifer developed deep pneumonia and there was internal infection of the lungs and windpipe . . . and was taken into the intensive care unit at the Royal Sussex County Hospital, Brighton. When she regained consciousness she told doctors she had taken fifty barbiturate tablets and was mainlining – injecting drugs into the bloodstream – three times a day.

I couldn't imagine anything worse than injecting yourself. I still can't. To this day, I can't fathom how she was doing this without me noticing. I never saw a needle or powder or foil or liquids or any of the stuff you associate with heroin. I told Granny this.

'Obviously this is what she was doing when she went out,' Granny surmised and I agreed. All those times she was out for hours or nights on end, she was high on heroin.

'So why was it different this time? Why did this time kill her?' I asked.

Granny had obviously been thinking about it too.

'Maybe the question is: why didn't all those other times kill her?'

I wonder when I would have discovered the truth if I hadn't seen that newspaper by chance during my art lesson. It was yet another example of my grandparents 'protecting' me. But look where it got them. I'd been denied closure at the hospital, then at the funeral. I'd appeared to be coping better than expected – better than them, in fact. But it all had to come out eventually.

For weeks I was horrible, hitting, shouting, refusing to do anything but rail, question, accuse – and cry. Finally the tears had come.

It felt good to have such an emotional release, but no sooner had the tears dried than the vicious circle began again and I was looking for answers. Whereas Granny had channelled her anger towards the mythical figure of my father, I just blamed her.

'Why didn't you tell me the truth?'

'Why didn't you stop her?'

'Why didn't you let me say goodbye?'

I was out of control, completely screwed up and thirsty for blame. Someone had to be responsible. I needed that, I needed an outlet. And, I'm ashamed to say, for an unpleasant few weeks, it was my grandparents.

Grandpa did his best to hide away. I'm sure he thought he'd been tested as much as he ever would by Mum's behaviour and her unnecessary death. But I was something else. There I was, a guest in his own home, accusing him and his wife of not caring. No army training had ever prepared him for this.

'That's not true, Cathy!' he shouted.

'Then why didn't you save her?'

'I tried. We all tried.'

'Then why did she have to die?'

'Because,' Granny interrupted quietly, 'she didn't want to be saved.'

Every few days we'd have the same argument. The same accusations, the same answers. Even when we weren't arguing, I didn't have a civil word in my head. Doors were there to be slammed, books just things to be thrown whenever I felt like it.

I was awful, I know that now. I had no right to talk to them like that. They'd lost their daughter – no parent should ever experience that – and in the most stomach-churning circumstances. They would have done anything to have saved her: they'd bought the flat, after all. They'd recognized the problem and done what they could. And now here was a foul-tempered child accusing them of not doing enough.

I'm amazed we ever got through it, but we did. You can only stay angry for so long. I just needed to let off steam, shed the tears I'd bottled up for too long. It wasn't Granny and Grandpa's fault, I knew that. Nothing was. They were victims, just like me. *No*, I realized with great sourness, *there is only one person who deserves the blame for this. Mum.*

TEN

I Was a Handful

It wasn't just losing their daughter that tested Reg and Daphne Beavis. As far as Granny and Grandpa were concerned, they'd raised their family, watched them grow up and moved on to plot their retirements together. Now here they were, saddled with an eight-year-old at their time of life. On top of that, Grandpa had been forced to take early retirement to get the money to try to save his daughter. He'd bought the flat, done as much as he could. And now Jenny was gone – and so was his job. In the end, he took a part-time job in advertising. Anything to get out of the house.

In hindsight, it can't have been easy for either of them. Being grandparents is one thing – and I'd always loved staying with them at weekends or random week nights, either with Mum or alone – but taking on a parental role is something else entirely. That's when rules come in. And I was not a child used to rules.

Time had little meaning when I was living with Mum. In this new, scary world, I discovered that everything ran by the clock. There was a time for breakfast, a time for lunch, a time for evening meals. There was a time for school, a time for playing, a

140

time for church, for Brownies, for cleaning my teeth. There was even a time for bed. That was the hardest one of all. After a lifetime of falling asleep, eating and playing when I felt like it, fitting into this regimented structure was difficult.

I wasn't the only one who lived by the clock. My grandparents did too. After Grandpa's military background, it was probably the only way he knew.

For example, Saturdays began with homework, if I had any, before I was allowed out to play with friends in the woodland or park at the back of the house. There was a pitch and putt course, which was always fun, especially if you could get on without paying, and there were tennis courts where I would later practise when I was part of the school doubles team. Sundays were even more rigid: after church it was my job to clean all the brass in the house, while Grandpa chopped the vegetables and Granny prepared the weekly roast. Afterwards Grandpa always washed up, while Granny and I retired to the lounge to play cards, with some classic Sunday afternoon Bing Crosby or Omar Sharif film playing in the background. Grandpa never played, but he would come in and do the *Telegraph* crossword until he fell asleep. Then, at 4.30 on the dot, it was time for high tea – and scones! Then the radio would come on for the evening or we'd listen to the Carpenters on Granny's old eight-track player. It was a lovely, calm atmosphere and I really appreciated all the effort my grandparents were making.

If only things weren't quite so regimented . . .

I wasn't a wild child, exactly, but I was used to my independence. I'd always come and gone as I pleased, just as Mum had done. I could wire a plug, peel vegetables, light fires. I could lay kitchen floors, for Christ's sake. In effect, I'd been living as an adult for as long as I could remember. All that came to a screeching halt at Tremola Avenue and, I admit, it was hard to go from a lifetime of semi self-governance to a world where Granny insisted on brushing my hair, I wasn't allowed out in the dark and touching sharp knives was forbidden because they were too dangerous for someone my age.

My grandparents were only trying to give me back some semblance of a childhood, but I couldn't see that. All I could see was that they were imposing rule after rule after rule and taking away the one thing I'd always had: my freedom.

Initially it was a rough ride. I was a handful and I thought their curfews were silly. They probably came down on me hard at the start, but you can understand why. They'd lost one child to indiscipline. They were damned if I was going to go down the same carefree route.

Whatever our early teething problems, I know their hearts were in the right place. When my grandfather died, Granny gave me a box of his letters which included Grandpa's claim to become my guardian. In it he says, 'I am a fit and capable man on early retirement and able to offer a good home and background to the said minor. I am in receipt of a pension of £4,000 a year and own capital property worth approximately £30,000. Said minor has for some years been very close to me and my wife because of my daughter's illness and incapacity prior to her death. I am confident that my wife and I will provide a good home and education for Cathy.'

He also goes on to say he would 'allow reasonable access for the petitioner to the said child'. It's all so formal and, when I first read the letter, I struggled to make out who was who. I was obviously the child, but who was the 'petitioner'? And then I came across another letter, from my father. So he was the petitioner and he had requested access. I was a bit shocked by his demands: 'I would ask that reasonable access should be defined as being allowed to take my daughter out for one day a month, following three days' notice.' One day a month? In all honesty, I can't recall seeing him at all during my younger years.

My grandparents took all responsibility, then, and became my surrogate parents. I don't know if you ever appreciate at the time the people who do the most for you – and children, of course, take for granted the fact that someone will be there for them. In an ideal world, out of sheer gratitude alone, I would have been the perfect child. For a while, and to a certain extent, I was. But it wouldn't last.

Because of Grandpa's early retirement, he wasn't exactly flush with cash. I didn't appreciate that at the time and, approaching my ninth birthday, I decided it was time to finally get rid of my biggest embarrassment.

'Can I have a new bike, please, Grandpa?' I begged.

He thought about it for less than a second.

'No,' he replied, 'but I'll get you another tyre!'

And he did. What other nine-year-old wakes up on their birthday to unwrap a black tyre and wheel? In hindsight, of course, he did the right thing. I'm the same now. My son isn't spoilt. Tough love is the only way to go. But no child appreciates it at the time.

Apart from my grandparents' rules, school quickly became the mainstay of my life. I couldn't get over the way it just continued to be there, day after day. I'd never had structure in my life. Getting to grips with timekeeping and homework deadlines took a while, but once the penny had dropped I was a new person. Whatever it was in me that enabled me to survive the unwanted attentions of men like Mark, Brian and their mates had made me stronger. School was nothing compared to that. Just as I'd actually enjoyed making the bongs and joints and taken pride in caring for our flat and for Mum, I totally embraced schoolwork. It was a challenge, there was a logic to it and I could see the path I needed to take to make progress. That was enough for me. I love a challenge.

Not being able to read or write is a bit of a disadvantage when you join a school late – especially if everyone else can. Unsurprisingly, I was bottom of the class from the moment I stepped through the doors of Saltdean Primary School. But, I'm proud to say, it didn't last. Set me a challenge and I will meet it. If I can, I'll beat it. That's how I am now and that's how I was then. Whether it was rolling joints or playing glockenspiels in the sand, I wanted perfection and I was prepared to work for it.

Everyone in the class was above me, but there were these two brainboxes, Peter Haslem and Jeremy Kempton, who were head and shoulders above everyone. Once I'd got my feet under the table, there was only one target. I thought, *I'm not having this. I want to beat them.*

So I knuckled down and I worked and I worked and I worked and, by the end of the first year, I'd almost done it. I was in the top three for just about everything, just fractionally behind these two in most subjects. It was quite an achievement. These lads were singled out as potential Mensa candidates, so I was thrilled to be first among the ordinary kids!

I wouldn't say I was naturally gifted, but I am definitely a grafter. I really thrived on applying myself, which was just as well because Grandpa insisted on the highest standards. He was very strict. If I made a mistake in my homework, especially once I'd gone up to senior school, I rewrote the whole thing. He wouldn't tolerate crossings out and, of course, after a while I grew to despise them as well, so I would just start again. I didn't mind. The strive for perfection burnt bright.

It wasn't just Grandpa who was pleased with my progress. I was in the headmaster's office every single week to get a gold star for the quality of my work. And if there was a new hall display, you could guarantee one of my stories or pictures would be up there. I was completely unrecognizable from the illiterate little girl who'd had to be escorted screaming from the premises.

If I wasn't doing homework, I'd be customizing my books. We are an artistic family and I'd think nothing of spending all my free time decorating the covers of my exercise books with colourful borders or intricate flower designs. It was the same diligence that I'd applied to making pom-poms for Mushka back at Telscombe Cliffs, although I tried not to think about that.

Mum was rarely far from my thoughts, but I had to select the memories. Too many, in hindsight, were soured by this new knowledge of drug-taking. Despite my best efforts, I'd begun to wonder, *If it was so dangerous, why did you do it? Why risk your life and leave me all alone?*

But it wasn't hard to sift out the good memories. Mum never told me off or made me do much that I didn't want to. Life with her was fun. Just being with her made me happy. She was all I needed. I just wished I had been enough for her.

Outside school, my thirst for perfection – and, I admit, hunger for winning – was there in everything. When I was young Granny would take me to Brownies. After that I couldn't wait to join the Girl Guides. I loved everything about it, but what really thrilled me was collecting the achievement badges – for reading, sewing, helping, you name it. The target was thirty-three badges, which nobody got. I'd managed thirty-two by the time I left. One more and I would have qualified for the Queen's Guard. I wasn't particularly disappointed to have missed out because it was working towards a goal that really excited me. In any case, I did get to go to a massive Girl Guide jamboree and I always had a really great time.

I loved a challenge. I was soon picked for the school tennis team and no sooner had Grandpa taken me for swimming lessons at Roedean School for Girls than I was begging him for more and more practice time. Six months after my first lesson I represented the school in a competition. I obviously had a really competitive streak, but Granny was the one with the high aspirations for me.

'You'll have tea with the Queen one day,' she told me one morning as she teased my hair into its usual top-knot. 'It's your destiny.'

Of course, as a little girl, I wanted to believe that, so when Granny insisted I learn the correct way to break open and butter a scone, I listened and copied devoutly. It wasn't just afternoon tea she was concerned about. I was schooled in all manner of etiquette, all in preparation for that day when I would dine with royalty – and marry a certain type of gentleman. Our Sunday afternoons were already packed, but somehow Granny found time to teach me how to speak correctly, how to carry myself upright with books on my head, how to eat fairy cakes, even how to get in and out of cars with grace. It was like being at a Swiss finishing school.

The final piece of her jigsaw, she thought, was ballroom-dancing lessons. 'For when you take a twirl around Buckingham Palace.'

The original *Come Dancing* programme was on television at the time and, as a nine-year-old, I used to love watching those glamorous couples spinning around the screen. What little girl wouldn't dream of wearing dresses like that? So Granny made me some wonderful outfits and I started classes. Like everything else I'd set my mind to so far, I excelled. I won badges for my foxtrot, my cha-cha, my paso doble. You name it, I danced it.

A year or two later I wanted a new challenge. This time it would have nothing to do with preparing me for meeting the Queen. To her credit, Granny didn't baulk when I announced I'd like to take up judo, even though she'd really enjoyed dressing me like a dancing princess. But she did make me choose.

'We've only got money for one class. It's either judo or dancing.'

I had plenty of little trophies for ballroom, so martial arts it was. A year or two later, the familiar story: myriad colourful belts hanging up in my wardrobe. Such a desire to win at everything.

No sooner had I learnt to read than I wanted to do it all the time. There wasn't an Enid Blyton or Nancy Drew book in the village that I didn't devour. The more I read, the more I wanted to enact the adventures. Kids used to play outside unattended all the time in those days, so gangs of us would run around the local coppice pretending we were detectives, leaving clues and shadowing each other. I was pretty much a tomboy, I suppose. I even built and raced go-karts.

Church still played a large role in our lives, despite Grandpa's epiphany. He was still a warden and we still attended every Sunday. I was a little star of the choir and Sunday School and helped Granny with the flowers and, even though I wasn't sold on the religious aspect of it all, once again I found myself thriving on the routine. I loved tasks, I loved trying to better my previous work – and everyone else's. When the church held a fête, I would spend weekends knitting and sewing and cutting and drawing and making as much as I could to sell. Whenever there was a craft show, you'd find me manning a stall, flogging my own little stuffed animals or table decorations. I was such a sweet little girl – I wonder sometimes where she went!

I loved keeping myself busy. After all those years of just hanging around with Mum, rarely having anything to do apart from household chores, I really responded to a full diary. I suppose I had Granny and Grandpa to thank for that, for packing my early life with events and inspiration. And I found myself realizing that Mum had had exactly the same opportunities. What had made her throw it all away?

By the time I finished at Saltdean Primary I had achieved just about everything I could. When it came time to move up to Longhill Secondary, I was genuinely excited. I must have thought my reputation as an achiever would count for something there. I was wrong.

It was a classic case of big fish/little pond syndrome. At Longhill, though, several little ponds merged and I very quickly realized I was out of my depth.

Whereas Saltdean was a lovely village school whose pupils played nicely together in the copse after class – as I did most afternoons with my friends Peter, Debbie and Sally – some of the other schools didn't have such a good reputation. The kids from Woodingdean were like creatures from another planet. Granny warned me they would be rough and she wasn't joking. The girls wore make-up and even the boys had pierced ears. Attitude, though, was the main difference. If there was a chair and a child from Saltdean and one from Woodingdean wanted it, Woodingdean would win. The same with books, sports gear – even dinner money. I'd been there a week before some kid even smaller than me demanded I empty my pockets. Bearing in mind some of the horrendous things I'd witnessed and experienced from people scarier than these, I'm surprised now how much it affected me. I don't think ballroom dancing would have impressed these kids, but why didn't I at least try my judo on them? I suppose part of my grieving process over Mum included putting as much distance as possible between 'new me' and the horrors of the past. That's not who I was.

Rough kids aside, it's a peculiar thing about school life that you rise to the top of one system then get moved back down to the bottom of the next, like a game of snakes and ladders, but with more at stake. I'd gone from teacher's pet at primary to the bottom of the pile at secondary. And when I say 'bottom' I mean the very bowels.

Kids have an instinct to attack anyone who stands out. The gang mentality takes them all over at some point. Sound different, look different, act different and you can expect grief from the masses.

And I looked different. A couple of years earlier I'd been so proud of the beautiful dresses Granny had run up for me on her sewing machine. Even when she said she'd knit my school jumper and crochet a skirt, I was touched. And then all the other kids saw my uniform was different to theirs and that was it. I was a marked girl – especially with Granny's latest old-fashioned hairstyle for me. But at least I didn't have to wear that stupid top-knot anymore!

The only saving grace was that there were two girls who were considered weirder than me. They were twins to start with, which would normally have been enough on its own, but they also had a surname that was just asking for trouble: Pratt. It was horrible really, but at least while they were being picked on, the older girls ignored me. It couldn't last, of course. 'Nice jumper' would be one of the least harmful insults to come my way, however sarcastically it was said. It was horrid, a really unhappy time. A lot of kids never recover from bullying at school. It affects their whole lives. As bad as it seemed at the time, however, I knew I'd be all right. When you've felt the cold steel of a knife blade pressed against your cheek, a few names and a bit of bullying isn't a problem at all.

Maybe, though, I would have been better off being scarred by the bullying. The threats and abuse I'd already suffered had, I think, dulled my attitude to violence. It had been such a large part of my life already that I didn't notice my reactions to it weren't as extreme as other kids'. I wasn't as scared, I wasn't as prepared to change my behaviour to please the bullies. At the time that worldliness protected me.

But that was also why I couldn't spot the signs when the greatest threat of all was staring me in the face.

My grandparents weren't too much help when it came to getting through my new school ordeal. 'Just concentrate on your work and the bullies will go away.' *Nice in theory* . . .

But that's what I did. Head down, I really applied myself to lessons and was soon in the top class for every subject. I won lead roles in school plays and decided to take my guitar-playing more seriously. I'd always enjoyed evenings spent noodling with Mum's old six-string. Soon, once I'd put my mind to it, I was in the school band on acoustic guitar. Our teacher was a great inspiration: his band, the Piranhas, had a hit record in 1982 with 'Zambesi'.

Being a swot didn't make me any less likely to be bullied,

of course, and in fact I got dog's abuse. But as I grew older, I persuaded Granny to stop making me dress like a doll and confidence soon followed. With self-belief came a rekindling of my desire for independence. I enjoyed being at Granny and Grandpa's, but I really wanted my own space. And, to be honest, they couldn't wait to have their retirement back for themselves.

In those days young people would collect bits and bobs for their 'bottom drawer' – things you would need for your first home – so that's what I decided to do. In order to do that, however, I needed money. At fourteen years old, it was time to get a job.

Typical me, though, I thought, *Why get one job when you can have three?*

The local fish shop took me on for two evenings a week, which was nice, although it made my clothes and hair smell like a chip pan. Then, on Thursdays and Fridays, I would go straight from school to help out at Saltdean's florist shop. But best of all was getting a Saturday job at Robert Dyas. You had to be sixteen to work there, which I told them I was, and I loved it because I could get staff discounts on their stock. Week after week, I'd spend my pay packet on things like cutlery sets, crockery, glasses, an electric blanket, a duvet, duvet covers – you name it and I had it stored under my bed or in my wardrobe, ready for the day I could leave. I had my Duran Duran posters on the walls and my 'bottom drawer' all ready to go. How many kids are thinking that far ahead?

So, there I was, juggling homework, three jobs and half a dozen hobbies, and I was flying. I was going great guns. I bought myself a brand new Claude Butler racing bike for £500 and took part in the London to Brighton race. I was healthy, I was wholesome, I was happy. Everything was rosy. Granny and Grandpa must have been so grateful that I wasn't displaying any of the tendencies that their daughter had shown. And then I came off the rails.

It all seemed to happen at once. Boys, alcohol, cigarettes – they all came a-calling and I gave each my fullest attention.

Boys came first and, initially at least, nothing much changed. My first boyfriend worked at Robert Dyas with me. He was eighteen years old and another bike fan, so we used to cycle everywhere, especially at weekends, when we both went out with the Brighton Cycling Group for thirty-mile rides. I loved the whole routine of packing sandwiches and a bottle of Coke into my panniers and setting off with a bunch of other healthy people.

We went out for quite a while and eventually nature took its course. Because I had told Robert Dyas I was sixteen, that's naturally how old my boyfriend thought I was. He would have been horrified to learn he'd slept with a fourteen-year-old – just as my father had a decade and a half earlier. In my case, however, I was already on the Pill, having been prescribed it to combat awful period pains.

It was another boy who set me on the path to alcohol. A really great friend of mine when I was young was a chap called Peter – one of my playmates from the woods. We were inseparable as mates for years and his parents were convinced we'd end up married. That never happened, but we did a lot of things together – including getting drunk for the first time.

Other kids had started talking about drinking and some-how we'd got hold of a bottle of vodka. Units and percentages meant nothing to us, so we just sat on a wall near his house and swigged it like it was Tizer.

I remember swinging my feet and trying to concentrate on them. The next thing I knew, I'd fallen off the wall and landed in someone's garden. In a rose bush. Thanks to the vodka, I didn't feel a thing, but to this day I still have a thorn embedded in my back.

When the bottle was empty we decided to go back to Peter's house. En route was a greengrocer's and, sitting out the front, pride of the display, were lovely-looking gala melons.

'I'd love one of those,' I said.

'Me too.'

So Peter grabbed this melon and off we fled. We thought it was the most hilarious thing in the world, but honestly, what a pair of chumps! Peter's house was only a hundred yards away and the greengrocer had known him all his life. There was no way we weren't going to get caught.

Convinced we'd outwitted the greengrocer, we ran into the house and tiptoed up the stairs so as not to attract any adult attention. But obviously we were both wrecked, so it must have sounded like a herd of elephants passing through. Giggling elephants at that.

The hilarity continued. Peter's room had a basin in it, which was just as well because shortly after I sat down to eat the melon – like an apple, skin and everything – I threw up. We both stared at the melony mess in the sink and Peter declared, 'Coffee! We need coffee.'

So back downstairs we crept, but there was his mum cooking dinner. I hid in the doorway while he tried to have a sensible conversation, waiting for the kettle to boil. In the end, he panicked and filled the cups with lukewarm water.

After that, I would go to the woods with my friends and drink there. Whereas a few years earlier we'd been searching for pits of abandoned pottery and convincing ourselves we'd discovered Roman artefacts, now we were content to drink cider or sherry in secret – and smoke.

A lot of kids were saying they smoked, but I don't think many did. It was like boasting you'd had sex – it was the cool thing to say, whether you had or not. But a few people did and I decided to give it a go. I remember, it was a John Player Black and it was absolutely disgusting, but I forced myself to persevere. I really wish I hadn't. Until recently, I smoked forty a day.

I was helped in those days by the fact that it wasn't just Robert Dyas – and my boyfriend – who thought I was sixteen. I could buy cigarettes and booze from anywhere, as long as I wasn't wearing my school uniform. When I realized how unusual this was, I saw an opportunity. I bought a packet of twenty, a box of Swan Vesta and went back to school and sold a cigarette and a match for ten pence. Before long, I was making enough to give up one of my evening jobs. Most importantly, it reminded me of those Sunday mornings spent looking for pound notes with Mum and the time we sold melon at the Bay City Rollers concert.

I've inherited her eye for an opportunity. It was a proud moment.

Speaking of Mum, while all the other kids were fabricating their sexual- or nicotine- or alcohol-based experiences, I never once joined in. If I'd revealed my skill at rolling joints and setting up bongs, I'd have been a legend. But I kept quiet. That was in the past. I'd done my best to forget it had ever happened.

I told even close friends that my mother had died of pneumonia, which is technically true. It's only been in the last few years that I've been comfortable enough to tell anyone the truth. Obviously I was more scarred by the experience than I was prepared to admit.

It's funny, looking back, how I managed to spin even something like illicit drinking and smoking so I came out of it looking more successful than anyone else. *Okay,* I thought, *you can't be a winner doing this – but you can do it better.*

So instead of buying the usual cheap brands like Rothmans or B&H, I always bought Dunhill. They were more expensive and, I reasoned, therefore classier. They were certainly more distinctive. And as for alcohol, I began keeping a bottle of red, a bottle of rosé and a bottle of white under my bed for when visitors called. I thought it was the height of sophistication to be able to offer a glass to girlfriends after school. None of us knew that these bottles, opened weeks earlier, were well past their sell-by dates, so would obviously taste rank. We thought we were so grown up.

While all this was going on, my body was changing too. I noticed people had stopped taking the mickey out of my looks and, actually, boys were queuing up for my attention. Girls, too, wanted to be my friend. I was Miss Popular and I loved it.

The more attention I got, the more I wanted. I started wearing make-up, agonizing over every little detail for hours before I went out. Best of all, I bought my first pair of shoes with my own money. The cool girls at school – probably the ones from Woodingdean – all wore high heels. I thought, *I'm going to get a pair of those.*

My experience of shopping was close to zero. Granny had made most my clothes and the rest we'd picked up at second-hand fairs in the community centre. As a result, I was often four or five seasons out of date. So wandering around Brighton looking for the perfect pair of heels with cash burning a hole in my pocket was never going to end with the bargain of the century.

But my naivety was exposed when it came to size. I didn't realize that stilettos started at three inches. I saw an amazing pair of six-inch heels and I thought that's what they all looked like, so I bought them. Who knows where I got them – it was probably a sex shop. All I do know is that, for the next two years, I would not be seen dead in anything lower. To this day, I won't leave the house in anything less than four inches.

Shoes accounted for, make-up applied, that just left my hair. The craze then was for highlights, which I got and would spend hours teasing until it looked just so. I loved it. For the first time in my life, I cared about the way I looked and I loved the results. Other people did too.

Something had to give though. There wasn't enough time in the day to cram everything in, so decisions had to be made. I couldn't quit work because I needed the money to escape. I couldn't stop my new fun socializing because I'd never been happier. Which only left school.

Almost overnight, I just switched off. School held no interest for me anymore. That part of my life was over. I was fourteen years old. Exactly the same age my mother had been when her life of troubles had begun.

Of course, I only discovered that later. Back then, in 1984, the only thing on my mind was escaping. I informed Grandpa that I would be leaving his home the day I turned sixteen.

'You will not,' he insisted. 'You have to at least sit your O levels.'

'You can't tell me what to do.'

'While I am your legal guardian, Wilson, I can.'

He always called me 'Wilson' when he was angry with me. Partly it was a return to his days commanding the troops. It was also a reminder to us both that I shouldn't have even been there. I wasn't a Beavis.

We argued for hours, but in the end I relented, even though his legal responsibilities would end on the day I turned sixteen.

In Grandpa's defence, he'd already seen Mum married on her sixteenth birthday, having thrown her life away – as he saw it – when she was the age I was then. I didn't know this. They kept it from me. But it was another parallel with the life of the woman I'd barely known.

Longhill let me take a few exams a year early, which I passed easily. What I really should have done, though, is sit them all then, while I still had some interest. By the time my proper exams came round, I had been doing very little schoolwork for a year. It was no surprise when the straight-A girl came home with Bs and Cs.

It's only looking back that I realize how upsetting this must all have been for my grandparents. They'd seen their daughter unable to avoid the slippery slope. Now history was repeating itself. I was making a lot of the same mistakes.

It was with history in mind that I approached Granny one morning and said, 'I'd like to contact my dad.'

I knew her feelings about him, so it was to her credit that she only put up a token fight.

'Are you sure, dear? Are you really ready? You know what he did to you and your mother?'

I'd heard it all before, but that didn't change the fact that I wanted to see him. In my mind, I needed to give my dad the opportunity to explain to my face why he'd abandoned me, as I saw it. I needed to hear him say it was all a big mistake and that he'd been searching tirelessly for me for thirteen years. That's not how it worked out.

I should have guessed that my father would not live up to my dreams when he suggested our meeting place. He knew a pub in Rottingdean, the White Lion, and thought we should meet there.

He was already seated when I arrived. I think we shook hands, possibly there was a hug. No kisses though. Not yet. I can't remember a single topic we spoke about for the simple reason that we didn't discuss anything important. Unsurprisingly, he didn't exactly rush to explain why he'd left Mum all those years ago or why he'd stayed out of my life for so long. And I had no desire whatsoever to ask him if he really had planned to put me into care.

There's plenty of time for that one . . .

In the meantime, we broke the ice with the standard uninteresting probes.

'How's school?'

'Fine.'

'How's your grandmother?'

'Fine.'

'And your grandfather?'

'Scary. What's your job?'

'I run a holiday resort in France. Have you got a boyfriend?'

And so on and so on.

One awkward hour later, we parted with the vague promise to see each other again soon. I was in no hurry to do it again and from what I could tell, neither was he. Only years later did I question why Dad thought it would be appropriate to meet a fourteen-year-old girl in a pub!

Granny wasn't happy when I reported how my meeting with

158

my father had gone. As much as she'd expected him to disappoint me, she still didn't like to see me get hurt. Not again.

At least our joint low opinion of Dad gave us common ground. On so many other topics we were at loggerheads. In fact, the atmosphere at home deteriorated quite rapidly. It was just a clash of wills, really. I wanted to leave and, despite my grandparents secretly craving their own freedom as much as I longed for mine, they didn't think I should, at least not until I'd finished my education. Then, they reasoned, they could, in all conscience, say they'd done what they'd sworn to do on my mother's death. But until then we were forced into an occasionally uneasy truce.

I wasn't really drinking heavily, so they never saw me drunk, and because Grandpa was a heavy smoker, they never detected smoke on my clothes. Arguments tended to be over stupid things – like the time I was helping with the Sunday roast.

It had all been going so well. Granny was carving the meat and I was next to her, trying to tease the hot baking tray of vegetables from its shelf. It was my fifth attempt and yet again the tray was refusing to budge. The heat was pouring out and I was getting flustered. I gave it another go and – same result.

'Bugger this stupid thing!' I said and slammed the oven door shut.

'What did you say?' Granny's voice screamed into my ear.

I was so angry at the oven I couldn't even remember what I'd said.

'Nothing,' I replied.

There must have been something else bothering her because Granny overreacted. She shouted, 'Liar!' then spun me round. The next thing I knew, the tip of her great big carving knife was an inch from my face and she was shaking uncontrollably.

'How dare you use language like that in my house!'

I was no longer listening. Whatever Granny's problem was, I didn't care. I couldn't take my eyes off the glinting blade. I knew she wasn't going to hurt me, but I couldn't stop thinking about the Stanley knife I'd faced years before. I lashed out. I couldn't help it.

'I'm not scared of you, you old bag!'

'What did you call me?'

'You heard.'

That was the one moment when I thought she was going to lose it. She shook violently for a few seconds, then spat the following words into my face:

'I wish I'd let your father put you into care!'

I couldn't bite my tongue at that.

'You vicious old cow!'

But she was already storming off. I can't remember what happened to the vegetables that day, but we never spoke of it again.

Although I couldn't have my freedom by leaving Tremola Avenue on my sixteenth birthday, I could do the next best thing. I bought a motorbike.

It was a lovely Honda MB 50, with a top box and – best of all – matching wheels! I couldn't have been happier. Now the whole world – or at least the south-east part of the UK – was my oyster. Eighteen years after my mother had fled to the Isle of Wight for an illicit weekend, I had taken my first innocent steps towards joining the same mods and rockers crowd. It wouldn't be the last time our paths crossed . . .

Of course, you can't buy a bike without the accessories. All the bikers at the time were wearing leather jackets with tassels, so I thought, *I'll have one of those.* I really thought I looked the business. Unfortunately, not everyone agreed.

Longhill School didn't care how you travelled there, but they did care what clothing was worn on the school premises. The headmaster – the very same headmaster who had had to deal with my mother, I learnt later – said my jacket did not conform to school policy.

'You'll have to leave it at home or not come in yourself.'

True, I was wearing it mostly because it was cool, but all bikers wear leather for protection. Underneath was my uniform. I couldn't see what the problem was. And neither, miraculously, could Grandpa.

'What are you doing home?' he asked when I arrived back early that day.

'I was sent home to change,' and I explained.

'We're not going to stand for this. I'm phoning the head.'

To my amazement, Grandpa rang the headmaster there and then and told him in no uncertain terms that my jacket was a safety measure and that as long as I didn't wear it on the premises there should be no complaint from the school. It worked. The next day I returned in full tassels.

The look was important. I had matching DM boots and snake-effect trousers for wearing at weekends. Gone were the days of cycling and fresh air. All I was interested in now was drinking and smoking and riding – and I wasn't alone. Every Friday night I'd ride into Brighton and drink at a pub called the Hungry Years. It's called the Charles Street Bar now and it caters for a different clientele, but in the 1980s it was where all the bikers hung out. So that's where my new boyfriend, Simon, and I liked to go in our biker garb.

Simon was a seventeen-year-old apprentice scaffolder by day, but he had the DMs, the leather jacket and the attitude. His hair wasn't that long, but otherwise he looked the part. Every weekend there was a heavy-metal disco upstairs until the small hours, so I wasn't getting home until very, very late. But, as far as I was concerned, my grandparents could have no complaints. Yes, I was out, but they knew where I was – roughly. I was usually courteous and I did my best to get along with them. After all, I only had to get through my exams and then it would all be over.

Spring 1986 finally came and I sat down to take my O levels. The level of revision I'd managed to squeeze in was laughable. How I wished I'd taken them a year earlier, when some of the questions would have meant something to me. But I did my best – that was a habit I could never break – and in the end I scored higher than a lot of people who'd worked hard. It was also important to me to keep my word to Grandpa. I'd said I'd take them and I was going to. When they were over, however, that was a completely different story.

I finished my final exam at one o'clock one Friday in June. An hour later I had filled a hired van with all my possessions, including everything from my 'bottom drawer'. With Simon at the wheel, I was ready to start life as an adult.

It wasn't a shock to my grandparents. They'd known my plans and put up with my flat-hunting stories for the last few weeks. Now the moment had arrived and we parted exactly as I knew we would. Granny gave me a squeeze and told me to call her if I needed anything. Grandpa just held out his hand. As I reached to shake it, he said, 'Good luck, Cathy.'

As we pulled away, I didn't look back once. Tremola Avenue was my past. I had my independence now. I was in control of my own life, of my own destiny.

No one will ever tell me what to do again.

ELEVEN

A Charming Man

I honestly thought this was the start of something new. Mark, Brian and those evil bastards who'd driven my mother to her death were long gone from my life. School was over – no more detentions or tellings off for no homework. And it was also 'bye bye' to Granny and Grandpa. There were no hard feelings, not from my side anyway, but I was glad to be out of their house. Out of their control.

Control, I realized, was what I'd always wanted. The hours I'd spent perfecting my dancing, judo, knitting, sewing, home-work, drawing – in the end it had all come down to me wanting to master the skill, to be the best. To take control of it.

Because that was something my mother had never been able to do. From the moment she'd fallen pregnant, her destiny was out of her hands. Reading through the box of correspondence that Granny had given me recently, I could see she'd had to fight even to keep me. It wasn't just her partner or her parents or her school who wanted a say in her life, it was the local council and even, for a while, the police. This wasn't a woman in control.

Mum had never had the whip hand at any point after that.

Apart from, perhaps, the time she worked at American Express, there was always someone calling the shots. Social services removed me, the police arrested her time after time and, of course, there were the men who abused her. I didn't know if they were the same ones who gave her the heroin or whether she had dealers unknown to me. Either way, that was where the real control came from. As far as I can tell, from the moment she began earning a decent wage at AmEx, she'd given in to the temptation of drugs. And when she lost her job she would do anything to get her hands on the stuff that would one day kill her. That was game over, as far as we were concerned. That was the point that Mum lost control forever. I swore that would never happen to me.

My new home was a top-floor flat in Lansdowne Terrace, Hove, which I shared with Simon, my boyfriend of ten months. We'd planned my escape from Tremola Avenue together. What could be more romantic? Two lovers loading a van and driving off into the distance. It was like a Hollywood chick flick. The reality turned out to be a bit different.

You think it's going to be amazing to live together, but what young teen ever imagines the drudgery of domestic life? He'd never had to wash up or cook or clean or shop for himself, and my experiences were long in the past. We'd certainly never had to worry about bills. We truly imagined just spending our days and nights making love and partying. How many young people have fallen for that?

It would have been easier with a bit more money. As an apprentice scaffolder, Simon was not bringing home much. I managed to get a job at the Prudential, which was courting school-leavers at the time, but that only paid about £60 a week.

Our rent was £52, so that didn't leave much for heating, food or luxuries. Candles became our light, kettles of hot water filled our sinks. We lived off tins of beans and dry bread. It was an eye-opener for Simon, but of course I'd experienced it all before.

There wasn't a shortcut to cost-cutting that I didn't know. The electricity meter ran off 50p pieces, but after all our other costs these were few and far between. Fortunately I had the next best thing. One of my acquaintances from the Hungry Years tipped me off about the money mould and even lent me his. Essentially it was an ice-cube tray, except instead of cubes, the ice came out in the shape of currency! I couldn't believe it would work, but the second I pressed the icy coin into the meter I heard the electricity fire up. The only problem was that you were soon left with a rusting coin box. Some people drilled a hole in the bottom to bleed the melted water out, but as soon as the meter inspector saw that, you were rumbled. For a while, though, it worked just fine.

Our only luxuries were our bikes. Mine was only a 50cc – the maximum engine size for a sixteen-year-old – but Simon had a 125. After insurance and tax, we didn't have a huge amount for fuel, but we made it pay. Gone were my weekends of cycling and fresh air and packed lunches with health freaks. Now everything was about leather and sweat and petrol fumes. And, God, I loved it.

By now I was practically part of the furniture at the Hungry Years. I knew everyone and everyone knew me. That's how it felt, anyway. In practice, there was a large crowd of bikers – the Rising Sun gang they called themselves – all dressed the same in tasselled or studded leather over denim, and I didn't know much more about them than their names and their engine sizes. Different people came and went all the time, but there was always a face or two I recognized, someone who would look after me if Simon wasn't around. As the only sixteen-year-old, and certainly the only young girl, I never had to buy a drink – it was wonderful!

I looked the part too. I was still spending hours getting ready to go out, striving for the same effect which as an adult now takes two minutes. But at that age you're absolutely convinced that every eyelash has to be just so. Every item of clothing, especially my beloved stilettos, had to be spot on. That attention to detail really appealed to me. And when I saw that everyone had patches on their denim jackets I leapt onto that bandwagon with gusto. Pictures of skulls, semi-naked women, rats and poisons – the darker the image, the better – all went onto my jacket. I didn't give a monkey's about the pictures, I just loved sewing them on, creating this work of art to parade around the pub, and soon I was adding sinister drawings and patterns to everyone else's coats.

I must have looked pretty good, if I say so myself, because I can't think of anyone else who would have got away with the stuff I did at the Hungry Years. Apart from the heavy-metal disco every weekend, there was a jukebox in the bar that everyone used to play their Iron Maiden, Motörhead and AC/DC favourites. Not me. The money I saved on drinks went straight into playing Perry Como, 'Rambling Rose', Neil Sedaka, old classics like that. If another biker gang had come into that pub, the Rising Sun's reputation would have been gone.

Actually, I don't know if there was much of a reputation. They weren't Hell's Angels or anything like that. There wasn't a leader as such. They just liked to feel part of a group, so they all had their Rising Sun emblems sewn onto their coats and stuck on their bikes. They were all just happy to spend their nights playing pool in the Hungry Years – where I was a bit of a shark, I kid you not – and their days haring up and down the coastal roads.

I loved anything on two wheels – the faster, the better. My little 50cc would be barely out of the blocks when some of these other guys were dots in the distance, so I'd just jump on the back of one of theirs and enjoy it that way. Looking back, if I discovered my son was doing that now, I'd go spare. We would be clocking 100mph up these windy roads, bombing along, weaving in and out of traffic, with not a care in the world. Then we'd hit the five-mile straight on the A27 to St Dunstan's and really put our feet down. That's when I'd be clinging on so tight I could barely breathe and the speedometer would creep up and up until it was ticking 160mph. Absolute lunacy. But absolutely the best feeling in the world.

I had no trouble finding a ride. These guys were all in their late twenties and early thirties, so having the sexy sixteen-year-old on the back was a bit of kudos for them. But it wasn't all cock fighting because Simon, or anyone who didn't have their own powerful machine, was also invited to ride pillion.

I wasn't the only girl in the group. There were a few women, mostly about ten years older than me, and all of them happy to get involved in the laddish games of wet T-shirt competitions, topless dancing and the usual bloke-pleasing antics. The era of 'free love' was very much in vogue in the Rising Sun. I've always been a one-man woman, so that wasn't for me. But as a teen, at the height of my nascent sexual powers, I found it all really erotic and fascinating. I felt so mature just being part of it.

I suppose, reading this, you're thinking: 'How did you not have an accident?' The answer is: I did. Ironically, it didn't come when we were racing with the Rising Sun. If it had, I probably wouldn't have lived to tell the tale. I was out with a couple of Simon's friends. Their bikes were only 125s, but that was still more powerful than mine, so I was on the back as usual.

We were in Peacehaven, pottering along, looking for some-where for lunch. Simon pulled alongside us to indicate there was a Wimpy coming up and that should have been the end of it. But as we fell in behind him, his back and our front wheels connected. The next thing I knew I was flying through the air – with the bike just behind me. I landed on my knees and didn't have time to react to the giant shadow bearing down on me. Fortunately, most of the bike missed me, but the exhaust settled straight on the open wound on my leg. It already had gravel and crap in it, now it was being seared by the heat of the engine.

From there it was a case of waking up in an ambulance and panicking. *Am I alive? Do my legs work? Can I still walk?*

They obviously gave me painkillers, but not enough. Worst of all, nobody answered my questions. I must have blacked out again because the next thing I remember is being in a hospital bed, cursing and screaming at the shock and the pain. Suddenly I heard a disapproving voice.

'I really don't think you should swear quite so much, darling!'

Christ, it was Granny! Where did she come from? How long had I been unconscious? It didn't matter. I was in too much pain to think about my language now.

'Fuck off!'

Bearing in mind that she'd threatened me with a carving knife when I'd said 'bugger', you can imagine what went through her mind now.

But it was okay. I was fixed up and allowed to leave and Granny came round every other day to change my bandages. She didn't have to do that and it was good to see her. Like a lot of families, we probably got on better once we weren't under the same roof. Looking back, her visits remind me of the times she used to arrive with food for Mum and me.

The only problem was, I had to have a couple of months off work. By the time I was ready to return, they said they would not be renewing my contract. That was it. Cast onto the scrap-heap at sixteen. I was confident I could find another job, but I couldn't help feeling uneasy. Sixteen years old and life was going wrong already. Just like Mum.

Without my job, life with Simon was suddenly worse. You don't like to think money plays a part in matters of the heart, but when you find yourself arguing about bills and all that nonsense, it does. We were so young. We didn't know what we were doing. Still, I hated the idea of walking out without a fight. I'd left Tremola Avenue to set up home with this guy. It would be a failure – a personal failure – if it didn't work.

Looking back, was this my teenage response to my father walking out on Mum? Was I attempting to rewrite history with my own life? Either way, I promised myself, *I will not give up on this relationship.* It would be a position I would take again – and live to regret.

But then fate intervened and presented me with a way out. We were in bed one night, sound asleep, when suddenly I was awoken by a fierce banging. There was shouting as well.

'Simon!' I said, startled as hell.

By the time he came round, I'd realized where it was coming from. An old metal fire escape ran up the side of the house and there was someone standing on it outside our bedroom window.

'Christ,' I said, pulling the covers up, 'it's a burglar.'

'I don't think so,' Simon said. 'Listen.'

Above the sound of my heart racing, I could just about make out the words coming from outside.

'It's all right, it's your neighbour from downstairs!'

'Thank God for that,' I said. 'Are you going to answer?'

Simon shrugged yes, pulled on some trousers and went over to the window.

A second later there was more shouting and a bloke I'd never seen before was suddenly standing at the end of my bed. He was long-haired, scruffy and absolutely out of his mind with rage and who knows what else. And he was waving a long, sharp knife.

'What have you done with it?' he screamed. 'Where have you put it?'

I just wanted to crawl back under the sheets, but he was crazy, slashing the knife into the air like he was already in a sword fight in his head.

'Put what?' I managed to say.

He claimed he'd left his window open and someone had taken his jewellery. It had to be someone with access to the fire escape.

'Anyone could get up there,' Simon told him.

He wasn't having it. 'It was you. I know it was. If you don't cough it up you're getting it.'

The way he was swaying and flailing that knife around, I knew he wasn't right in the brain. I'd seen it before at Telscombe Cliffs. He was high on something. Maybe he'd injected, I had no idea. I just knew that logic and reason and truth meant absolutely zero to him. There was nothing he wouldn't do at that moment.

At one point he accused me of hiding the jewels in the bed, so he ordered me out to check it. I was stark naked and even though he was too far gone to bat an eyelid, you never feel more

170

vulnerable than when you've nothing on. I honestly thought he was going to finish us off there and then.

Eventually, though, he calmed down. 'I'll give you twenty minutes,' he said. 'Bring it down to me and it's no hard feelings.' He went to leave. 'Don't bring it back,' he added, 'and I'll kill you.'

The second he was gone we bolted the door, slammed the window shut and both cried. We hadn't touched his jewellery. I'd never even seen him before. How the hell were we meant to return it?

'We need to call the police,' I said. The problem was, we had no phone and in order to get outside to the call box we'd have to get past that madman's front door.

Fortunately there was building work going on in the block next door and it was covered in scaffolding, so Simon, a natural where climbing was concerned, said, 'I'll jump over there and get help.'

That was a brilliant plan. But then, just as he was about to jump across, I said, 'What if he comes back? I don't want to be on my own!'

So in the end I went. I must have stood on that window sill for five minutes before I felt brave enough to swing across. Eventually I banged on the caretaker's door and he called the police, who arrived in minutes. After they'd interviewed me and Simon, they went to talk to the neighbour.

So what happened? Absolutely nothing. He denied all knowledge and the police said there was no evidence. They asked if I could identify the weapon, but it was a kitchen knife. There was no law about having one of those on the premises.

The only positive to come out of it was that we showed the neighbour we were prepared to call the police. He never bothered us again, but life there was ruined. I couldn't walk down the stairs without feeling sick at the thought that he might come out. And every morning we would find both our motor-bikes kicked over in the street. It had to be him.

It wouldn't take a genius to draw the parallels between enter-ing that building and coming home to Preston Park or one of our old flats, with that sick feeling in the pit of my stomach, worrying if those men would be there or not. I thought I'd put those days of fear and intimidation behind me. I was wrong. So I had to act.

I can't live here, I realized. But with no money and no job, where could I go?

The only saving grace in those days and weeks after the down-stairs druggy incident was the Hungry Years. Ever since I'd first stepped through the door, as an illegal fifteen-year-old, I'd had this sense of déjà vu. Then, out of the blue, it came to me.

Mum used to bring me here.

I didn't know why I hadn't remembered earlier, but it was true. I was taken there as a toddler, allowed to wander around the bar while strangers attempted to amuse me. Mum drank snowballs. Even though I didn't know what it was called back then, I could still clearly picture the yellow Advocaat and re-membered thinking how ladylike she looked holding it.

It gave me a little fillip, realizing Mum and I had the same tastes. Maybe I blocked them on purpose, but any other emerg-ing parallels between our lives did not enter my mind. If only they had, I could have done something about it . . .

The Rising Sun crowd were a big, brash mob. Your classic biker gang, I suppose. They played drinking games in the car park at Box Hill. Blokes would 'accidentally on purpose' spray beer over women's tops so they had to whip them off and it was all a great laugh – and probably scared the bejesus out of old ladies on occasion, by looking like the tabloids' version of typical two-wheeled trouble-makers. But they were nice guys really.

Nothing gave me greater pleasure than playing pool all night – winner stays on – and drinking and giggling with everyone and making them all listen to 'Oh Carol' on the jukebox. I couldn't get enough of their company and, because they were so much older than me, everyone seemed so exotic. On reflection, most probably had day jobs in banks and things and only let their hair down at weekends, but as an impressionable teen, I just thought they were all so worldly and experienced in things I'd never understand.

Of all the characters there, one guy began to emerge more than others. As I've said, no one really led the group. Members came and went and the faces changed quite regularly. But during that first summer as an independent woman, I realized I was seeing one face more and more often.

The first time I saw him I was playing pool, as usual. I noticed that a small crowd had gathered round one table. Always keen to be near the action, I drifted over. Usually everyone would be trying to chip in with their own jokes and stories, the usual one-upmanship you get in groups. But on this occasion everyone was quiet, listening to this bloke.

I'd never noticed him before. He was older than the rest of them, at thirty-something, and even seated I could tell he was quite short, about 5'7. He was slim, dressed head to toe in tight denim and his skin was really tanned, which I liked. Whereas everyone else in the pub had long, trademark, Samson-like biker hair, his was closely cropped. Even his leathers stood out from the pack. The vogue at the time was for tassels, studs and sewn-on patches – the more outlandish, the better. His jacket was more Lewis Collins from *The Professionals*, heavy and practical.

At first glance then, he was unusual, but certainly not eye-catching. So why did he have such an audience?

I pulled up a chair and realized why everyone else was so quiet. The stranger had such a thick accent that I could barely make out every other word. I don't think I'd ever heard a Scottish accent before and this Glaswegian brogue was almost impenetrable. The man spoke quietly but with passion and the more I struggled to understand him, the closer I leaned in and the more I became hooked on his every word.

At one point I caught his eye and he paused. Then he took another puff on his Old Holborn roll-up and carried on speaking about the wounds he'd picked up during service on the front line.

'I've still got shrapnel in my wrist,' he said, pulling up his right sleeve for his audience to examine, 'but the worst of it is in the back of my skull.' He reached behind to the top of his neck. 'Just here.'

'Does it hurt?' someone asked.

'What do you think?' he replied with a wink. 'I've got drugs for it, but the pain never really goes away.'

I really was rapt. It was like watching one of those Sunday-night documentaries Grandpa loved. But this guy wasn't on television, he was right here in the Hungry Years. Most of my friends had never been outside Sussex. This bloke seemed to have been everywhere. This was a man who'd fought for his country in Aden. I didn't know where that was, but it sounded important. As for the shrapnel embedded in his body – that just made him the bravest person I'd ever met.

At some point, the group broke up for more games of pool

and a bit of dancing, but when we all got on our bikes to go home I found myself seeking the stranger out to see what he was riding. I wasn't disappointed. He had an old Honda CM250 with drop handlebars – my favourite.

A few days later, I saw the man again. When I walked into the Hungry Years he was already at the bar. 'Can I get you a drink?' he asked. I was flattered. After all, I didn't even know his name. A few minutes later we'd found a table and I was learning even more about his incredible past. He'd risked his life repairing oil rigs and had held high-powered jobs, with hundreds of people under him. Everything he said sounded so glamorous and so, so grown up. The people he'd met, the things he'd done, the danger he'd been in – it was an intoxicating cocktail for a girl desperate for something better. And best of all, not one of his stories was about scaffolding.

To be fair to Simon, I wasn't exactly setting the world alight with my own conversation. It's not easy to compete with a war veteran and I felt embarrassed that I'd done so little with my life. I found myself telling him that my mother had died when I was young – I didn't reveal how – and that I didn't really know my dad. I even heard myself telling him about the frustrations of living at Tremola Avenue. He laughed and nodded in all the right places, but I was convinced I must be boring him. What on earth did I have to offer a man like him?

He had plenty to offer me though. When I told him about my money worries, he just shrugged.

'A girl shouldn't have to worry about money. I'd never let a girl like you worry about money.'

'But I like working,' I insisted. 'I just can't find a job.'

'I'll give you a job,' he said. 'I manage a hotel. If it's work you want, then I'm your man.'

I couldn't believe it. Was there no end to this man's surprises?

I've thought about this moment thousands of times and, honestly, it was never a case of love at first sight. But I can't deny there was a lot about this man that I found very attractive. So, when he added casually, 'There's a bed for you there as well,' I leapt at it. He didn't say if it was sharing with him or not – and I didn't care. The fact that it was in his power to offer me anything at all, I found very seductive.

My life with Simon was over. In truth, it had been since I'd met this man who was older than my father. We'd run our course and it was time to part. Simon couldn't offer me half the things this stranger had promised. Where were his war wounds or tales of outwitting the law in half a dozen countries?

I admit, I was intoxicated. I'd been looking for an escape route from the drudgery of life with Simon, a way out of the hellish flat I was too scared to be in on my own and a new job. Suddenly this amazing man was offering me all three.

That wasn't all he was offering me, but I didn't care. The whole package was too good to turn down. By the time the summer of 1986 had turned into autumn, I'd moved in with my knight in leather armour. I'd moved in with Peter Tobin.

TWELVE

The Signs were There

For the second time in six months I was in a hired van loaded with my bottom drawer treasures and a combination of suits from my short-lived job and my bike garb. As Peter and I pulled up outside the large chunk of seafront terrace that was to be my new home, I was excited by the prospect of a new beginning. No knife-wielding druggies, no immature boyfriends with irritating friends and no more tedious builders' tales. It was a new dawn.

Going into the block, I was surprised not to see a reception, but assumed we'd used a trade entrance. Even that seemed strangely impressive. *He has his own door!* The corridors didn't seem to be in the freshest condition and when Peter stopped and unlocked a door I thought, *Is this it?*

Then we stepped inside and my nerves vanished. It was a nice flat, lovely even, and certainly the best one I'd ever lived in. It had a big lounge, six or seven steps leading up into a kitchen and dining area and then you went down a corridor at the side and there was a bedroom and a loo at the back. The pièce de résistance, however, was the view from the dining-area window – miles of glorious beach and sea. I was literally speechless.

Standing there, staring out at the lapping waves, my head was filled with all the possibilities that lay ahead. Life was going to be fantastic. And, I was pretty sure, it was going to be with Peter.

If I'm honest, enjoying that view from a pretty impressive flat had probably doubled, trebled even, the allure of the man I'd impetuously decided to set up home with. One day I'd been living with Simon, the next here I was with a chap more than twice his age. But whereas Simon had been in almost as bad a position as me financially, my new partner could offer me a job and this amazing home. It all counted in his favour.

I still hadn't really got to the bottom of our sleeping arrangements. I presumed Peter thought we were a couple and I was prepared to go along with that. It sounds crass now, but at the time I thought, *It's the least I can do. He's doing so much for me.*

My other boyfriends had been chosen on the strength of their looks – and look how they'd ended up. I couldn't say I fancied Peter, but I was infatuated by the idea of being in a grown-up relationship with him. That in itself was enough for Peter to take on some allure in my eyes. My friends were doing A levels or hanging out with teenagers as skint as they were. He was offering me the chance of something different, something mature. Something my parents had never had.

I couldn't, then, hand on heart, claim I was blinded by love. Not at first. I was blinded by something though because as impressive as the flat turned out to be, when I saw the rest of the building the following morning, I only had questions. Our corridor was typical of the grotty décor throughout the place and, I'd been right, there was no reception – for the simple reason that it wasn't really a hotel at all. It was a doss-house for old men.

It had been a hotel at one point, quite a grand one judging by the remains of the original features, but that had been years ago. Then some landlord had converted the rooms into self-contained bedsits and begun charging the council to put people up there. Now its only occupants were retired, older blokes on pensions and benefits. It was honest enough, but it was hardly the Ritz.

If it's not a hotel, I wondered, *then how can Peter be the manager?*

Simple answer: he wasn't. At best, I could describe him as odd-job-man-cum-janitor. The old boys pretty much looked after themselves, so all Peter had to do was make sure the cleaner turned up, organize the annual fire check and fix anything that went wrong. Apart from that, there was a little bar in the hotel where Peter would serve the tenants their whiskies. It wasn't to be sniffed at, but no one would call him a manager.

Another thought occurred to me. *If Peter's not the manager and there isn't a huge staff under him, what job is there for me?*

He seemed surprised when I mentioned it.

'A job? You don't have to work.'

'But I want to work. You said you had something for me here.'

He thought for a moment.

'Yeah, of course. But you don't have to, you know.'

The silly young girl in me was flattered that he didn't want me to get my hands dirty. I saw it as him offering to look after me. That really didn't fit in with my need to earn my own money and control my own destiny, but it was almost sexy that he wanted to.

Even when I realized that there was no job as such and I'd only be helping out with the cleaning and doing a few hours behind the bar, I didn't care. I certainly wasn't going to make a fuss and storm out. After all, whatever my circumstances here, they were a damn sight better than where I'd been a few days earlier. If anything, I was flattered that he'd lied to impress me. Mainly though, I'd be staying because I didn't have anywhere else to go.

There was always Saltdean, but, just like my mother before me, the last thing I wanted to do was admit defeat. I couldn't face the disapproving glare in Granny's eyes or, worse, the idea that Grandpa would say those four damning words: 'I told you so.'

For years since her death, I'd wondered why Mum had never asked for help. Why hadn't she gone to Grandpa when we were living in fear, with no electricity, no heating, no food? Those questions had eaten me up for eight years. Why, why, why?

And now I knew. Mum's parents were proud people and they'd made her proud and, in turn, me proud. Too proud for my own good, as it turned out. But I didn't know that then.

But there was another reason why I turned a blind eye to Peter's false promises. I would never have admitted it then, but it's pretty easy to spot all these years later, isn't it? There was me, who hadn't known my dad until I was fourteen, abused by a string of evil men, and all the while my life had been crying out for a hero to ride to my rescue. It had been crying out for a father figure. And now I'd found him.

Everyone has 20/20 vision in hindsight. Apart from the father figure thing and my insistence on demonstrating the same character flaws that had done for Mum, there was another obvious clue to what was just around the corner staring me right in the face. I was making excuses for him

I thought nothing of it at the time. Peter had lied about his job. *That's fine*, I told myself, *he's just trying to impress me*.

He'd lied about being able to find me work. *No problem*, I

said, *he's just being chivalrous. He doesn't want his young lady to work.*

Two lies, two justifications. I know now that it's a classic trait of domestic abuse victims. They gloss over the problems and somehow dress up the bad things as inevitable. Often they convince themselves it was their fault. They were only small lies and he certainly wasn't the only man who's ever told porkies to get a girl into bed, but I should have seen that a pattern was emerging about the way he was going to treat me in the future. The signs were there.

Very quickly our life settled into a routine. I tried desperately to be the 'good wife', keeping the flat spick and span and making sure there was a meal on the table when Peter came in. Unfortunately, Granny had only let me help in the kitchen occasionally on a Sunday, so I had very little cooking ability. But I was willing to learn. *Anything for my man.*

Sometimes I worked at the doss-house, sometimes I didn't. For a while I got a job as a silver service waitress at the Metropole – a proper hotel. Even when I wasn't busy, contact with the Rising Sun guys fizzled out. Peter didn't exactly tell me not to see them anymore. He just used to find other things for us to do instead. After a while, I realized we hadn't been to the Hungry Years in weeks.

Funnily enough, I didn't miss them. Not at first. I'd look around our lovely flat and think how lucky I was, especially when I'd remember the places some of those other guys lived. In the past, a group of us would go back to someone's house or flat and even when I was caught up in the whirl of being a biker chick, I didn't like the way they lived. Every place would stink, usually of damp, and there would be empty cans and fag ends everywhere. I'd come from a world of linen napkins and domestic order. Now I was entering a world where clothes were strewn over the floor, table tops served as ashtrays and last week's curry remains littered every surface – and nobody seemed to notice but me. They treated their homes like they were squats, whether they were or not. Although they were great fun to be out and about with, that wasn't the life I wanted to lead.

Yet another reason, then, to be grateful for Peter.

As the group faded from our lives, another figure – somewhat grey, lean and stooped – emerged. John was one of the residents at the doss-house. He was old, about seventy, and was always shuffling around in his crepe-soled shoes. But from the way he and Peter talked, it was clear they shared years of history. They were both from the same part of Scotland, I think, although how they ended up together in Brighton was a mystery. Although he'd been a newcomer to the Hungry Years, Peter told me he'd been in Brighton for ages because of his previous marriage. In fact, he said, his stillborn daughter from that relationship was buried in a local cemetery and he'd already bought the plot next to hers for himself. It was such a tragic story, I never had the heart to ask for more information.

He'll tell me when he's ready.

I'd often see John and Peter walking up and down the streets together or going for a drink or watching the world from a bench.

It's only looking back – there's that hindsight again – that I realize it must have been Peter's idea that we put a bit of distance between the bikers and us. Eventually I figured out that he'd been a pretty transient character, not really that close to any of them and not, I didn't realize till later, even a member of the Rising Sun gang. I, on the other hand, had been at the centre of that community for a couple of years. I'd done my growing up with them. I knew everyone and they knew me. Only a paranoiac would ever think that their partner was actively trying to steer them away from seeing their friends, so obviously that thought never crossed my mind. But that is exactly what he was doing.

Peter's greatest skill was manipulation. As I mentioned, he never told me to stop seeing the gang. Sometimes he put obstacles in the way – like arranging for us to go somewhere else on a weekend or giving me a few hours' work. Other times, if he could see I was wavering about going, he'd just let slip a few snide remarks one of them had said about me.

'You know he thinks you're cheap, don't you?' he said about one guy I'd known for years.

I fell for it.

'What do you mean, cheap?'

'It's not fair for me to say,' Peter said, suddenly coy. 'He's not here to defend himself.'

'I'll be the judge of what's fair. Just tell me what he said.'

'Okay, but you didn't hear it from me.' He paused and looked at me lovingly. 'Are you sure you want to hear this?'

'Just tell me.'

'Okay, he says you're the local bike. You have been since you were fourteen.'

'That's a lie!'

'I know, pet, I know. I told him that. I said, "If I hear you say that again there'll be trouble."'

There were plenty of conversations like that. At the time, I'd be ready to march down to the pub and declare open season. But then I'd usually think, *Sod them*. The upshot was, I wouldn't see anyone – which is, of course, what Peter had wanted all along.

So why, I bet you're asking, did I listen to him?

183

CATHY WILSON

It's a good question and it has a very simple answer: because I honestly thought I'd got the better deal in this relationship! I'd seen the women flocking round Peter at the Hungry Years. Girls always came over to him when we were out; I'd seen it with my own eyes. And, from what I could tell, they all had a lot more to offer than I did. They were older, more mature; they knew how to treat a man.

I had so much to learn, I knew that. When I came back to the flat one day and found Peter having coffee with a woman I'd never seen before, I was angry. That quickly became jealousy – *Why is she here, in my home, with my man?* But then, when Peter explained this Lucy woman was just a friend, no different to John, I just felt stupid. I was so young. I'd had no parents to show me the ways of the world.

That's obviously how proper grown-up relationships work.

There were times when I considered myself literally honoured to have been chosen by Peter. So that's why, whenever he suggested something, I listened. I hung on his every word. Even when he tried to change me.

The things about me that he'd said turned him on – my short skirts, stilettos, bright-red lipstick – were the first things to go. I don't know how he did it. Those were the things I most associated with my own identity. I'd cultivated that look over years of posing and preening and shopping and experimenting. Yet somehow they all gradually disappeared from my fashion repertoire.

The heels went first. I suppose he felt more comfortable without me looming over him, but he never admitted that. He was clever. He said, 'I've got you a present,' and handed over a shoe box. More excited than you could imagine, I ripped it open – and found the ugliest pair of flat shoes I'd ever seen.

184

The me of a few months earlier would have laughed in his face and thrown them back at him. The new me, the one so desperate to be mature enough for this worldly man, didn't want to disappoint. And so I took the shoes and put them on and didn't look back.

When you're young and you think you're in love, you want to please your partner, don't you? It's natural. If you don't, then you're in the wrong relationship. So when he mentioned how much he liked longer skirts, I found myself digging around for something a bit more respectable. I hadn't worn anything below the knee for years, but I did it for Peter. Making him happy made me happy, just as it had done with Mum.

A couple of other changes happened for different reasons. Without regular work, I had no income. Peter gave me money for shopping, but made it clear that times were tight. He never actually said, 'Don't waste your money on lipsticks and mascaras,' but I would have felt a selfish cow if I had. So, gradually, as the staples of my make-up bag were depleted, the colour vanished from my face. As for maintaining the highlights in my immaculately coiffed hair – forget it. I couldn't justify that, not when he was being so kind to me in the first place.

If you'd asked me at the time, I would have sworn there was never any pressure on me to dress down. Even when he would pore over every till receipt, scrutinizing where every penny of his cash had gone, I chalked it up to a generational thing or maybe even a Scottish habit. He was checking the shops hadn't ripped him off, I assumed. It would never have occurred to me to imagine he was checking up on me. What sort of person would even think of such a thing?

It took about two months. By the turn of the year I'd gone from hot young thing to a plain Jane in sackcloth and sensible shoes. I was like a bad caricature of my former self and the worst thing was that I couldn't even tell. When I looked in the mirror I didn't see this dowdy, mousey-haired teenager staring back. I only saw the proud, happy partner of the wonderful Mr Tobin.

To this day, I don't know if Peter had a plan with me or whether he was acting on pure instinct. I don't know if he schemed from the start to make me utterly dependent on him, to rob me of any shred of self-esteem or independence, or whether that's just how he was. For all I know, he did that to every partner.

When I consider all the things that happened seemingly randomly, it seems inconceivable that it was pure chance. He must have been pulling the strings from the moment we met, spinning plates in the air one at a time – and he was so damn smooth I never even noticed. It was a war of wills and I'd surrendered before it had begun.

I know now that changing my appearance was a control thing. He didn't give a toss about my hair or my skirts or my tight tops or my heels. He probably liked them. But what he really loved more than anything was proving that he was the boss of me. If he could take those things most precious to me, the very characteristics that I thought defined me, and make me give them up, then he could do anything to me. That was his logic – and that is exactly what happened.

Everything was so subtle, so cunning. It was like being mugged and not realizing it until the pickpocket has left the country. Whatever he did, however extreme it seems to me today, there was always a reason for his behaviour. I could always come up with a justification. Maybe he planted the idea, but it was always my own call. I came up with the excuses all on my own and didn't I feel clever for that.

He engineered everything. Getting me to change my appearance would never have worked if we'd kept in with the Rising Sun crowd. I would never have agreed to ditch my leathers if I was still knocking around in those circles – the bikers would never have let me get away with those shoes and dresses. So he'd steered me away from them, chipping away, whispering how I was better than them, how they didn't deserve me, how I was too mature for those reprobates. I was so hungry for approval, I lapped it up. Was he a master of human nature or did he just spot that my ego would respond that way? I think it was a bit of both. Anyway, it worked. He played me like a puppet. Every day that passed, he exerted more and more control over me.

Of course, I didn't see any of this. If I had, I would never have fallen for his next trick.

The way Peter explained his lowly job at the old folks' place was simple and perfectly logical – and, of course, he came out of it in a sympathetic light.

After so many successful years making a fortune in various different and exciting industries, his war wounds had finally caught up with him. The shrapnel was sliding further into his body and inflicting more pain. Ultimately, he was too ill to work. As for his money, well, he admitted he'd been married before, but she'd run off as soon as he was too ill to work, wiping out all their savings. So now here he was, an injured war hero, doing the best he could in Brighton, looking after pensioners.

It was a story to make anyone's heart bleed. I had nothing but respect for the way he'd got his life back on track. I didn't even begrudge him milking the benefits system for every penny he could squeeze out.

'They owe me,' he said. 'After all I've done for this country.'

I was compelled to agree. *He put his body on the line and now he's paying for it with his health. It's the least the government can do.*

Even that was a massive change for me. A year before, the idea of accepting dole money or disability allowances or any of those handouts would have been anathema to me. That was Grandpa's pride seeping through again. He'd been offered financial help to look after me but had refused it. 'No one is going to tell me I can't afford to feed my family,' he'd said. As much as I learnt to respect his principles, if he hadn't been so stubborn I would have been able to do judo *and* ballroom dancing.

So once again, without even seeing the sleight of hand, I'd given up another piece of my personality and replaced it with a slice of Peter's. My pride at pulling my weight and my desire to work had gone up against Peter's raging sense of entitlement and hadn't even landed a punch. I hate myself for it now, but I just gave in. Another cherished belief handed over and trampled into the dust by the master manipulator.

Living off a disability pension meant Peter was always disappearing to the doctor's for check-ups and tests. Usually he'd return with the largest bag of pills I'd ever seen. Some of them had names like Amitriptyline and Triazolam, but I didn't have a clue what they were for.

'Do you take all of those?'

'Every one,' he said. 'Until next month when I get a new batch.'

God, I'd had no idea he was so ill. I'd never heard him mention his pain since that first day in the Hungry Years. *The poor love must be so brave,* I thought, *keeping it to himself.* And what pain must he have been in to warrant this vast amount of drugs? I didn't have any answers. All I could say for sure is that I was more determined than ever to look after him. He deserved it.

One day Peter returned from his trip to the GP with the usual medication, but I could tell there was something wrong. It was in his face, in his body language, it even seemed to come out of his pores.

'Are you all right?'

'Oh, don't you worry about me, hen, I'm fine,' he said, but clearly that was a lie.

If my man's ill, it's my job to know, I told myself. The amount of pride I derived from seeing through his protestations of good health was ridiculous. It was affirmation, me proving that I was a good girlfriend.

I had to wrestle it out of him, or so I thought, but eventually Peter told me to sit down with him. Worried as hell, I obeyed. Every second that he sat there, in silence, I felt the fear rise in me. *What on earth is he going to say?* I'd gone from pride to anxiety to abject terror in the blink of an eye.

'I saw my doctor today and he gave me the results of a test I had done last week.'

'Test? What test? You never told me you were having a test? What's wrong?'

'I found a lump,' he said, so quietly that I had to lean in, hanging on his every syllable. 'In my testicle.'

I gasped. I couldn't help it. The tears were already in my eyes, waiting for their cue.

'It's not . . . ?' I couldn't bring myself to say the word.

Peter nodded. 'It is. I'm sorry, love. I've got cancer.'

Wow. When a bombshell like that hits, you can either bury your head in the sand or go crazy. I went crazy, completely into overdrive. I wanted to know everything about this perfidious disease. I wanted to completely mother my man, fulfil his every whim. And I wanted to show my love for him more than ever. We had to fight this together. We were a team.

'Are they going to cut your balls off?' I asked.

Of all the questions! But that's what they did to women with breast cancer. I figured it would be the same for him.

Peter shook his head. 'No, thank God. The doctor thinks he can treat it with a laser. I won't lose anything.' He paused. 'Except . . .'

'Except what? Come on, you can tell me. I'm here for you.'

He picked up my hands and stared directly into my eyes. I felt like he could see into my very soul.

'The thing is, Cathy, when they use the laser, they'll kill off my reproductive ability. I'm so sorry,' he said, crying now. 'I won't be able to give you children.'

That was in January 1987. By the start of February I'd done some serious thinking. This was the man I intended to spend my life with. This was my war hero, my lover, my worldly gift of a man. *At some point in the future,* I rationalized, *I will want to have his babies.* That wasn't going to be possible, though, was it? So why not have them now?

Christ, I was much too young for children. My mother's problems had begun, it pained me to admit, when she'd accidentally fallen pregnant with me. Yes, she and Dad had got married. Yes, I suppose they were in love for a while. But they had been too young, too immature, too out of their depth to make it work. If their pregnancy hadn't exactly ruined their lives, it had certainly shaped them. And Mum's life, of course, had been ruled by the hold her blackmailers had over her while I was around. I was the knife they'd held at her throat, the sharp stick that made her do everything they demanded.

No, I told myself. Mum had been unlucky. She wasn't in control. Not of her body, not of her life. Not like me.

A few days later I told Peter I wanted to have his children.

'Really? But you're so young. It will change your life forever.'

'I know. But I want to do it.' I kissed him. 'For you.'

He hugged me tighter than he'd ever done before and we both cried.

And then, in March 1987, I announced I was pregnant and Peter couldn't have been happier. It wouldn't take me long to discover why . . .

THIRTEEN

I'll Try Harder

From the moment I became pregnant, everything altered. And not for the better.

Even before my little bump began to show and then grow and grow, it was all I could think about. My child had my full attention, my entire focus. Suddenly Peter wasn't the most important person in my life. My unborn baby was. And he didn't like it one bit.

'Where are you going?' he asked when he saw me getting ready to go out one morning.

'To the doctor's,' I replied. 'It's only a routine check-up. Nothing to worry about.'

'Well, if it's nothing to worry about, it can wait till after you've done some cleaning.'

I stared at him, searching his face for a sign that he was joking. Nothing.

'Are you serious?' I asked eventually.

'Well, this flat's not going to clean itself, is it?'

Too tired to argue, I took my coat off again and got out a brush to sweep the floor. Then, as soon as Peter had gone out,

I shoved the broom back in the cupboard and rushed out. If I hurried, I might still make the appointment.

It was only on the way back that I thought about Peter's behaviour. He was obviously anxious about the baby, I decided. I needed to remember that I wasn't the only one my pregnancy was affecting. I needed to be more sympathetic to him.

That was easier said than done. A few days later, during dinner, I brought up the subject of where our baby was going to sleep. I'd been thinking about it for ages and hoped that would be the cue for Peter to say we could go out shopping for bassinets and babygrows. I couldn't have been more wrong. He threw his cutlery down and looked like I'd insulted his mother.

'Shut the fuck up, woman!' he exploded. 'You're obsessed.' Then he pushed his chair back and stormed out of the flat. *He's just nervous about the baby,* I reassured myself. But that didn't stop me crying myself to sleep that night.

I truly hoped Peter would snap out of whatever was troubling him, but if anything he just got more and more angry. I couldn't do anything right. If there was a newspaper out of place, it was my fucking fault. If he couldn't find his watch, I must have fucking moved it. Everything was 'fuck' this or 'fuck' that, which I absolutely hated. Even worse, it was usually followed by some insult directed at me. 'What the fuck have you done with my keys, you stupid bitch?'

I'd gone from his 'princess' or 'beauty' or 'pet' or 'hen' to any number of vile insults. I didn't know where the anger was coming from. It was so shocking, so violent, I could only think of one explanation: had I done something wrong?

Just by asking the question, I was unwittingly falling deeper into his clutches. Think about it: he was swearing at *me*, calling *me* names, and I was the one wondering if I'd done anything wrong. No rational person would think like that. When you're in love, you're not rational. And when you're pregnant, people might as well be talking a foreign language. Logic goes completely out the window.

Not once did I think, *He needs to look after me now, I'm carrying his child.* The only thoughts passing through my head were things like *He can't help it. It's the pressure of his illness. The drugs are making him talk like that. It's the stress of going under the laser.* I even found myself thinking, *Is this what Scottish men are like? Is it just their way of talking?* You name it, I made an excuse for it.

I could have done with some support early on because those first days of pregnancy were tough. I suffered from chronic morning sickness and struggled to get around for a while. This is the time I should have been resting, being waited on by my partner. Peter, unfortunately, hadn't read the script. This was the period when he suddenly decided he needed me to work in the bar and clean the building. It was almost as if he didn't want me clogging up the flat while he was in there during the day.

Then, out of the blue, I was told I'd spent my last night in the flat. The owners announced they wanted to convert Peter's pad into a paid residence, so he was being relocated to a flat in a little cottage around the back of the building. I thought it sounded nice, although it was weird that I only got a day's notice. 'Surely someone would have told you earlier?' He denied it. What else could I do but get on with packing – alone? Two months pregnant and there I was stuffing crates and shifting boxes around the flat. Criminal, really.

Always willing to look on the bright side, I decided that our new home was just what we needed. We could draw a line under our recent trials and tribulations. This was a fresh beginning. *Another* fresh beginning.

If anything, though, Peter's behaviour in the cottage was even worse than before. His friend John was a regular visitor, especially on a weekend, when he'd come over for a few beers. Shortly after we'd moved home, John was there and Peter had finished his beer. He could have asked me for another one, he could even have got up and fetched a tin himself, to save my poor legs. But he didn't. His response to discovering a depleted glass was 'Empty again? Where's that fucking useless bitch?'

I was about ten feet away. I heard every word. The sudden viciousness of it was like a kick in the abdomen, an explosion of pure hatred. The way he looked at me sent a shiver down my spine. Worst of all, he didn't care that I'd heard.

Again, I put it down to fear of losing his testicle, but it did hurt. I would have done anything for that man and he was beginning to treat me like dirt. It was horrible, but, I decided, there was only one way to fix things. *I have to try harder to make him love me.*

I'd always got on well with John, but I could barely look him in the eye after that.

While I seemed to be getting more attention from Peter's harsh tongue, attention of a more intimate nature had pretty much dried up. I didn't know if that had something to do with the new flat or whether it was because of my growing bump, but my sex life was non-existent from the moment I first stepped into that cottage. I tried to seduce, I flirted and I even begged, but Peter wouldn't touch me. He made it clear that it wasn't right to be having sex while carrying a baby. I knew that wasn't true, but he succeeded in making me feel guilty.

One way to try to please him was to be a better housewife. I was no cook – a lifetime of uncooked roasts and non-rising cakes had taught me that. But I had an enthusiasm to master it which was complemented by my desperation to do anything for my man. I'd passed my home economics O level, but what good was that in the real world? If you needed a pineapple upside-down cake or mince pies, then I was your gal. But anything practical, anything you might actually want to serve for an evening meal, like roast lamb and mashed potato, was completely beyond my ken. But I tried.

One morning I said, 'What would you like for tea tonight?'

Without hesitation: 'Pork chops.'

'No problem. I'll buy some today.' So I did. I hopped on the Honda and was at the shops in no time. On the way back I was aware of that silly smile on my face that said, *I'm happy*. Any opportunity I had to do something special for Peter gave me a warm glow. For all my noises about independence, when it came to relationships, I was already a traditionalist. Peter brought home the bacon, such as it was, and I looked after him. I wanted to. Like so many other things in my life, you can trace it directly back to my own parents, can't you? If Mum had had a man to look after, all her troubles would never have happened. I was convinced of it at seventeen and I still believe it now. So I was excited. I couldn't wait for the evening.

Unfortunately, I didn't know how to cook chops and I'd never seen a recipe book, so I had to wait until Peter came home to ask.

'Just grill them,' he said and went off to read his newspaper.

Fine, I thought, and turned the grill on. I was in my element. This was what my man was used to. This was what his other partners had done. This was how they'd looked after him. I honestly got a real kick out of it. I just hoped I compared to them.

I was about to find out. Five minutes later I called Peter to the table.

'Hope you like it,' I said earnestly, serving his large plate of meat and boiled veg. He grunted – his usual reply when he was reading, but then he did have a lot on his mind – and I turned back to the kitchen area to serve myself. Before I'd even reached the oven, the wall in front of me exploded. I screamed and dived for cover.

Is the house falling down?

'You stupid cow! Are you trying to fucking poison me?'

I stared at the wall, stunned to see the remains of meat, gravy and veg smeared on it. Had he just thrown his plate at the wall?

No. He'd thrown it at me.

It turned out I'd seriously undercooked the pork. Peter had taken umbrage at that. Rather than ask me to put it back under the grill for a few more minutes, the red mist had descended. I really was lucky not to have crockery wounds in the back of my head. As it was, there were flecks of carrot and pork over me. As the full picture of what had just occurred gradually unfurled in my uncomprehending brain, I began to cry.

I did my best. I didn't mean to do it wrong. Why did he try to hurt me?

Cowering against the door of the still-warm oven, arms wrapped protectively over my head, I sobbed and sobbed. I just couldn't work it out. *Who throws their dinner just because it's a bit underdone?*

I was down there for just a few seconds, then I knew what I had to do.

'You shouldn't have done that!' I shouted at Peter, who was still sitting at the table. 'That's it, I'm leaving.'

I turned and ran towards the bedroom. It would take me

about a minute to grab enough emergency things. Before I got to the door, Peter was there. He was amazingly light on his feet for his age. His arm blocked my escape.

'Don't hurt me!' I begged and he looked genuinely shocked at the idea.

'I would never hurt you, silly,' he said softly and reached out to take my hand. I flinched. 'Babe,' he added, 'I'm sorry about that. You know how I get about food. I've had a hard day. The shit I've had to put up with. I'm sorry you were on the end of it.'

Still I didn't move. 'You could have hurt me. You could have hurt our baby!' The last words I virtually spat at him.

'Cathy, Cathy, Cathy! God, no, how could you think such a thing? I'm appalled. I just threw it at the wall. Look, I'm sorry, so sorry, you have to believe me. It was aimed at the wall, not you.'

He could see me wavering.

'Come on, babe, we'll clean it up together. It was just an accident.'

And that was it. A line was drawn under it in his head. For him, the big concession was helping me clear up his mess. I couldn't understand what had just gone on, but I went along with it. What choice did I have? I was pregnant with his child. I was penniless – and I was proud. I honestly think that was the moment I realized that I didn't and couldn't love him. But, more than ever, I was determined: *I'm going to make this relationship work.*

For a few days afterwards Peter couldn't have been nicer. It was as if he'd been shocked by his own destructive behaviour and had resolved to change. He didn't swear at me, put me down or even so much as joke about his meals. It was bliss. I really thought the future would be just fine. And, in any case, it was finally time for his operation. *He's got a lot on his mind. Of course he needs to let off steam.*

We went down to the Royal Sussex together and Peter was put in a bed to be prepared for his op. Doctors and nurses flitted in and out like waiters bursting through kitchen doors. Several of them smiled at my obvious baby bump and then one commented on it.

'Yes,' I said, 'I was really worried I wouldn't be able to conceive before the operation.'

'Why was that so important?'

'Because of the side effects. The fact that he won't be able to have children anymore.'

The doctor stared at me like I was speaking in tongues. 'What do you mean, this operation will stop him having children? It won't do anything of the sort.'

Now it was my turn to look confused.

'Peter said that after you laser his testicle, he'll be sterile.'

'No, no, that's completely wrong.'

'Well, that's what he thinks.'

The doctor puffed out his cheeks and scratched his chin. 'I can assure you, Mr Tobin has had it explained to him half a dozen times. He knows as well as I do that, at worst, he'll be one or two per cent less fertile. I promise you, he'll be able to conceive as well tomorrow as he would be able to today. And,' he nodded again at my tummy, 'there are obviously no complaints in that department.'

The doctor disappeared again and I was left to mull over his words. He must have been trying to cover his mistake. Peter obviously hadn't been told what the procedure would entail, otherwise we would never have tried so hard for a baby. Or would we?

Was there a chance that he did fully understand everything? No, of course not. I was angry at myself for even thinking it. What possible reason would he have for tricking me into getting pregnant? We were going to be together forever. There was plenty of time for a family.

The doctors were happy with the operation and, when Peter was finally allowed out, I raised the subject with him. I thought, *I'll know from the look on his face whether he was conning me or not.* But he responded as I knew he would: with utter incredulity at the doctor's claims.

'That's not true, hen. They told me it was all over for me and kids. Why would I lie about something like that?'

I didn't know. It was too far-fetched an idea to entertain for a moment longer. But I was still left thinking, *I'm seventeen years old and pregnant when I don't have to be.*

There was no way I could ever reveal that to my grand-parents.

I was so confused about Peter, I didn't know what to think. Whether he'd lied to me or not, I knew my options were vanishing by the day. In particular, I realized, without money, I was trapped. Peter was as fastidious about bill-checking as ever and as I wasn't allowed to work, I had to think of a new solution. That's when I hit upon the idea of teddy-bear kits. I was familiar with all the craft shops in Brighton, so I spent an afternoon buying equipment to sew a teddy bear from scratch. By then I'd designed a cute-looking bear, but that was only half the story. I then deconstructed it and made a pattern of the pieces. Once I'd replicated that a dozen times, I had twelve kits containing wadding, eyes, little bow ties – basically everything you needed to make the bear of your dreams. No more going into a sewing shop for two metres of fabric when you only needed one. I'd done it all for you.

I loved doing that. I was a real craft junkie. Once I'd finished, I gave them to Peter and he flogged them to the doss-house residents for their grandchildren. It didn't bring in a fortune – and Peter kept every penny anyway – but it kept my brain active and it showed me I did have the power to take back some control of my life. Unfortunately, I would need to do that sooner than I'd hoped.

Without the fear of his operation to occupy him, I honestly thought Peter would be a changed man. One day, then two, then three passed without incident. As we neared the week mark, I studied his every move, looking for a sign that he might erupt. But it didn't come. And then, a fortnight after Peter had been given the all-clear, I burnt his toast. And all hell broke loose.

'Fucking stupid, useless bitch!'

'It's only a bit of toast. I'll do another one,' I cried. 'Calm down.'

A second later, Peter had his nose pressed against mine. 'Don't you dare tell me to calm down. Have you got that, bitch? Never!'

I'd got it. I promised I'd never say it again and we moved on. I cried, he cried, I said I was scared, he apologized and promised it would never happen again.

It was maybe a week later when Peter found a smear on the lounge window.

'Come here,' he roared.

What now? I thought. But over I went, the dutiful woman.

'This was here yesterday,' he spat, literally shaking with fury. 'What the fuck do you do all day?'

'I didn't do the windows yesterday,' I explained, desperately trying to remain calm. 'I'll do them today.'

'You'll do them now.'

'I can't, I'm doing—'

But I never finished that sentence. He grabbed my dress so violently I nearly fell over. Then, dragging me furiously forwards, he began to rub away at the smear. I thought my dress was going to rip to shreds. *But*, I thought a few minutes later, when he was sobbing and pleading for my forgiveness, *at least he didn't use my face.*

Two weeks and two really unpleasant episodes. Still I persevered in my role as the accommodating spouse. I was like a woman possessed. Whatever Peter did, I was determined to rise above. I would prove myself the better person – and I would give our unborn child the security of a happy family life. But then he threw a screwdriver at my proud baby bump – and the rules changed.

I can't even remember what had provoked it. He'd been doing odd jobs, which is why he had his tools to hand. One minute we were talking, the next he'd flung his flat-head screwdriver like a circus performer throwing knives – and it was aimed straight at my tummy.

I screamed, dived out of the way and cowered as the tool ricocheted off a cupboard and landed on the floor by my feet. I leapt up, more angry than I'd ever been in my life. It was one thing to attack me, hurl abuse in my face, call me every name under the sun. It was another to put my child at risk.

'That was your last chance!' I screamed, but Peter didn't hear. He was halfway out the front door by the time I'd opened my mouth. There would be no tears from him this time, no grand apology as his tender hands cupped my cheeks. It was just as well. As far as I was concerned, he'd tried to hurt me for the last time. I threw a few things into half a dozen carrier bags and fled downstairs to my bike.

I didn't know where to go, but I knew I couldn't go back to Granny's. She'd been so good when I'd broken the news about the baby – 'Whatever you do, we'll always be here for you' – but it would just be embarrassing to go there now. I couldn't. That really had to be the very last resort.

Instead, I ran into a newsagent and grabbed a copy of the *Brighton Argus*. I ringed all the places with bedsits to rent and drove to an out-of-the-way phone box, where I hoped I wouldn't be interrupted for half an hour or so. Then I got out a handful of 5ps I'd been squirreling over weeks from my shopping change and started dialling.

I didn't know how long it would take or how many coins I would need. All I could think about was getting as far away from that tyrant as possible. I tried to hold it all together to make the calls, but I don't know how convincing I sounded. But that wasn't the reason landlady after landlady turned me down. The second I admitted I was pregnant – and they all asked – that was it, end of transaction, on to the next number. It was the same story every single time.

'I'm sorry, dear, I don't think young babies would fit in here. It's not that sort of place.'

I can't remember what ran out first: my money, my ringed numbers or my patience. By the end, though, I was in floods.

I'm ruined. Nobody wants me. What the hell am I going to do?

Half an hour later, tear marks still etched on my face, I found myself knocking on a door in Tremola Avenue. Granny stared at me for a second, then, without a word, threw her arms around me and ushered me into the house.

'There's a bed here for as long as you need it,' she said.

I'd never loved her more.

*

That should have been the end of it. That should have been the point at which Peter Tobin exited my life. That should have been the point where this book stopped.

But there was another chapter to come. Many chapters, in fact. When I came down to breakfast the next morning, after the most relaxing night's sleep in ages, I stopped, miserable with shock. There at the kitchen table with Granny and Grandpa was Peter. He looked like butter wouldn't melt, but as soon as he saw me, his face changed. If he'd mastered the emotional apology at home, in public it was a genuine tour de force.

'I've been an idiot, pet,' he said.

I didn't say anything.

'I don't deserve you, I know I don't.'

Still I said nothing. Peter didn't seem fazed. He just ploughed on.

'You've got to come back, baby. I need you. You know I do. I can't cope without you.'

'You'll cope just fine,' I said, surprising myself with how confident I sounded.

I was enjoying myself. Peter looked like he was about to burst into tears.

'You don't mean that, pet, I know you don't. Think of our baby. That little mite needs two parents. We owe it that, you know we do.'

Bastard!

He played his joker and I folded. A minute earlier, I'd never wanted to see Peter Tobin again. Then he punched below the belt and I knew I had no choice.

What sort of mother would I be not to give my baby a chance at a proper family?

He knew the answer as well as I did. I couldn't even look at

Granny as I packed my bags and climbed once again onto my Honda. For the sake of my baby, I was giving him another chance. The chance my parents had never given me.

That was one of the last times I rode my bike. At my next check-up at the doctor's, I complained how hard it was to get about on it. The old boy nearly coughed his false teeth out.

'You shouldn't be riding a bicycle at your stage!' he exclaimed, absolutely horrified.

'It's not a push bike,' I explained. 'It's a motorbike.'

I thought he was going to hyperventilate. 'No, no, no, that won't do! You can't be risking yourself and your baby on one of those death traps. I absolutely forbid it.'

So that was that. I could have ignored him, but he was right. What's more, he fell precisely into the 'father figure' category – so, basically, whatever he said, his word was law as far as I was concerned.

The final trimester of my pregnancy was upon us in no time. Long gone was the morning sickness. In its place were really strong cravings. Bearing in mind that I'm a vegetarian now, and have been for more than twenty years, it's incredible to think I was addicted to pork pies. Without my bike, I would waddle the mile down to the shops in my hideous, shapeless Mothercare tent of a dress, buy a pack of six and they'd be eaten before I was home. Luckily, my other craving was plums, which hopefully cancelled out the pies.

Peter could have gone to the shops for me. It would have taken him no time on his bike, but he didn't offer. I didn't ask – it was my duty, as I saw it. But as I got bigger, the walk took longer every day. I'd set out after breakfast and barely return in time to do lunch. Then it was time to clean the cottage and do the laundry. The place was a lot smaller than the hotel accommodation, so it only took ten minutes to lick it into shape. The washing was another matter. We didn't have a machine and Peter wouldn't waste money on a laundrette. Every day I had my arms in a sink of bubbles and hot water, scrubbing and rubbing. The rounder my tummy got, the further away I needed to stand, until in the end I could only reach the bottom of the sink by standing side-on.

It was agony on my back, but if Peter said we couldn't spare the 50p needed to get it done by machine, then so be it. I had no choice. The cleaning was another matter though. I knew I did a bloody good job – the flat was so pokey, it was harder to miss a surface than give it a wipe. But I noticed that whatever I did, Peter wasn't satisfied. Sometimes he would be around during the day and would see me with a duster and brush. If he went out, though, he was convinced I didn't bother. The first thing he'd do after coming home was run his finger over the table or window sill. And woe betide me if he found dust.

Usually it was easier to say I'd been too ill to clean – that seemed to calm him. But one day I thought, *Sod it, no. I've cleaned this shoe box of a place from top to bottom every day for four months. It's bloody spotless.*

And I told him so.

I don't know how I'd expected Peter to react, but I didn't see this coming. He leapt at me, screaming, 'You fucking liar!' and grabbed hold of my neck. I thought he was going to punch me, I honestly did, but I didn't dare cover my face. I needed both hands to protect my bump. That was the only thing that mattered.

It obviously didn't matter to him though. Gripping my neck as tightly as he could, he rasped into my ear, 'This is how you fucking clean' – and he slammed me against the wall, dragging my face along it like some cheap feather duster.

The whole ordeal probably lasted no longer than ten seconds from start to finish. Afterwards he was contrition personified. He was sorry, he loved me, he prayed the baby was okay. I'd heard it all so many times I could virtually have said it with him, but this time I didn't respond. I just stood, quivering, crying at the way he'd shoved me with no regard for our baby.

I have to get away from here.

Once again, however, my history held me back. My parents should have stayed together. That, I told myself, would have prevented all the bad things happening. That would have been enough to keep my mother alive. By the time I'd calmed down, I knew I wasn't going anywhere. My baby was only three months away. I had to make things work with Peter. Whatever the cost.

But, I thought, *I do need to think about emergencies.* If this behaviour continued once the baby was born, I would disappear. I would not put our child at risk. That was a promise. With that single thought, however, my motorbike went suddenly from perfect getaway vehicle to completely inappropriate.

That's no good for a baby, I realized. *I need a car.*

Before I could get a car, however, I needed to learn to drive. I went straight out and phoned BSM and said, 'I need to be able to drive in the next two and a half months – and I can only afford about six lessons.'

That didn't go down too well. I think they thought I was taking the mickey. But I was dead serious and I explained my reasons. I needed to be qualified when my baby was born. I wouldn't get a chance to learn after that. I just sensed it. The guy explained that I'd be hard-pressed to pass, but if I wanted, I could take lessons in an automatic and only qualify to drive those kinds of vehicles.

'Perfect,' I said.

207

Like everything else in my life, once I put my mind to my lessons, I knew I would succeed. Because I will always succeed – or die trying. Driving was just another skill to be mastered, like maths or ballroom dancing. Sure enough, two months later, I was the proud owner of a driving licence. Best of all, I already had my own wheels.

At the same time that I'd started my half a dozen lessons, I'd also looked at buying a car from the local paper. I picked up an old Austin Allegro for £250, but as soon as I got it home, I thought, *I bet this would have been worth more if it had been spruced up a bit.* That gave me an idea, so I spent the next day polishing it, blacking the tyres and filling in the odd bit of rust with Autosol and then I put it back in the paper for sale at £350. A few days later I accepted £325 for it, which I was more than happy with.

This is easy money, I realized, so I did it again. And again. And again. All I ever did was pick up grubby-looking vehicles and smarten them up a bit. I didn't touch the mechanics or make any improvements. I just tidied and cleaned and sprayed and tarted – and I pulled in about £100 for every one. Shifting two or three of those a week gave me a pretty tidy profit. That was the point when Peter became interested. He said I'd better let him look after the money. That was his contribution, while I did all of the work.

With a driving licence, I felt I'd won back some semblance of control of my own destiny. That was important for me. Even though I'd pledged to work at my relationship with Peter, it was crucial that I claw back some of my old individuality. I was a traditionalist, yes, but I didn't like being a kept woman. I knew my new arrival would be dependent on me for everything, which wouldn't work if I depended so much on someone else.

By the time I was seven months gone, however, there was no way I could drive. That put me in the unenviable position of having to ask Peter to be on standby.

'The baby could come any moment now. We need to be ready.'

So my bag was packed and I told him to make sure the car was always topped up with petrol. I didn't want anything left to chance. But it did mean relying on Peter – the very thing I didn't want to do.

On 15 October I thought it had all started and I was going into premature labour. I remember the date because it was the night of the Great Storm in the south of England, when the weatherman Michael Fish told us there was no hurricane coming. There bloody was, Michael – and by the time we reached the Royal Sussex it had already put out the hospital's power. The whole place was bathed in the eerie glow of lamps running from the emergency generator. When you've got life-saving machines to worry about, getting power to lifts isn't a priority. Unfortunately, since the maternity wing is a thirteen-storey block, that did mean I had to do some uphill walking. On the plus side, I was only seven months down the line and not nine, so it could have been worse.

I was shown into a consulting room and a doctor came out and reminded me how humiliating having a baby can be for a woman. It's not a very dignified experience, with all the nurses and students and doctors discussing you like a special offer in a shop window. The consultant strapped this Davy lamp to his head, like a miner, and went down to explore. I was there for ages, but eventually he said, 'You're fine, false alarm. You can go home.'

Thank God for that. I don't want to have a baby in a power cut.

The real thing wouldn't take place for another two months. Knowing it could happen at any time within a five- or six-week window is pretty stressful and it was hard to think about anything else. But for one day in November I did allow myself a bit of time to think about me.

My eighteenth birthday was a pretty happy day, not least because my grandparents had a special surprise for me. When Mum died, Grandpa had sold the flat and her various belongings and invested £1,000 in a bond for me. It had matured and was now worth £4,500.

'There you go, Cathy. Happy birthday – and spend it wisely!'

I don't know if it was the hormones or some other pregnancy-related thing, but as soon as that cash was in my hands I only had one thought. Motorbikes.

I hadn't ridden mine for a few weeks, not since the doctor's orders. But that didn't mean I hadn't been thinking about them. Peter had stopped me looking like a biker chick, but that is what I still was at heart. Not only could I identify every model on the road, but I also dreamt about my ideal machine. And now, with Mum's money in my pocket, I could buy it.

The Kawasaki LTD 450 was a truly wonderful model and not for the faint-hearted. It had king and queen seats, dropped handlebars and it could go like a bat out of hell. Unfortunately, just at the moment when I was able to afford my dream bike, Kawasaki announced they were ceasing production. As stockists all over the world sold out, I'd be lucky to find one anywhere.

We didn't have the internet in those days and phone books were so cumbersome, but there was always word of mouth. The bike shop in Brighton put me in touch with one in Margate, who gave me a number for a guy in Rochester. I was so nervous when I rang him.

'Do you have a Kawasaki LTD 450?'

'You're in luck. I've got the last one imported into the country.'

'You hold on to that. I'll be there in an hour!'

I don't know what I must have looked like, but, doctor's orders or not, I squeezed into my old bike leathers, climbed onto my Honda and shot off.

It was love at first sight. A brand new F reg, with a burgundy tank – I could just picture myself haring along the coast on that beauty. The fact that the baby would put a stop to a lot of my freedom didn't enter my head – or if it did, it was shoved aside. I'd cross that bridge when I came to it.

They wanted four grand for the bike, but I knocked them down to £3,750. We both got a good deal though, because I spied an older version of my new baby. *Peter would love that,* I thought. So after a bit more haggling and by throwing my Honda in as a part exchange, I bought that one as well.

I gave Peter a call and told him what I'd done. He was really pleased and told me to wait. An hour or so later, we both drove home, pleased as punch, on our new steeds. Easy riders, wind in our hair. For those sixty minutes, life had never been better.

It's funny – all I could think about when I bought my bike was sharing my exhilaration with Peter. I still didn't see him as bad news. He was my partner, my lover and the father of my unborn child. After everything, I still wanted to spoil him. I must have had feelings for him still. And I would move heaven and earth to keep my unborn child's family together. That's how Peter ended up with his own bike.

My crazy bike fever sated, once December began, I had just one thing on my mind. I was ready. Whenever the moment came, I was locked and loaded. The same, sadly, could not be said for Peter.

It was Sunday 20 December 1987 and Peter had invited his mate John round for an early Christmas roast. John used to come over most Sundays, actually, but this one had a bit of tinsel to it. I got up, dressed and was making my way to the kitchen when it hit me.

'Peter!' I called out. 'It's starting!'

He appeared in the doorway.

'We need to get going,' I said, but he didn't budge.

'Let's not be too hasty. Remember last time. I think we should hang on an hour or two until you're really certain.'

That made sense. In fact, I was relieved to have Peter there. He had been through childbirth before. He knew all about false alarms. He could recognize the signs. *I need to trust him.*

Two hours later there was absolutely no doubt. It was happening.

'Peter,' I said, barely able to contain my excitement, 'it's coming. The baby's coming. Can you drive me up there?'

He just stared at me like I hadn't spoken.

'Peter, for God's sake. We need to go!'

Now he moved. 'No, no,' he said. 'That won't do. John's expecting a roast. You're not going anywhere until you've cooked that.'

'You can't be serious.'

I could tell from his face he was. There was no way I was leaving that pathetic excuse for a kitchen until I'd served up something resembling a Sunday roast. Not if I wanted to get out in one piece. He didn't say that, but he didn't have to. The only way I would be walking out of that front door would be with his blessing. My worst nightmare had come true. I'd allowed someone else to take control of my life – and look where it had got me.

So there I stood, for two hours, leaning against the side of the counter to try to ease the contraction pains while John and Peter sat and drank beer at the table about ten feet from me. They didn't even offer to peel the fucking potatoes.

With every passing minute, the pain got a little bit worse and my sniffing turned to snivelling, which turned to sobbing and full-blown howls. I was in extreme discomfort, wailing and hollering like a tortured banshee, part anguish at the pain and part mortification that I had such an uncaring partner. But I knew that, didn't I? I'd known that for a while. Now, though, wasn't the time to think about it.

Somehow I powered through the pain, the last half an hour spent doubled over, waiting for the chicken to cook. Every so often, John would say something kind about me and Peter would shoot him down.

'Don't pay any attention to her. She's a bloody attention-seeker, that's what she is.'

They seemed to take forever to eat their lunches, then I whisked the plates from under their noses and began to wash up. Finally, eight hours after I'd asked to be taken to the hospital, I said, 'Peter, for God's sake, we have to go now.'

I'll never forget his face for as long as I live. He smiled smugly, like he was about to unveil the greatest joke ever, and said, 'Fine – but we'll have to walk. There's no petrol in the car.'

If I'd known we weren't driving anyway, I could have left on my own hours earlier, even if I'd had to climb out a window. Peter must have been aware of that too. That's why he'd kept quiet. He'd been playing me all along.

*

I wish I could say that was the most Peter let me down during my labour, but it wasn't.

There were a lot of horror stories in the press at the time about women who'd had epidural injections in their backs and lost the use of their legs. I wasn't worried about the pain of childbirth at all, but the idea of being paralysed terrified me. So I said to Peter, 'Whatever else happens, promise me you will not let them put me in for an epidural. Give me a full general anaesthetic and knock me out completely. But don't let them go anywhere near my spine with a needle.'

'Leave it to me,' he said.

We reached the Royal Sussex at about seven and eleven hours later I'd exhausted six canisters of gas and air. I was high as a kite and still nothing was happening. Somewhere through the haze, I made out some panicking tones. Lots of people were coming in the room saying, 'The baby is distressed.' It turned out that he had got hold of his umbilical cord and had it clutched in his hand. He was cutting off his own oxygen supply. My baby was going to die.

I remember someone saying that they were going to perform an emergency Caesarean. *That's okay,* I giggled to myself. *A quick jab in the back of the hand and I'll be asleep.*

I must have switched off then because the next thing I remember is opening my eyes and seeing Peter looming over me.

'They're going to give you an epidural. I've signed for it.'

It took a few seconds for the words' meaning to sink in. An epidural? Luckily for everyone else, I couldn't speak. But in my mind I was screaming.

I've only ever asked one thing of you in our entire time together, Peter, and it was to stop them giving me an epidural. And you're letting them do it. I don't want to spend my life

214

without any bloody legs. Jesus Christ, how are you allowing it to happen?

An hour later, however, at 7.05 a.m. on 21 December, I was still in my bed, exhausted but absolutely delirious. I hadn't had a Caesarean or an epidural. Nature had taken her course. The only thing I'd had was a beautiful baby boy.

'Welcome to your new home, Daniel.'

FOURTEEN

Think of Daniel

The baby changed everything.

I'd never hated anyone more than I did Peter for betraying my wishes about the epidural. I'd read so many horror stories and the idea of some doctor trying to inject into such a precise spot on the small of my back while I was writhing around in agony had terrified me. After the torture about John's precious Sunday roast, it was the final straw.

And then Daniel had popped out, naturally in the end, and I was in love with everyone. Especially Peter. In fact, looking at him as he held our little boy, I didn't have a negative thought in my brain. I didn't see the man who'd sworn at me, hurled things at me, slammed me against walls and turned me from leather queen into dowdy frump. I didn't see anything other than the man who had given me my child. *Without him, I wouldn't have my bundle of joy.* We were a family. Together we could take on the world.

Peter and I struck a deal before the baby was born.

'If it's a girl,' I said, 'I want to call her Jennifer – after my mother.'

'And if it's a boy?' Peter said.

'If it's a boy you can choose the name.'

So that's how our son came to be called Daniel. I don't know if Peter was aware of it at the time, but the meaning of the name is 'God is my judge'. Years later that would seem particularly prescient.

Being born so close to Christmas, Daniel was virtually whisked straight from the hospital to my grandparents' house on 25 December, to share the big day with them plus my mum's sister Anne, her husband Geoff and their children, Theresa and Jonathan. After a pretty harrowing few months, it was such a relief to relax among family. Even though I was acutely aware of not being married, I still felt proud at bringing a bundle of joy into Tremola Avenue. After all the harsh words that had been exchanged during the last days of my life there, it was good to spread some joy for once. There's nothing like a baby at Christmas. It was the best present ever.

Welcoming Daniel into our little cottage, however, I saw it with fresh eyes – a mother's eyes.

This won't do. It's not big enough.

Peter agreed, although for different reasons.

'I don't want to be hearing crying all day and night,' he informed me coldly.

'How are we going to stop it?' I asked innocently, as though my more mature partner had the secret to child-rearing.

'*We're* not going to stop it. You are. It's not my job.'

It was as though Peter's contribution ended with choosing the name. He wouldn't feed Daniel, he wouldn't bathe or burp him. He would barely hold Daniel, unless I genuinely couldn't physically do it at that moment. I had to have both hands full before Peter would help, and only then if it suited him, like if I was trying to carry his dinner and mug of tea. He was happy to go for walks with us, as long as I pushed the pram, but really that's about as close as he liked to get.

It sounds awful, but I actually had nothing to judge Peter against. There'd been no male role model when I was growing up. For all I knew, this was exactly how dads were expected to behave. My own grandfather, after all, deferred to Granny on virtually all matters of child-rearing. So, as unhappy as I was at bearing the full brunt of responsibility, I didn't immediately think Peter was being a particularly bad dad.

He's done it before, I thought. *This must be normal.*

I, on the other hand, was eager to learn. But where could I look? These days new mums can go to classes and there are books and DVDs you can buy. The majority of women, though, still draw most of their childcare information from their own mums. Obviously I couldn't do that. I knew nothing and I was reminded of it again and again. I hated that. I've always been able to master anything. Give me a puzzle and I'll complete it, a school topic and I'll memorize it, a game like pool and I'll master it in no time. This baby lark, though, was unknown territory for me. It seemed like every second of the day I was confronted by another situation that terrified me, another reminder that I didn't have a clue what I was doing.

I didn't know when Daniel should eat and sleep, whether he should lie on his front or his back. I didn't know if he was too hot or too cold. It was all trial and error. I looked to Peter for guidance, but he was only interested in one thing, as I found out on the first night when I curled up next to the sleeping baby in our bed.

'No way, Cathy, this isn't how it works. The baby sleeps in the cot. We sleep here.'

'But I'll have to feed him in an hour. I don't want to be getting up all night.'

I shouldn't have disagreed.

'I don't want the fucking thing in here!'

He's just tired, like me, I thought and immediately blocked the outburst from my mind.

As a result, exhaustion kicked in. I thought I'd been tired lugging my groceries up the hill during the last weeks of pregnancy, but this was a new level of torture. No wonder interrogators use sleep deprivation. By the end of our first month, I would have admitted to anything. I just wanted to rest.

But I couldn't, not with Peter. If Daniel wasn't being held, fed or played with, then he had to be in his cot. That was when I should have had forty winks. As soon as I had my hands free, though, I was still expected to clean and cook. Before Daniel had been born, Peter would spend long chunks of the day at home, so I knew his work at the doss-house wasn't that taxing. But the second we had a baby to look after, I didn't see him except at meal times. God knows where he went or what he did. I was too tired to even think about it.

The only saving grace was that he didn't bother me sexually. It had been a crushing blow to my confidence when he rejected me night after night while I was pregnant. I was big, four stone heavier than I had been – I'd put on fifty per cent of my weight again. Despite my ambivalent feelings towards him, I still had physical needs, needs which he refused to meet. I think pregnancy even heightens your sex drive, but he refused to touch me. I thought it would be different when the baby was born, but thank God it wasn't. The second my head hit the pillow, there was only one thought in my mind: sleep.

In my waking hours, though, another thought began to

plague my zombie-like state. Grandpa and Peter might have shared similar views on childcare, but with my grandparents that was part of a package: Granny raised the kids, Grandpa brought home the bacon. That's where the similarities with Peter ended. Not only was he not lifting a finger around the house, he didn't seem to work much either. There was certainly no money coming in that I could see.

I didn't like it. As a fourteen-year-old I'd held down three jobs and sold cigarettes on the side. I was used to having money because that was what bought you independence. It might have been okay for Peter to drift along, maybe even for me to go along with him for a while. But I was a mother now. It wasn't good enough.

What could I do though? I was so tired and any sort of proper job was out of the question until Daniel was much older. Then, one day, I picked up the local *Argus* paper again and began to look for cars to trade.

It was a lot harder doing it with a newborn strapped to my front, but the money was good for fairly straightforward work. I did it for about three months and I would have done it for longer. But my self-preservation gene, dormant for so long, had well and truly kicked in and I had a plan.

Peter announced one day that we had to leave the cottage.

'Why?'

'The hotel wants it.'

He still called it a 'hotel', even though I knew the truth.

'But what about your job?'

'What job?' he said. 'I haven't worked there for ages.'

Talk about a bombshell. If he wasn't working there, then where the hell did he go during the day? Where was his money coming from? It was always questions with that man, but I was too focused on my own project to dwell on it. If anything, it just made me more determined to proceed.

Peter had tried to take my car-sales money off me to 'look after', as he put it, like he'd always done. This time I said no. I needed it to pay rent. On a tea shop.

I don't know where the idea had come from. Desperation drives you in odd directions. I needed an income, I needed a new roof over our heads and I needed something I could do with a young baby in tow. This is what my brain came up with.

I found premises in Portslade comprising a little restaurant space with a flat at the back. It was perfect for what I wanted and, on a peppercorn rent, it was affordable. I found a shopfitters from which to buy the counters, tables and chairs and took myself down to Southampton for the actual stock. I figured that if you want to sell tea, don't go to a middleman – get it at source. There was a wholesaler at the docks who took everything as soon as it came in off the ships, so I strolled around sourcing pots of exotic-sounding herbal teas, Earl Grey, and everything else I needed. This was years before fruit teas became trendy and there was a strong chance it wouldn't work. People might just turn their noses up at anything that wasn't PG Tips. But I was sure I'd identified a gap in the market and I wanted to exploit it. I even bought extra tins of tea leaves and teapots and cups, so customers could actually buy the tea I was serving them and the crockery it came in.

When The Olde Tea Shoppe, as I called it, was finally ready to open, I was happy. I'd thought of everything. Almost.

I just needed Peter to look after Daniel while I made it all happen – and he refused. He had no job, nothing to do, no plans and no real disability. But he absolutely dismissed out of hand any notion that he should be involved in caring for his own son.

Fine, I thought. *I don't need you. I don't need a man in my life.* The less he wanted to do with Daniel's life, the better. That meant no interference in my decisions and more time for me. It was fighting talk and I meant every word. I was eighteen years old and I really didn't need a bloke in my life, especially that one.

But Daniel did.

Again, the haunting parallels with my own life loomed large. However much I barely tolerated or disliked or even hated Peter at times, those feelings paled into insignificance next to my determination to keep my son's family together at any cost. I may not have loved Peter, but I did love being in a mature relationship and I was hellbent on making it work, whatever the cost to me. My son was not going to grow up without a father, as I had done. That was the priority. That was what I had to ensure never happened. And that, ultimately, would be our downfall.

If I'd thought I'd been exhausted before, opening my tea shop taught me the true meaning of the word.

My alarm was set for six in the morning, but most days I was still up from one of Daniel's night-time feeds. Then I would wash the cot blankets and sheets and his nappies – still no washing machine, all by hand – and have it out on the line by half six. Then I would make breakfast for me and Daniel, then it was time to clean the flat – that chore didn't disappear just because I was working and Peter was at home – and finally I was able to think about work. Before I could open the shop I needed supplies, so, with Daniel strapped to my front, I would walk down to the local supermarket to buy gateaux and other treats I could slice up and sell. Then, at nine o'clock, I was finally ready to open.

Luckily, business was good from the start. People complimented me on my Chinese rice-pattern crockery and the lovely atmosphere I'd created while having a slice of cake with tea served in a pot and made from tea leaves not bags. And, of course, most of them couldn't help but admire the sleeping baby strapped to my chest. Even when Daniel wasn't sleeping, when he was hungry or restless and noisy, I had no choice other than keep him there. It killed me, knowing his dad was so close and yet so unwilling to lift a finger for his boy.

It didn't take Peter long to find an excuse not to help. The flat had a cellar, which he said he would use as a workshop. He was going to convert part of it to house a Scalextric track for Daniel, he claimed. At one point he even suggested installing a little kitchen, so I could prepare food for the café there rather than use our flat's kitchen, which, the first Health & Safety inspector informed me, was illegal. But I didn't care what he did down there. He could have been masturbating to pictures of the Queen for all I knew. I was just happy knowing where he was – and that he was out of my way.

I cried myself to sleep some nights through sheer tiredness. But I'd got into a nice rhythm. I was with my son all day, I was making money and I was doing it all by myself. I was independent and I was in control.

Then, out of the blue, Peter said we had to move out, we had to give up the flat, the business and the profit. And why? To put our names down on the council house list. It was unbelievable. I honestly thought he'd gone mad.

'Look, we've got a baby – we'll get a nice council house, no problem,' he said.

'But we've got a nice place now.'

'This is a shithole. We've got a kid. They'll give us a fucking palace.'

'But why do we have to give up the tea shop?'

'Because you're earning too much. Council won't give us a penny if you're earning. You've got to stop it now.'

I'd love to pretend that conversation never took place, but it did. Most embarrassing of all is how seriously I took him. I think that was partly because I hadn't seen him this animated about anything for ages. Suddenly there was a spirit to him and a flicker of life behind the eyes. As his partner, as the mother of his child, that really spoke to me. I can't really explain it, but on some sort of primeval level I found myself being motivated by his desire. My man had a plan and – as stupid as it was – that moved me. I hadn't felt this impressed by him since those nights in the Hungry Years, when he'd seemed to have the whole world in his hands. Maybe I had low expectations, but I found myself seeing him once again in a more positive light.

The more Peter dressed it up as this big, fantastic idyll, the more I came round to it. But he was clever. He'd wait until I was virtually dead on my feet, desperate for a nap or to take my shoes off for five minutes. Then he'd start the whispering, the off-hand remarks, the little glimpses of how our future could be.

'In a council place, you'd be able to sleep.' That sounded good. 'You'd have time to play with Daniel.' That was even better. But it was when he suggested 'You'd be able to be a proper mother' that I really sat up.

Wasn't I being a 'proper' mother working every hour God sent to provide a safe home and food for my son? Wasn't I a proper mother for not letting him out of my sight for a second of the day? For Christ's sake, for most of it we were tied to each other. Was Peter telling me that wasn't the behaviour of a proper mother?

It's only looking back now that I see he was playing me like a violin. There was nothing wrong with my mothering. And it certainly wasn't his place to criticize. But a new mother is a fragile beast, easily knocked off balance by the slightest suggestion that she could do more. All new mums take everything personally. And so, stupidly, I agreed to his scheme. I put my business up for sale, sold it as a going concern for £10,000 and walked away. I was eighteen years old, a new mother and I'd made and sold a successful business in the space of nine months. That felt really good.

But I'd also just given away my hard-fought independence. The moment we left Portslade, Peter was back in control.

As soon as I clapped eyes on our new home in Windlesham Gardens, I knew it was a mistake. I'd been promised a palace. What I got instead was a studio flat.

'This can't be right,' I said.

Peter went straight on the defensive. 'We're at the bottom of the pile, what did you expect?'

'But it's not big enough! Where's Daniel going to sleep?'

He pointed to the wall furthest from the small kitchen area. 'We'll put the cot over there. What's the problem?'

He couldn't see it. Or wouldn't. We'd given up a lovely little place for a cramped shoe box of a flat. It was smaller than some of the dives I'd stayed in with my mum. Really horrible and not at all the dream family home I'd been sold.

He's done it again. When would I ever stop falling for his lies?

It was too late now. As much as I hated myself for being so gullible, all those bridge lessons with Granny had taught me to play the hand you've been dealt. But even so, I honestly couldn't understand what Peter had been thinking. It was as if he didn't see Daniel at all. Or me for that matter. He wanted a council flat and he got one. He probably hadn't even filled the form in properly, to say we were a family. That's how low down in his priorities we were. He didn't seem to mind that we had to share a bathroom with people from eight other bedsits. I've still got a photo of Daniel in our kitchen sink. That's where he had to have his night-time bath. He seems happy enough in the picture, but I felt so guilty. It's not the lifestyle I would have chosen for my son.

Given the choice, there were a lot of things I would have done differently for my son. In an ideal world, for example, he would have had grandparents who doted on him. I couldn't even give him that. Daniel was nine months old when my father and his partner came to see him.

It was just going to be a flying visit. Dad and his girlfriend worked abroad for half the year. They were getting the ferry from Portsmouth and had decided that Brighton was a convenient stop.

I'd seen my father a handful of times since that first awkward meeting in 1984. I couldn't say we'd really made progress. We'd never discussed Mum. I couldn't honestly see the point in continuing the relationship, but, once again, I put Daniel's needs first. Some parents make better grandparents. Maybe my dad would be one of those. I owed it to my son to find out.

Having guests at our pokey Windlesham Gardens flat was stressful enough and the idea of cooking them a roast was doubly so. Realizing that it would also be the first time Dad met Peter just added to the pressure. What if he swore at me in front of my father? What if he criticized me or rejected my dinner or launched it at the wall? I'd die of shame.

Please let him behave.

But Peter was on his best behaviour. My meetings with Dad

had usually been stilted, awkward affairs. Not this time. Peter took full control. I realized I hadn't seen him be so effortlessly charming since those early days in the Hungry Years. The anecdotes, war yarns and good-natured humour tripped off his tongue once more, and our guests lapped it up. I was happy. He hadn't let me down. I wish I could say the same for my dad.

Once Peter took over the hosting duties, I fled to the tiny kitchen area. It was too small to prepare the simplest of meals, really, so why I thought it would be up to the task of a roast for four I don't know. The Belling oven was so tiny that I had to roast the chicken upside down. And as there were only two rings, vegetables were kept to a minimum. Dad came over to make small talk with me and watched as I struggled and failed to fit half the things I'd prepared into the limited space. I tried to be pleasant, to not carry any lingering resentment, to give him a chance. But I couldn't.

I just thought, *How can you stand there and watch your worn-out daughter sweat herself stupid trying to fit a quart into a pint pot?* Surely he could have said, 'Forget it, I'm taking you out.'

But he didn't. He'd come for a roast and he was going to get it.

The food was fine, in the end, and we got on okay. Dad and his girlfriend made an effort to play with Daniel, but I couldn't help feeling it was too little, too late. Dad had had a chance to rescue me from the misery of cooking and he'd blown it. Just like he'd blown every other chance with me. They left singing Peter's praises – and vice versa – but I was in no hurry to see them again.

That episode over, I tried to get to the bottom of Peter's obsession with the council house. It didn't take long to crack it.

Maggie Thatcher's government had passed legislation entitling council-house dwellers to purchase their properties for a fraction of their value after a certain period of time. This was Peter's dream. But to buy the place, you needed to be in the scheme to start with.

It was so ridiculous. I said to him, 'If we'd kept the tea shop we could have bought our own place in a couple of years.' He shook his head, not even listening.

'This is the best way. Trust me.'

He's mad. But, again, I owed it to Daniel to try to make it work.

I found that by moving a wardrobe next to the sofa bed, I could hive off a piece of the open-plan room and give Daniel the illusion of his own space. He could still hear everything and the light would still reach him, but psychologically it felt like a different room. The problem was, though, that at nearly a year old, he still wasn't sleeping through the night. My GP was less than helpful. When I told him the crying was making me pull my hair out, he said, 'I can give you some Valium for that.'

Valium? I wanted to help my boy sleep, not sleep through it myself!

Then he recommended a book by a woman called Gina Ford, which taught you how to train your child to sleep – using tough love. This would involve letting Daniel cry himself out, leaving him alone for just long enough to work out: *There's no one coming so I'd be better off sleeping.*

There were two problems with this. One, Peter went berserk at the slightest whimper from our child. Much more than that and he'd storm out of the flat – just as well, given his temper. And, two, just to make things worse, Windlesham Gardens was a residence the council reserved for single mums in trouble.

The whole shitty building was packed with poor women on the run from abusive husbands or recovering from problems. They needed all the help they could get. What they didn't need was a woman choosing to let her child scream for nights on end. I just couldn't do it to them. So Daniel continued to sleep badly and I continued to attend to his every demand. Anything for a quiet life.

God knows how long we were at that place. It felt like a lifetime, but was probably only a couple of weeks. Peter might not have been too fussed about our requirements, but the council seemed to be. Someone noticed that there were three of us and we received the keys to a new place in Chadbourne Close. On the plus side, it was a one-bedroom. On the downside, it was largely unfurnished.

Actually, there was another positive. All this moving around had given Peter a new lease of life. The more desperate our situation appeared to me, the easier he found it to adapt and to keep himself busy. Sometimes this meant him coming home with things like a large cockatiel in a brass cage, which just added to the mess. Other times, though, like when I pointed out that we needed a sofa and a cooker that worked, he said, 'No problem. The church will give us that.'

I didn't know when he'd done it, but he'd been down to the local Catholic church – he claimed that was his religion – and signed up for their charity scheme. Within a couple of days of moving in, they'd found us the things we needed.

When I pointed out that the place still looked like it was from another century, Peter had a solution for that as well. 'The council will give us £400 to tart it up,' he said, genuinely happy at the idea of something for nothing. I don't know where he got his information from, but it was spot on.

So down we went to Homebase, or whichever shop the vouchers were for, chose some paint and wallpaper, took it all home and started to decorate. I shouldn't need to say that I did it all – while Daniel played in his cot or crawled around. Peter had a knack for disappearing whenever there was work to be done. I didn't care though. As much as I wanted him in Daniel's life, I was always happier when he wasn't around.

Once again, though, I enjoyed the work. Even the muscle-ache and stench of paint couldn't stop me looking at the end result with a whole bunch of pride. I'd never hung wallpaper before, but now I could. Another skill I'd mastered by default, another reason never to rely on a man in the future. Especially that man.

Then a funny thing happened. 'That man' said we should get married.

Peter's Glaswegian accent was so heavy that I struggled to understand everything he said. In fact, I used to joke that the reason I married him was because I didn't understand the question.

But I understood it perfectly well and everything it meant. And still I said, 'I do.'

Can you imagine the turmoil? On the one hand, I hated to think further ahead than tomorrow if it meant Peter was still in my life. If only he behaved with me with the same effortless charm that had wowed my father, then it might have been different. But he seemed to keep the charming side of his personality under lock and key. I knew it was there, though, and the fact that he couldn't be bothered to get it out made me resent him more and more. I could have put up with the insults, the tantrums and the aggression much more easily if only he'd made an effort.

On the other hand, a world in which Daniel was denied access to his father – as I had been – was inconceivable to me. That was my driving force. My fondness for Peter may have seen better days – sometimes it was all I could do to remain civil to him – but I still wanted the dream that every girl has. I wanted my white dress, I wanted my husband, I wanted the father of my child in his life. And, more than anything, I wanted Daniel not to go through life as a 'bastard', as Grandpa undoubtedly called him. That had been shameful enough for me. I wouldn't visit it on my own child if I could possibly help it. So I said yes.

For the next few Sundays I found myself enduring hideously long and pious sermons, just to be seen as good practising Catholics. Then, when he was happy we'd put enough hours in, Peter went off to arrange the wedding. A short while later, he returned, swearing and cursing.

'What's the matter?'

'That fucking priest.'

'What about him?'

'He won't marry us.'

He refused to tell me why. I got the feeling it was my fault somehow. They'd seen through my fake Catholic credentials. For a moment I felt guilty that I'd ruined Peter's dream, even if it was a dream I'd only become aware of recently. He was happy to let me beat myself up over it. Eventually, though, the truth emerged. The priest had said it was against his beliefs to marry a divorcé. It was Peter's fault for being married before. He was the reason we couldn't get married there – and he'd let me take the blame.

I thought that might have been the end of it, but Peter defiantly found a Methodist minister who said yes. 'They'll marry anyone,' he said.

231

As underwhelmed as I was by the whole spectacle, it was still my wedding day. It was still every girl's dream occasion. I had to be seen to be making an effort. Then I realized it was an opportunity to rekindle old relationships and I perked up.

We had a joint hen and stag night, with everyone congregating at Chadbourne Close. My grandparents came, along with my aunt Anne, her husband Geoff and their children. I was also delighted to see my old vodka-drinking buddy, Peter, plus my other school friends Debbie and Sally. I suppose it was down to Peter Tobin that I'd drifted out of touch with all of them, but this was a day of reunion. Sally lent me her husband and his Daimler for my wedding car. I felt like a princess in there. When they all returned the following day everyone was on my side of the church apart from John, Peter's old friend. For the first time in a couple of years, I didn't feel alone.

I had £500 from Granny to organize everything – the party, Peter's Moss Bros suit, the rings. My wedding dress, a knee-length, lacy cream dress which Granny also paid for, came from Debenhams. It was the first time in ages that I actually felt like a woman – and it felt amazing, even though I was in flat heels as usual, so as not to tower over my groom.

It was a nice day, I have to say. We got a few gifts, including, pride of place, a sewing machine from Granny. Grateful as I was, I made a mental promise not to dress my own son as far out of date as Granny had dressed me.

There was no honeymoon and, thankfully, Peter didn't come near me. But at least Daniel was no longer what my grandfather would call a 'bastard'. Just like Mum and Dad, Peter and I had done the right thing eventually. And I was determined our marriage would last longer than theirs.

*

I wonder now if the marriage had proved a wake-up call for Peter. If he'd thought he'd cut me off from my past, then the wedding, small as it was, showed he'd failed. There were my closest family – my father excepted – and three old school friends. It was a reminder to me that they were there if I needed them. I think Peter saw that too. You could interpret everything that happened next as his attempt to get me away from them. He didn't want me – I know that now. But he didn't want anyone else to have me either.

In the meantime, we had to get by in this tiny one-bed. No sooner were we married than I said, 'We can't stay here. One of us has to get a job.'

'I'm not fucking getting one,' he snarled, that sense of entitlement shooting to the fore. 'I'm on disability.'

'Well, I'll get one then.'

He shrugged.

'Make sure you get enough to pay for babysitters then.'

'What do you mean? You can look after Daniel. You're not doing anything else all day.'

That didn't go down well. He pushed his face up so close against mine I thought he was going to bite me. 'That's your fucking job. See that you do it.'

I was a nervous wreck for hours after. I tried to hide it from Daniel, but I was scared. I hadn't seen that side of Peter – that violent tendency – since Daniel was born. I thought it had passed. I was wrong. It was back and, based on past experience, now that he'd done it once, he would do it again. It was about to get worse.

But it's all right, I stupidly told myself, *as long as he only threatens me – and not my son.*

For a while afterwards, just seeing him reminded me of his

contorted face during that last burst of anger and I felt sick just being in the same room. But then he shocked me.

'I've been thinking about what you said.'

'About getting a job?'

'Fuck that. No, this place, you're right. It's too small. I've registered us on the council exchange scheme. We'll be out of here in no time.'

I never gave a second thought to what he spent all day doing, but obviously a minute or two had gone into researching the rights of council-house tenants. I shouldn't have been surprised. He could have written a book about benefit claims. Apparently you could advertise your council property to other tenants and, if both parties agreed, just swap homes.

'Who's going to want to swap a bigger place for this?' I said. 'You'd have to be desperate.'

I was right.

Obviously there was no one in Brighton mad enough to trade with us. Nor Kent, London, any of the Home Counties in fact. The nearest council with anything like a potential swap was in Corby. I didn't have a clue where Corby was.

'It's in the middle of the country,' Peter explained.

I thought anything further than London was the North, so the middle sounded close.

'Okay then,' I agreed, 'let's take a look.'

Corby turned out to be a lot further away than I'd realized. The further we travelled in the second-hand Metro Peter had come home with one day, the more I wondered what sort of person would consider giving up a three-bedroom house for a one-bed flat. Maybe they were downsizing and wanted to be near the coast?

Or maybe, as it turned out, they'd destroyed one home and were desperate for anywhere else.

Where we were living in Brighton wasn't anything like five-star, but it had fresh air and a sea view from the end of the street. This was like driving into hell. We parked on the outskirts of this grim-looking housing estate and I didn't want to get out of the car.

'Come on, it'll be nice inside,' Peter insisted, so out we got and set off down a warren of gloomy, narrow paths. I'm sure the whole place had been designed originally to provide green space for children to play in without cars. What they'd actually ended up with was pavements full of hypodermic needles, bottles, fag butts and graffiti, stinking of urine, dirty nappies and leftover rubbish. The idea of pushing my baby's buggy round there every day made me feel sick, so my mind was made up even before we reached the house.

Let's just say, I don't think it was a hasty decision. We couldn't knock on the door because it was hanging off its hinges. Two panes of glass were broken in the lounge window and there was graffiti all over the walls – and inside was even worse. There was a threadbare carpet, a mattress on the floor in one room, rubbish everywhere and, most revolting of all, piles of dog mess dotted around. I'd never seen anything like it. Even in Mum's worst days, she wouldn't have lived like this. Somehow, among all the crap, a family of four was living there. It would have been a squeeze, but I could see how they thought our tiny flat would have been an improvement.

We looked at other places: one in Lincoln and another in Portsmouth, both horrible, although nothing like Corby. I'd pretty much given up on the idea and was making tentative noises once more about working. That must have scared Peter because, out of the blue one day, he announced, 'I've found it. The perfect house.'

'Really?'

'Really,' he said, and handed me a sheaf of photographs. They were of a nice, neat three-bedroom house. The décor wasn't to my taste, but it seemed well-presented, lovingly so, in fact, and the views from the top windows were of fields and grass.

'It looks too good to be true,' I said. 'What's the catch?'

'There's no catch,' Peter insisted, but he was lying.

The catch was that the house was in Bathgate, Scotland – about thirty-five miles from Glasgow. That's why he only had pictures of it – it was too far for him to travel to view. There was no way I wanted to go to another country, of course, but he wouldn't let it drop. The opportunities, he said, would be ten times better up there.

'But you don't want to do anything, opportunities or no opportunities.'

Then he went down the healthy route, talking about the fresh air and the countryside, but I just said the sea air was probably better for you.

Finally he came up with the argument he knew I couldn't beat.

'Think of Daniel,' he said. That old chestnut.

'I am thinking of Daniel!' I snapped. 'I don't want him cut off from his great-grandparents.'

'Yes, but my family live up there. He'll see my mum and dad, my sister and brothers, my nephews and nieces.'

'Since when do your family live there? You're from Glasgow.'

'Get away,' he laughed. 'Where'd you get that idea?'

'It's what you told me.'

He had, several times, along with the fact that he had six siblings and plenty of nephews and nieces.

'Scotland's all the same to you English, isn't it? No, I'm from

Livingston, I told you that. It's about five miles up the road from Bathgate. Think about wee Daniel and his big, new, happy family. Doesn't he deserve that?'

The bastard! I couldn't argue against anything to do with Daniel's happiness – as well he knew.

For the first time I thought about what the south coast could offer Daniel. I rarely saw my grandparents more than once a month and Aunt Anne just a few times a year. Maybe it would be nice for Daniel to spend time with more relatives his own age.

So that was it. Peter hired a lorry and we loaded it with our belongings, including, pride of our collection, the cooker and sofa from the church. All the overspill, like our pet cockatiel and clothes, went with me and Daniel in the Metro. Then we set off for Scotland in convoy, with Peter and his mate John in the lorry, then me and Daniel and, behind us, my friend Debbie in her Escort. She'd said she wanted to come up to help me settle in, but it was a long old drive just to help me unpack. It was almost as if she were worried she'd never see me again.

FIFTEEN

And Then I'll Kill the Kid

From the moment I arrived in Bathgate, I couldn't wait to leave.

The house in Robertson Avenue was nice enough. The pictures hadn't been tampered with; it really was as cute and homely as we'd been shown. A decent semi-detached on the final cul-de-sac of an estate, with ample parking out the front and amazing views of cow fields on two sides, it was actually as pleasant a place as you could hope for. No graffiti, no dark, drug-filled alleys. There were no people around either. This was un-usual for an estate: everyone had jobs, they were at work. They weren't dossing around like the layabouts who'd filled that place in Corby or our neighbours in Brighton. These were respectable people who cared about their environment. In fact, you would never guess to look at it that we were on a council estate at all.

Inside, the three bedrooms were decent sizes, the lounge was very comfortable and there was even a washing machine! Apart from the horrible pink and blue colour scheme throughout, it was pretty near perfect. On paper, then, I should have been perfectly content. So why did I feel like a mouse about to nibble the cheese on a trap?

I'd been all right as late as packing the lorry and setting off. I might even have been excited. Then we'd reached our first motorway and I began to have kittens. I'd never driven on anything bigger than an A road before and here I was trying to follow Peter's truck, with Daniel crying and a cockatiel squawking in my face. It was horrible, a real baptism of fire. Then, as the hours began to trickle by and we were still in England, major doubts really began to descend. What was I doing? Why was I allowing myself to be taken so far from the town and the people I knew? How had I let this happen?

Of course, if you'd asked him, Peter would have said it was my idea. I was the one who'd wanted the bigger house, the one who'd said I needed help looking after Daniel. Here was the answer to my problems. A cute house in a picturesque area on the doorstep of the extended Tobin family. It was exactly what I'd requested.

Except it wasn't. I had a lot of time to reflect during that marathon journey to West Lothian. I knew I hadn't asked for this. Peter had done all the running and, as usual, had manipulated me so I felt like it was my decision. Of course, I'd wanted to get out of that flat, but not to come here. However it looked to him, I'd given in because I thought it was worth a gamble, to see if it would make him happy. That had to be worth a shot, didn't it? A happy Peter might be a nicer Peter. He might just take an interest in me again without swearing and scaring. He might just start to play a role in his son's life too.

There I was again, making excuses like every other battered wife. And I still didn't see it.

Even the weather tried to tell me to go back. The moment we pulled off the M8, it was like stepping into a dark tunnel. The fog was so thick I could hardly see the lights of Peter's lorry ten feet in front of me or Debbie's car behind. We could have been anywhere, but it seemed familiar. With a shudder, I realized, *If we had some scary music, it would be like driving into a horror film, that part just before the killer strikes.*

Even without the soundtrack, that thought was more prescient than I realized.

I assumed Peter would find a job and his mum and brothers' families would be round all the time to socialize and maybe even help out. I think, in all the time we were there, I visited his sister's home once and called for one brother at a tenement block in Glasgow – but he was out. The sister and her family were nice enough, but my strongest memory is of how uncomfortable Peter looked while he was there. He refused to sit down, preferring to hover nervously in the corner of whatever room we were in. It was weird. *If you can't be yourself in front of your family, when can you?*

That was the extent of our contact with the Tobins. I never met his mum and his dad's name never once came up. As for the promises of babysitting, no one ever came to our house. In fact, after Debbie and John had both left us, I didn't see another face at our door for at least a month.

Peter had been polite enough to Debbie while she was helping me to get the house straight. Her departing Escort was still within earshot, however, when he said, 'You won't be seeing her again.'

I said, 'I beg your pardon?'

'You heard. She's poison. I don't want you seeing or phoning her unless I say you can. Understand?'

I didn't and told him so. Then he called me every name under the sun and threatened to smack me. Suddenly I understood perfectly.

It was only then that I realized I hadn't been on the sharp end of Peter's tongue for a while. Admittedly, we'd been busy. Once the exchange had gone through, we suddenly had to sort out packing, vehicle hire, new doctors, utilities – all the usual things that go hand in hand with a move. And, stressful though it had been, Peter hadn't lost his temper once. Not with me anyway. Seeing how easily he slipped into his old ways scared me. Not because of the words – I'd heard those a dozen times before. No, what terrified me was the nagging suspicion that he'd been on his best behaviour for a reason.

It's like he planned to bite his tongue until he got me up here – alone.

I hadn't seen Debbie much over the last few years, so not calling her wouldn't make her suspicious for quite a while. My grandparents, on the other hand, had been worried enough about me going up to Scotland. If I didn't ring them, they would marshal the air force to find me.

'You can't stop me phoning them,' I told Peter firmly. He acquiesced, but only on the condition that it was no more than once a week – and he could see and hear me. Every call I made saw him perched on a chair right next to me. I don't know what he was so paranoid about. I was never going to tell Granny or Grandpa anything. It was too embarrassing. I wasn't going to heap any more shame on our family.

I had to admit, if it had been Peter's plan to cut me off from the rest of the world, it had worked. In Brighton I probably wouldn't have spoken to Granny much more than once a week anyway, but the option was there. And if I didn't have money for the phone I could get a bus or walk or drive over. I didn't appreciate the value of that until it was taken away. Only on the drive up, along those seemingly endless roads, did it really sink in. It's how my mother must have felt when she was abandoned in Stockport.

I'm on my own.

In the rare moments on that drive when Daniel and the bird weren't demanding my attention, I entertained an idea so far-fetched I laughed at it. Was it the council right-to-buy dream that was really driving our move? Or was Peter upset that I'd taken control after Daniel was born and opened the tea shop and made a success of it – and proven I didn't need him? Was it simple jealousy that made him persuade me to shut up shop and start at the bottom rung of the council-house ladder? Did he just want me dependent on him again? And was that why I was now driving all the way to Bathgate, to a place where I would have to rely on him more than ever before?

I don't know how my Metro stayed on the road while I was thinking this. The idea was so big, so preposterous, that it obsessed me for mile after mile. But then I thought, *That's ridiculous. No one would think like that. No one would be so insecure – and so manipulative.*

And anyway, I decided, desperately looking for a bright side to the situation, didn't it just mean that Peter loved me so much he wanted me all to himself? That was a good thing, wasn't it?

By the time we'd settled in at Robertson Avenue my can-do attitude had kicked in. *I'm here now. I have to make an effort.*

I took Daniel to a mother and baby group a couple of mornings a week and enrolled him in swimming lessons – basically any activities that were free. I wanted to get a cat for him as well, but when Peter came home from the pet shop he had two guinea pigs instead. It wasn't exactly what I wanted, but a pet's a pet at that age, I supposed.

And that, pretty much, was my new life. I now had a bigger house to clean and a garden to look after for the first time as well, but apart from that there was absolutely nothing to do. Peter loved it, but it drove me spare. Day after day, night after night, we'd just sit in the lounge, watching telly. I was itching to get out and do something, but he was comfortable where he was. It just felt so unnatural to me. A year earlier I'd been running my own business. Before that I'd made a decent profit turning round second-hand cars. I'd even made a few quid flogging teddy-bear templates. I loved – still love – to be busy and making money is an instinct for me, but Peter wouldn't let me follow it. And he still refused to work.

It was the same excuse as before. He was not getting a job – 'not after what I've done for this country' – and I could only go to work if I earned enough to pay for Daniel's childcare.

'Don't be ridiculous,' I said, yet again. 'You're sitting here all day. What else are you going to do?' I instantly regretted asking. He flew off the sofa and had his hands round my throat.

'Don't you ever tell me what to fucking do, you cunt!'

I tried to fight him off, but he was too strong. His hands were like steel on my neck. Nothing I did made any impression. I couldn't even scream. As soon as I opened my mouth, his grip tightened, choking any sound back inside. Then I saw the dark rage in his eyes. He didn't look human. That's when the panic set in.

That's when I thought, *I can't breathe. He's going to kill me.*

Then, as suddenly as it had started, it was over. Peter called me 'cunt' again and stormed out, still swearing.

I wasn't listening. I was clutching my throat, willing it back to health. I could still feel where Peter's fingers had clamped my flesh. The skin was so sore and when I coughed it felt like I was trying to swallow razor blades.

CATHY WILSON

I didn't cry. There was no point. I wasn't upset, I was angry – with myself. Had I really thought that the abuse and the violence would be left behind in Brighton? He'd only behaved recently because he'd wanted something. Now he'd got his way, the true Peter was coming out again. I needed to get used to it.

How has my life become such a mess?

I was in the middle of nowhere – no, not even the middle. I was in the furthest reaches of nowhere and I had no friends, no money. I really felt stuck, adrift, desperate. And so, when the inevitable apology came an hour or so later, I begrudgingly relented.

'I love you so much, hen,' Peter said. 'Don't let this ruin everything.'

Immediately the pressure was on me to make amends.

'You hurt me,' I replied, without looking at him.

'I know, I'm sorry.' He put his arms around me and pulled us together. 'It will never happen again. I swear it. Do you hear me? I swear it.'

I pulled away. Apology or not, I didn't want to be touched.

'Come on, pet, don't be like that. Don't ruin our fresh start.'

Me ruin it? I wished he'd just go away.

'It's all right,' I said. 'I shouldn't have upset you.'

That was what he'd been waiting for. I'd apologized to him. Just like a good battered wife should.

To fight the boredom, I decided to start the redecorating. The kitchen needed it most, so I told Peter what wallpaper I wanted and eventually he let me go and buy it.

'I'll want to see change and the receipt,' he warned as usual.

I didn't even question it anymore. That was just the way things were. On those occasions when I was given too much change, though, or if I spotted a coin in the street, it would go

244

straight into my pocket. Never my purse because Peter always checked that.

It was a slow process, especially as I had to do the decorating during Daniel's nap times. But I got there. A week later I was the proud owner of a smart new kitchen.

Peter didn't have a good word to say about it. He complained about the mess while I was doing it and he moaned about the colours when I'd finished. He couldn't have been more un-complimentary if he'd tried. Still, at least Daniel and the guinea pigs seemed to enjoy running around now that it was all fresh and clean.

It turned out the guinea pigs were enjoying it too much. When they weren't scurrying around under my feet, I'd noticed that they liked stretching over the skirting board on their hind legs. It looked cute. What I didn't see, however, was that the reason they were doing that was to be able to nibble the bottom of the new paper. Sod's law, it had to be Peter who noticed it first.

'What the fuck?' he shouted and before I could even register what he was talking about, he flung open the door and hurled one of the guinea pigs like a cricket ball up the garden. I gasped as it smashed against the shed and didn't get up again. That's when I realized Daniel had seen everything.

'Stop it, Peter, for Christ's sake, you're scaring him!'

But he wasn't listening. With another fierce lob, the second guinea pig sailed into the air and over the fence at the bottom of the garden.

'Come here, Daniel, darling,' I said and led him quickly out of the room. The sooner I got the cockatiel to distract him, the better.

I didn't give a toss about the torn wallpaper and I couldn't see why Peter cared so much either. I was the one who'd put it up and would have to repair the frayed edges. What really bothered me, though, was seeing how invisible Daniel was to his father in that mood. It was like he wasn't there. And that scared me more than any threats or smacks against me.

A lot of people were feeling the brunt of Peter's temper, not just me. He was so aggressive and so unpredictable. Being in his company was like carrying a grenade without its pin. You never knew when he was going to explode. I remember, for example, him taking me to the supermarket. The bill was only six pounds and Peter handed over a tenner. When he got his change, he immediately started shouting at the cashier. No warning, no arguing first, just pure eruption.

'You fucking lying bitch, I gave you a twenty!' That was it, he was off, laying into her for giving him the wrong change – which was a lie anyway because I'd seen him give her ten pounds. I still don't know if it was a mistake or he was trying to con her. What I do know is that being scared of him had just been taken to another level. If he could turn on a stranger like this in a public place, there was no telling what he would do to me in the privacy of our own home.

I don't know if that was the catalyst or whether it was the next time he body-checked me into the wall or the time after that, when he hit me across the dining room before falling to his knees and begging forgiveness. All I know is that, at some point, I finally woke up. I was depressed, I was bruised from his fists, I was lonely and, worst of all, I was scared to be in the same room as my own husband. The moment I admitted that, it felt like a huge weight was lifted from my shoulders. As they say, admitting the problem is the first step to finding a solution. Now I had admitted my problem, I realized the solution was staring me right in the face – and it had been for a long, long time.

I need to leave.

Suddenly I wasn't scared of him anymore. In one fell swoop, one clear-cut decision, I retook control of my own destiny. From now on, it was just a matter of sorting out the practical issues. Like packing, leaving and finding somewhere else to live. First though, I had to tell Peter.

We were all upstairs when the right moment came. He seemed in a decent mood, the sun was shining, everything appeared to be in place. Following him into the bathroom, I said, 'Peter, I'm not happy. I can't go on with this. I want a divorce.'

He stared at me for a few seconds, then smiled and nodded.

He's agreeing, I was relieved to think. But then his face changed. It was like a thunder cloud had parked over his head. From smiles to a face knotted in rage in a matter of seconds. It was utterly disturbing – and it was about to get worse.

Without a word, Peter barged past me and ran across the landing to Daniel's room. Before I could follow, he reappeared carrying our son.

'Peter, what are you doing?'

He didn't answer, but slowly walked towards me until he reached the top of the stairs.

Oh my God!

'Peter! Put him down!'

He didn't move. Holding a confused Daniel at arm's length over the staircase, he said, 'I'm only going to say this once. If you leave me, I will fucking hunt you down and kill you.' Then he shook Daniel so hard I thought he was going to drop him by accident. 'And then I'll kill the kid.'

'Put him down! Put him down! I'm begging you! Give him back to me, please!' I was screaming, hysterical, but I didn't dare go forwards. Daniel was distressed and crying, but Peter was cool as you like, just staring, daring me.

'Okay, okay,' I said. 'You win. I'll stay. I promise.'

He considered it for a second, then nodded and swung Daniel over to me. Then, without even looking back, he skipped down the stairs as calmly as if he were being called for breakfast.

When he was safely out of sight, I fell to the floor, clutching my son harder than I ever had before.

'What have I done?' I sobbed. 'What have I done to you?'

Daniel didn't answer. He was still frozen with fear.

Everything changed after that. Every aspect of our life got worse.

I was suddenly under twenty-four-hour surveillance. He confiscated my car, motorbike keys and purse, so I couldn't go anywhere or do anything. I had a Bradford & Bingley account book with about eight grand in from the tea shop sale, but that disappeared as well. If we needed food, he accompanied me to the shops, swearing his way up and down each aisle, putting half my choices back on the shelves and refusing to lift a finger when it came to carrying the bags. I couldn't go out to the boot of the car without him following.

If he went out he locked every door and window and took my house keys, so I was a prisoner in my own home. The worst part about that was not knowing when he would return. Every engine in the cul-de-sac, every footstep on the pavement sent a chill through me. I was soon jumping at my own shadow. If it weren't for trying to be brave in front of Daniel, I would have gone mad.

Degrading though it was, being in solitary confinement was better than having Peter there with me. Now he no longer bothered trying to soften his language and attitude. Every other word was 'fuck' and he didn't have to be in a bad mood for me to get both barrels. Sometimes I swear he would attack me for fun. After a while, I managed to tune it out. But then he started doing it in front of Daniel.

'Where's my tea, bitch?'

'Clean this fucking pigsty, you lazy shit.'

'What the fuck's this shit on my plate?'

It was as vicious as it was relentless and I was suddenly aware of every evil syllable. I'd always sworn to prevent my son from seeing his mother hurt, as I had witnessed my own mother being abused. And I'd failed.

Daniel saw me thrown to the floor if Peter's dinner was late, smacked across the mouth if I dared to speak out of turn and crushed under his weight against the wall if there was a single toy out of place. I hated Daniel seeing it, so I'd fight, desperate to make it look like a game. But that wasn't good enough. Peter wanted to see me in pain; that was the point of it. The violence wasn't about hurting me – like so many of his actions, it was about controlling me. The longer I kept smiling for my son's sake, the harder he pulled my hair and twisted my arm and held my throat. Till, in the end, I had to give in and cry and beg him to stop. That was all he wanted. He needed me to be dependent on him. He couldn't do it financially and he knew that. So the only means left to him were brute force and threats.

Once I'd had the idea that the move to Scotland had been devised to separate me from anyone who could help, it just wouldn't leave my mind. Slowly, as I was beaten and cowed into submission every day, it grew stronger. Then I thought, *If he's capable of sacrificing my successful business to feed his paranoia, what else has he done?*

I flicked back over the events of our life together. The wedding – was that just another way to control me? Did he believe all that marriage vow crap about 'honour and obey'? Did he think that if I became Mrs Tobin I would legally have to bow down to him?

Before I could find an answer, another thought blew that one clean out of my mind. What about Daniel?

That whole not being able to have children story must have been a lie. The doctor had assured me that Peter understood the repercussions of his op and I'd chosen to believe Peter instead. The more I dwelt on it, the more I felt my face begin to burn with shame.

I'm just a puppet to him.

But why had he lied? He hated having a baby in the house and refused to lift a finger to look after him. Why would he have been so desperate to have a child with me? It didn't make sense. He couldn't have gone to all that trouble just so I would be more reliant on him, could he? I knew, of course, that he could. He was capable of things I'd never imagined in my worst nightmares. But there was another reason.

Peter had wanted Daniel to use against me, just as Mark and Brian and those scumbags had used me against my own mother. Peter recognized that I had an independent streak the day we met. That had scared him and he'd sought to tame me. Aggression and bullying at the flat and cottage hadn't worked. I'd always bounced back, dusted myself down and been ready for the next battle. Peter knew it would take a special weapon to control me – and in Daniel he'd been handed it.

The more I raked over the past with these fresh eyes, the more I cried. I wouldn't have given up Daniel for the world, but I was as guilty as Peter for bringing him into this violent and loveless marriage. If you marry without love, you deserve what you get. I'd been naïve and flattered by Peter's attentions and what he could offer me. Everything that had gone wrong, I'd found an excuse for. The truth was there, but I hadn't listened. I should have walked, rescued Daniel from this hell he hadn't asked to be born into.

The only good news I could draw from my situation was that Daniel was a lot younger than I had been when I'd witnessed the attacks and bullying against my mother. He was barely two. I prayed they wouldn't scar him, as I was scarred seeing her being set alight and raped in front of my eyes.

Sexually, at least, Peter had left me alone since we'd arrived in Bathgate. In fact, we had barely had sex at all since I'd started to show at around three months pregnant. A year ago it had really bothered me. A woman wants to feel desired by her partner. I'd struggled to shift the four-stone pregnancy fat and I blamed that for his lack of interest.

Now, though, I was grateful. I couldn't imagine anything worse than him touching me. Ironically, I too found myself using Daniel as a means to an end. Focusing on his poor sleeping, I would take Daniel up to bed around half seven, read him a story and do my darndest to fall asleep on his little single bed. The way I saw it, Peter loathed child noise so much he'd never rouse me if I was in Daniel's room, in case he set the crying off. My son, unwittingly, was protecting me, like a car alarm or, I was sad to appreciate, a human shield. Even though there was no danger to him, I felt bad using him like that. But it worked. I was amazed how often I got away with that, actually. By the time I'd emerge, it would be morning and Peter wouldn't be surfacing for a couple of hours.

I thought I was being so clever, making sure I wasn't available for sex at night. I assumed Peter didn't have the appetite of a younger man, so all I had to do was keep out of his way. I was wrong. There was nothing wrong with Peter's libido. He was just saving it for someone else.

One night I put Daniel to bed and did my usual thing of snuggling up next to him. Usually I'd sleep through the night. On this occasion, I woke. My head felt incredibly cloudy, but I could hear voices downstairs, so I went to investigate. Peter was there with a woman, a slim, young blonde. She was dressed casually, in jeans, trainers and a sports top, but I knew this wasn't right.

'Who's she?' I asked him.

'This is Lisa.'

That didn't help much.

'What's she doing here? It's late.'

Peter glared at me. 'That's none of your business. Fuck off back to bed.'

I did as I was told, but instead of going to our bed I made my way back to Daniel's room. I was struggling to keep my eyes open, but it seemed important that I stay awake. Ten minutes later I was sure I heard two sets of footsteps making their way up the stairs. It was hard to tell. I felt as if my ears were packed with cotton wool. It was very disconcerting, but not as disconcerting as picking up the unmistakeable noises of Peter having sex – and a woman screaming.

I didn't dare investigate. I put a pillow over my ears and desperately hoped that Daniel wouldn't wake up. Then I closed my eyes and gave in to the unusually powerful urge to sleep.

The next morning Lisa was gone and Peter didn't mention anything. A few nights later the same thing happened, except this time Lisa arrived before I'd put Daniel down. I felt a lot more alert than I had the last time I'd seen her. Ignoring the risk, as soon as Peter went to the toilet, I said, in no uncertain terms, that she wasn't welcome in my house.

The girl shrugged. 'Not up to you, is it? You're not the one paying me.'

Paying her? What for?

Then Peter returned and told me to get rid of Daniel and come back. I said I wouldn't.

'All right, the kid can stay as well.'

I was out of there before he'd finished speaking. When I finally made my way back downstairs, I froze in the doorway. They were already having sex. Peter saw me. 'Come in and watch. You might learn something.'

Typical of him, the bastard. I tried not to look at the vicious way he was smacking the girl's back and bottom with every thrust into her or pulling her hair and making her scream with pinches and arm-twists. She was squealing like a cornered animal, begging him to stop, but he didn't listen. He never listened. At the end of it she looked frightened and cold. He just looked hungry.

I'd seen enough and turned towards the stairs, but Peter had other ideas. I hadn't seen him move, but suddenly he was holding my arm, digging his nails into me like his life depended on it.

'Get off, you're hurting me!'

'Shut it, bitch,' he shouted and even while I was still trying to free my arm, he began tearing at my dressing gown.

'What are you doing? Get off me!'

But he wouldn't. I fought and I fought, but he was too strong. My gown and then my night clothes were ripped off my back and I was forced down onto my knees. It had taken seconds and it just proved how he saw me: I was nothing. No one. Something to use and discard.

I tried to stand up, but his grip on my neck just tightened. I thought about collapsing and rolling away, but he was one step ahead of me. One fierce tug of my hair and I wasn't going anywhere – not unless I wanted my scalp ripped raw.

I was terrified and so confused. It was Mum being raped at Telscombe Cliffs again. That's all I could think. I'd always wondered why she didn't fight and now I knew. She couldn't. Men are too powerful, even one standing at 5'7. There was nothing I could do.

Then it began. There was no attempt at preparing me, no thought for any pleasure I might have or anything I might need to be ready. Peter just forced himself into me, roughly and noisily. The more I cried and begged him to stop, the more he seemed to enjoy it. The more I said he was hurting, the tighter he gripped my skin and the more viciously he pounded my body. At that moment, I wasn't his wife. I could have been anybody. For a second, I thought it wouldn't have even mattered if I'd been dead, but that was wrong. Peter needed me alive because he seemed to thrive on my screams.

When he finished, it took me a few seconds to realize he had. I was so sore and was bleeding so much that I hadn't even noticed the pain stopping. Trying not to be sick, I scooped up my clothes and ran for the door. Only then did I notice Lisa on the sofa, watching with a blank expression. Had she seen everything? Why hadn't she helped me? I didn't know and at that moment I didn't care. I thundered up the stairs and didn't stop running until I'd reached the sanctuary of Daniel's room. I was safe. A broken woman, but safe for now. Just when I'd thought Peter couldn't degrade me anymore, I'd reached a new low.

It was a few days before I could walk without pain again. The physical agony was actually the least of my worries. Every twinge I had reminded me of the ordeal I'd been subjected to. It was everywhere; my entire body was a reminder of that night. It was a day or two after the attack that I realized something.

He hasn't apologized.

That was important. No matter how unpleasant or hurtful or spiteful he'd been in the past, Peter had always been quick with his regrets. Forty-eight hours after raping me in my own lounge, it was as though he'd forgotten the whole episode. That wasn't a good sign. For some reason, he no longer felt the need to say sorry. Did he honestly think he'd done nothing wrong? Or was he so confident in his power over me that he could no longer be bothered?

Over the next weeks and months, there were several new faces in the house. Sometimes Lisa, sometimes other girls of my age or maybe younger. My memories of them are admittedly vague, like I'm trying to see through a fog. That's often how it seemed at the time too. Sometimes it felt like I was living in a dream. It was a vile thing for Peter to do in my own home, with his son around, let alone me. It was as if he was saying, *I can do better than you.* They all looked like they could do with a decent meal and a few hours in the sun. And they all acted as though they weren't there by choice. Not in front of Peter, of course. When he was there, they couldn't do enough for him or to him. I think, to be honest, he was their meal ticket.

When so many unpleasant things are happening your mind tries to block them out. Consequently, I can't say for sure how often there were strange women in the house. I do know it felt like at least a couple of times a week. Sometimes I was forced to watch them; sometimes they were forced to watch me be subjected to Peter's violent fantasies. Other times I'd wake up in Daniel's bed, heavy-headed, convinced I could hear yelps and yells and I'd roll over and pray that I was being left out tonight.

I knew he was hurting the other women, because he hurt me. If anything, I suspected he held back with me. So why did they keep returning for more? I couldn't understand it. Then I realized, *Maybe they think the same about me?*

The truth was, I had no choice. I couldn't have left if I'd wanted to.

Not all Peter's visitors were female. One day he announced he was going out.

Thank God. A few hours on our own.

'Don't go getting any ideas, though,' he said, 'because I've got eyes everywhere.'

With that he sneered a half-laugh and left. I was just about to pick Daniel up when a thought occurred.

He didn't lock the door!

Excited, I ran up the hall and turned the handle. I was right. Unlocked. It flung open. And there, walking up the path, was a stranger.

I didn't know this bloke from Adam, but he was nice enough. A bit rough, but friendly. He just said Peter had asked him to look after me. After what I'd seen Peter do to those women in the house, I was terrified of what 'look after' meant.

Has he hired me out? I wouldn't have put it past him.

But he had literally just come along to make sure I stayed where I was. It happened again and again. Whenever Peter popped out, more often than not, this guy would turn up. God knows what was in it for him because he'd only get a cup of tea for his troubles. Then we'd watch the telly or sit in the garden or I'd cook while he played with Daniel. It was utterly surreal and, I suppose, quite a threatening thing if you think about it. I shudder to think what he might have done if I had tried to leave.

It could have all been bluff or it could have led to a world of pain. All I know is, after the initial shock, I didn't bat an eyelid when he turned up. I was just grateful he was nice. But that didn't stop me planning my escape.

Peter must have thought he was so clever. He'd terrorized me to the point where I was putting up with all sorts of physical and mental abuse and yet he knew I was too proud to tell anyone. But, just in case, he monitored my phone calls to Granny and I was under round-the-clock surveillance. I had no money, no privacy, no pride. I was broken and utterly dependent on him. He'd won. I was completely under his control. Or so he thought.

Peter made one mistake. However much he trod me down, however close he came to breaking me with this relentless regime of violence and degradation, there was one fact that kept me strong. I was a mother.

The bastard could do whatever he wanted to me, but there was no way I was going to give in and endanger my son's life for a second longer than necessary. Ever since that moment on the stairs when I'd realized how Daniel was just a poker chip to Peter, I'd been ready. I had my secret bag of 10ps, scrounged and found, and I had my plan. I just needed the opportunity.

Then, one afternoon, just after five, Peter came over to me in the kitchen. The onslaught I braced myself for didn't come.

'I'm going to a car auction. I'll be an hour and a half.'

He'd recently started buying and selling cars, like he'd seen me do in the past, although this auction looked to have caught him off guard because he was in a hurry as he left the house. And he forgot to lock the door.

Normally I wouldn't have budged. My minder would be just

arriving. Not this time though. There was something about the way Peter had been rushing around. This was a last-minute arrangement. He looked flustered, anxious to get out in time.

I bet he's forgotten about me.

It was a gamble, but one I had to take. If I got it wrong and my prison warden caught me, then there would be hell to pay. But if I was right . . .

Just the idea of freedom put a spring into my step. I flew round the house, grabbing clothes, toys, essentials – as many things as I could stuff into a holdall. Then I scooped up Daniel, put my emergency stash of coins in my pocket and went to the front door. And I froze.

What if it's a trap?

It would not have surprised me one bit to see Peter standing on the other side, just waiting. As I stood, transfixed, by the door, I could picture his face, smug and angry at the same time. I could imagine him gloating that he was too clever for me. And I could picture every single blow that he would rain down on my head and my face and my body to teach me a lesson.

It was too much. I felt sick. I couldn't go through with it. The risks were too great. And then I felt Daniel wriggling in my arms and I knew the risks of staying were even greater.

Come on, Wilson, I ordered myself. *You have to do this.*

I yanked open the door and – nothing! He wasn't there. I'd never felt such relief. But now the hard work began. I literally ran as fast as I could manage with my child and luggage until I was out of the cul-de-sac. Only when I was deep in the heart of the estate did I stop fighting the urge to slow. But I dared not stop altogether. I had to get off the main road before Peter came home. If he discovered me there would be repercussions to end all repercussions.

Eventually I reached a bus stop. It was such an anticlimax after the sprint, but I had no choice. I couldn't afford a cab. My heart was still racing when the first bus pulled up. I threw our stuff onto a rack and hurried to the back. Now the nerves began in earnest. It wasn't just the exercise making my heart pound a hundred times faster than usual. I'd never felt so nervous. The enormity of what I'd just undertaken kicked in and panic followed. Before, on our street, I could probably have explained it away as taking a walk, getting some fresh air. It was implausible, but there was a chance he would swallow it. But if he caught me now, he'd know I was trying to escape.

And what was it he'd threatened when I'd said I wanted to leave? I hugged Daniel as hard as I could and tried to relax. This was only the first step.

Another bus and a long walk later, we arrived at Glasgow's coach station. I'd been planning this for so long, I knew I had just enough cash for two tickets to Portsmouth. Granny and Grandpa had recently moved into the area to be nearer to Anne and her kids. There was nowhere else in the world I wanted to be more right then.

When the teller handed over our tickets, she must have thought I was on something. I remember staring at them like they were made of gold. To me, they were more valuable than any precious metal. They were our escape route out of hell. As I lugged everything out of the booking office, I just prayed I'd get the chance to use them.

Our coach was scheduled to depart at half past nine. I looked for the station clock and my heart sank. Eight o'clock. Ninety minutes stood between us and freedom. I have never felt so scared in all my life. The threat of being hanged from Brighton's 'Cathedral' was nothing compared to what I was going through at that moment. Not even having a knife pressed against my cheek came close to the crushing dread that Peter was probably at that very moment on his way.

He's going to find us. I know it.

I could just picture it. He would have been home by seven. He would have noticed the door was unlocked and gone tearing in, swearing and shouting the odds as usual. Then he would have discovered us gone and put it all together.

He'd work it all out. 'I've got the bitch's car keys, her bike keys, her bank books and purse. What's the cheapest way out of town? A coach.'

It was obvious. He knew I had no friends. He'd cut me off from my past and stopped me having a future. The coach was my only option. He had to be on his way. And I knew exactly what he would do when he found us. I could picture it as clearly as if it had already happened. The car would sweep in, screech to a halt and he'd be out, snarling and shouting and swearing, car engine still running, door still wide open. He'd grab me by the hair and he'd batter me with his fists and anything he could lay his hands on. That would be it. No discussion, no arguments, just pure retribution.

Just thinking about it now makes me cry. I was fighting waves of tears at the time. Daniel looked so worried, but I just couldn't stop. I kept saying, 'It's all right, darling, Mummy's just being silly.' But seeing his little face and remembering Peter threatening to drop him down the stairs if I disobeyed overrode any other emotion. I knew, with all my heart, that if Peter reached us before the coach arrived, he would kill us. Of that I had absolutely no doubt. The whole scenario played out in my head again and again. However hard I resisted, he would drag me off that plastic bench in the bus shelter and kill me there and then.

He wouldn't care who was watching or trying to stop him. And then he would turn his attention to Daniel.

I was sick with nerves, my head spinning with question after question. Was I doing the right thing? Was I risking my son's life unnecessarily? Should I have stayed to try to make it work with my husband? Should I just phone him and apologize and ask him to pick us up before it's too late?

That thought honestly popped into my head. The longer I sat there, the more panicky and ridiculous my ideas became. Deep in my heart, I knew I was doing the right thing. It wasn't a risk at all. It was the only way to save my son's life.

After the longest ninety minutes of my life, the National Express coach arrived and we climbed on with all the other nocturnal travellers. If I'd thought my ordeal was over, I was mistaken. It was nine hours to London Victoria. Nine hours of staring out of the window, paranoid that every set of headlights overtaking us would be Peter's van or my old Metro, dreading each pit stop in case he stepped on. While everyone else on the coach slept for hours on end, I was awake the entire journey.

Finally, we reached London. Daniel was tired and hungry, but I only had one ten pence piece left and I needed that to ring Granny. She didn't complain about the time, especially when she heard my news.

'We'll pick you up when you get to Portsmouth,' she said calmly. 'Don't worry. Everything's going to be all right.'

I wanted to believe her. But until I'd heard where Peter was, I couldn't relax. How could I? That monster was capable of anything.

He's probably planning something horrible right now, I thought.

I was right – but he wasn't planning it for me.

SIXTEEN

His Home is Here with Me

The phone was ringing as we stepped inside the front door. Grandpa answered, while Granny helped me with my bag and Daniel.

'Cathy,' Grandpa called out, 'it's for you. It's a hospital.'

I was so tired, my initial reaction was: Daniel! Then I relaxed. He was fine, he was with me. So why were they calling and how did they find me there?

'Hello,' I said gingerly.

'Hello, Mrs Tobin, it's Edinburgh Royal Hospital here.'

'Is something wrong?'

'Mrs Tobin, I'm afraid I've got some bad news about your husband.'

'Oh my God, what's he done?'

'I understand you two have had an argument. Peter's obviously very upset because he has taken an overdose. He's asking for you. I think it would be for the best if you came up to see him.'

I remember that phone call so vividly. I was sitting down in my grandparents' lounge and I was shaking like a leaf through

262

exhaustion and nerves. I hadn't managed a wink of sleep because I was so terrified about what this man would do to me – and now this anonymous doctor was expecting me to walk back voluntarily into the lion's den?

'That's not going to happen. He'll kill me.'

'I don't think he's in a position to kill anyone,' the doctor replied. 'He's very ill.'

'Look,' I said, trying not to sound completely callous to this stranger, 'do you think the overdose will be fatal?'

'No. I think your husband is more in need of psychological help than anything else.'

I could see it all. He'd just taken a handful of Amitriptyline pills that had been prescribed for his so-called depression and had called an ambulance before he'd gone under. Anyone can do that. He had no intention of dying. It was all about control. More mind games, more power games, more control games. It was just another trick to get me where he wanted me. But he'd underestimated me. He thought I cared about him enough to check that his health was okay.

He must be more ill than they realize if he thinks that.

My grandparents' new place only had two bedrooms so, as welcome as they made us, it could only ever be a temporary fix. They didn't have to tell me that. Energized after a few hours' nap, I made two very important phone calls. The first was to Portsmouth council. An hour later, I left Daniel with Granny and went to register as homeless.

It's amazing the effect that not being with Peter had on me. It was barely twenty-four hours since I'd been screamed at for not tidying well enough, as usual, and I'd just taken it like I always did – but here I was, almost back to my old self, determined, industrious and armed with a strategy. The resilience of the human spirit is a marvellous thing. He hadn't killed my independence, I realized. He'd just chased it into hiding.

Of course, knowing Peter was five hundred miles away having his stomach pumped gave me some breathing space. I wasn't jumping at shadows anymore. I knew I'd have to face him some day, but, I swore to myself, *It will be on my terms.*

I do have Peter to thank for one thing though. If he hadn't indoctrinated me into the benefits culture, it would never have occurred to me to ask the council for help. People like Peter have their phone number on speed dial. If they need a new light bulb fitted, it's a call to the council. Well, now it was my turn to be helped. I wasn't workshy or claiming a penny. But I did need somewhere to stay.

As I entered the council offices, I remembered how I'd tried to find lodgings to escape to when I was pregnant. The private landlords had all refused to house me. If only I'd known about the 'system' then. Everything could have been different.

I'm sure Grandpa hated the fact that I was going cap in hand to the authorities because I certainly did. But I'm glad I swallowed my pride because they acted swiftly and gave me the address of a B&B in Southsea's Nightingale Road which offered temporary accommodation. Because I was not a Portsmouth resident, they would only pay for it for six weeks, to give me time to get back on my feet. After that, I could apply for the housing benefit programme.

None of the downsides bothered me. In fact, I glazed over during half the conversation. I was so grateful they were giving me anything. All I could think was, *I've done it. I've got my own place. I'm free.*

My second phone call that morning had been just as

important as the council one. This time, there was no financial gain to be had, although it would provide me with something equally valuable. My identity.

I'd spoken to my friend Debbie only once since she'd left me in Scotland. But the moment she heard my voice say, 'I'm back,' she said she'd drop everything to come round. She was a good friend. I didn't have to tell her anything, she said. She was just glad I was safe. Actually, it felt good to get some things off my chest, but I only told her a fraction of the truth. The pain of what Peter had made me do and – worse – what he'd made me become was too raw to discuss. Remembering it was like reliving it. Peter was the past, as far as I was concerned. It was Debbie's job to help with my future.

Debbie helped me settle into Nightingale Road. The room was basic, but adequate, with a double bed and two singles crammed in. There was also a two-ring hob and a sink, which passed as the kitchen. I didn't care. At that moment, I would have been grateful for a cardboard box and a shop doorway.

I only had a bag of clothes and toys, plus various bits Granny had given me, so moving didn't take long. Then Debbie said, 'Okay, that's the flat done. Now it's time to sort you out.'

'What are you talking about?'

'I'm talking about that tent you're wearing.'

Oh. With no exercise and no motivation in Scotland, I don't think I'd shifted a pound of my pregnancy excess. I was massive and the hideous polyester, A-line, ankle-length skirt I was wearing was doing me no favours. In Scotland my appearance had been the least of my worries. I'd been encouraged to dress drably for so long that it didn't register anymore. But away from Peter's all-pervading influence, I suddenly saw myself with Debbie's eyes and felt disgusted that I'd let myself go like this. Where were my stilettos? I used to be so proud of my legs. How had Peter made me not even care about myself anymore?

Debbie could see that I was upset, but she had a plan. 'Come here,' she said and pulled out a pair of nail scissors from her bag. Then, while I stood open-mouthed at the idea, she hacked away at my dress until it rested above my knees. By the time she'd finished, we were both laughing at the raggedy line her tiny scissors had made. But, my God, what a release it was.

'I can see my legs!' I said. Okay, they weren't as slim as I remembered, but psychologically it was a reminder that I was a woman and it was okay to dress like one too.

I was so happy with my new look. We went out for lunch, Debbie's treat, and I didn't care if anyone looked at me oddly. That skirt was a statement of intent. *I'm going to get my old self back.*

It took a month or two of firm dieting, but the weight fell off. Like everything else, I put my mind to it and made it work. When I finally achieved my aim of getting back to a size eight, Debbie appeared again to celebrate with me. We drove down to Brighton and spent an afternoon trying on outfits in a fetish shop. Then, back home with a bottle of wine, we poured ourselves into our new latex mini-dresses and hit the local nightclubs.

If I had to put a date on when I finally regained my independence, that night in Portsmouth would be one of the candidates. Watching a dancefloor full of blokes drooling at me and Debbie, buying us drinks, flirting like crazy and getting nowhere made me feel like a million dollars. I thought, *This is who I am!* I didn't want any male company, but just knowing I still had 'it' went a long way to banishing the meek, unattractive washer-woman I'd become over the past few years.

That was an important night in my recovery. There was

another date, however, when I would really come of age if I handled it right: the next time I saw Peter.

I think it says a lot about Peter that he didn't give up on me. If you'd beaten and humiliated and bullied a woman so much that she left all her possessions behind and fled the country, wouldn't you be too ashamed to see her again? He obviously didn't believe he'd done anything wrong, though, because as soon as he could, he arrived in Portsmouth.

I knew the day was coming. I knew Peter wasn't the sort of person to just give up and walk away. He would consider me unfinished business. It was only half-time in the game of control, as far as he was concerned. Still plenty of time, in his mind, for him to be the winner.

Even though I was expecting it, my blood still froze when Granny told me, 'Peter rang – he wants you to call him.'

For a while, I considered not returning his call, but what was the point? He'd just leap into his van and track me down eventually. I didn't want to be looking over my shoulder for the rest of my life. *No*, I thought, *I have to face this head on*. At least that way I could do it on my own terms.

In the days leading up to Peter's arrival, Granny and Grandpa were beside themselves with nerves and even talked about having a man in the flat for protection. I genuinely couldn't see what the fuss was about. I felt a completely different person to the broken wretch who'd done a moonlight flit weeks earlier. I looked different and I felt different. I was stronger. The weight had lifted from my shoulders and I was standing tall again. I had my family five minutes up the road and my own two-room flat – on housing benefit – in Middlesex Road. I'd reset the clock to 1986 and I was ready to take on the world again. Peter was no threat, as far as I was concerned. He'd only ever hurt me when we'd lived together, when I was under his control, and that was never going to happen again. He didn't bother me and he didn't scare me, not anymore. He was nothing to me – just like I was convinced I'd meant nothing to him during those rape fantasies. So why was I letting him come?

In an ideal world, I would not have let Peter Tobin within a hundred miles of me or my son. But that wasn't fair on Daniel.

I don't think anyone with a normal background could ever appreciate just how much value I placed on giving my son two parents. Unless you've known the aching chasm of loss in your life, unless you have a gaping hole in your heart where your mother or father should have been, you'll never appreciate the lengths I was prepared to go to to keep both Daniel's parents in his life as much as possible. It was like an obsession for me. I was possessed with the promise I had made Daniel to give him the two parents I had been denied. In simple terms, I genuinely believed that any father was better than no father.

For a while, I honestly thought it could work. The second Peter stepped through the door, he hoisted Daniel up and played with him more lovingly than I'd ever seen in the past. That counted for a lot with me, so by the time he turned his charm in my direction, I had warmed slightly. When Peter suggested taking our son to the beach, I thought, *Why not? You have no hold over me anymore and Daniel will like it.*

So that became our life for a while. Every couple of weeks Peter would drive down from Bathgate and we'd have, I have to say, a really nice family time in a park or on the beach. We even took the hovercraft over to the Isle of Wight. We'd never enjoyed a single family day like this before I'd left. Yet here he was, riding on mini steam trains with his son, while I sat on a bench and waved. It was sad. It was like the night Peter had charmed my father and his partner. He obviously could turn it on at will, but just chose not to.

I was happy to see Daniel enjoying himself. I even smiled to see Peter having fun with his son. But Peter, as ever, had another agenda, which soon became clear.

'Come back to me, Cathy,' he said one day as we strolled along the beach. 'Come back to Bathgate and we'll give it another go. We owe it to Daniel.'

That line didn't wash with me anymore.

'No, I owe it to Daniel to give him two parents and that's what I'm doing now. He doesn't need us back together.'

'But I do!' Peter exclaimed. 'I need you, Cathy. I want you. I love you.'

Once upon a time, those last three magic words would have been enough to cast the spell that saw me packing. Not anymore. I was immune to Peter's powers. He had nothing I wanted.

'You weren't very nice to me before,' I explained. I didn't want to pick at old wounds, but, on the other hand, he needed to know where I stood.

'It's my depression,' he said. 'You know how I suffer.'

I had to laugh. 'I know how you like to say you suffer. I know you like the tablets.'

'Cathy, I've changed. You've got to believe me. Come on, come back with me. Give me one more chance.'

How many times had he said those words to me? And how many times had I fallen for it? But not anymore.

'No, Peter. My life is down here now.'

When straightforward wooing didn't make an impression, Peter went to phase two of his plan. I was surprised to step out of my flat one day to find Peter unloading some of my belongings from Scotland from his van – including my motor-bike. It was a genuinely thoughtful thing to do.

Of course, then he went and ruined it. In Peter's mind, that should have been enough for me to be swept off my feet and say, 'I've been stupid. Please take me back.' When I didn't, he asked again for the hundredth time. For the hundredth time, I said no. He was asking so regularly that I didn't even feel mean anymore. I just couldn't take it seriously and I think that night he realized it. On his way out of my building, he stopped to use the communal toilet. A few minutes later I heard a commotion in the hallway. There was screaming coming from the bathroom. When I got there, the door wasn't locked.

Which meant I had a perfect view of Peter, in the bath, with blood streaming from his wrists.

He was shouting, 'There's no point living without you, Cathy!' but I just wanted to laugh. Obviously I was meant to be won over by this act of sacrifice. But the thing about blood is that it often looks worse than it is.

'You're a joke,' I said. I know it sounds cold, but he'd tried this stunt the night I'd fled Bathgate and he seemed to come through that one okay. To be on the safe side, I ran outside to dial 999. After I'd asked for an ambulance, I added, 'You'd better send one from St James's.' That was our local nut house, after all. As far as I was concerned, that was the place where Peter needed treatment, not A&E.

Amazingly, the doctors who arrived agreed and Peter was taken to St James's for two days of recovery and tests. He had a full psychiatric assessment while he was there. I don't know what they discovered, but it was obviously nothing that worried them because he was soon released.

It was another few weeks before I let Daniel see Peter again, but soon after that we were back to once or twice a fortnight. I'd dismissed the suicide attempt almost as soon as it had happened, electing to concentrate on wanting the best for Daniel. Watching him enjoy a fun and loving relationship with his father at last meant the world to me. It helped that Peter appeared to be really trying to be nice to both of us. The wrist-slashing episode aside, I have to say, we did have fun together once again as a 'three'. Nothing gave me greater pleasure than seeing Daniel happy. As long as he perceived that I trusted Peter with him, that was okay by me. In fact, as the weeks and months passed, I soon realized it was a perception I was beginning to share as well.

Life in the spring of 1990, I have to say, was good. I had a bit of social security money coming in, I had my friends and family round the corner and Daniel and I even had a home with separate rooms. We still had to share a bathroom and kitchen, which were pretty grim, to be honest, filthy and full of cockroaches. But, with a bit of imagination, I had made our rooms feel like they belonged to us. While Daniel slept at night, I decorated the fireplace with hand-painted pictures of flowers. Then, during the day, we'd collect sticks from the park to spray silver and create a lovely display. They were just cheap, small things, but they really made a difference. After so long, I really was happy. And proud. I remember looking at Daniel sleeping one night and thinking, *I've done a bloody good job here.*

What is it they say about pride coming before a fall?

After a few weeks of visits and lots of happy times, I could see Daniel was more comfortable with his father than he'd ever been in Scotland. So when Peter suggested one day that the pair of them go out to the park and then maybe to McDonald's for a treat, I thought, *Why not? It will be good for both of them.*

And I needed the break. Single-parenting is tough on everyone. You tend to snatch babysitting offers when they come.

'Make sure he's back for bath time at six.'

I felt a bit guilty enjoying an afternoon at home by myself and after three or four hours I was ready to have my son back. But six o'clock came and went. Then it was seven – and I was panicking.

Have they been in an accident? Is everything all right?

I needed to phone someone, but we didn't have a landline and I was scared to leave the flat in case they returned. By half seven, though, it was decided. I grabbed my purse, left a note on the door and ran out to the nearest phone box.

My first call was to Grandpa. He obviously didn't want to worry me, but he said, 'You could call the hospitals, but you really need to tell the police.'

I could barely see the dial on the phone for tears as I made call after call. They weren't in any hospital in the area – thank God. So where were they?

The police said they'd be round in five minutes.

I was in such a state by the time they arrived, I don't know how they understood a word I was saying. After months of believing I was back in control of my own life, Peter had brought me back down to my knees at the first attempt.

All I could think of were his words on that staircase in Robertson Avenue: 'If you leave me, I will fucking hunt you down and kill you. And then I'll kill the kid.'

Oh God, what have I done!

It was the worst evening of my life. Going over and over everything that had happened in the last few years didn't help, but I couldn't stop myself. I'd been so desperate to put the past behind me, to start anew, that I'd forgotten that history can always teach us something. My own vanity, that relentless desire to prove that I was free, had blinded me to the truth and now there was a chance my son could be paying the price.

Then, at midnight, there was a knock at the door. Two policemen were standing there and obviously I thought the worst.

'It's all right, Mrs Tobin, we've found your husband and son. They're at home, in Bathgate. Your husband has asked if you would call him.'

Bathgate? Now I knew they were safe, I could afford to be angry. What the hell were they doing there? Peter had obviously had no intention of taking Daniel to the park or McDonald's. As soon as my back was turned, they'd jumped into his van and driven the whole day up to Scotland. Even hearing the policeman's words, I couldn't believe Peter had actually kidnapped his own son.

What's he playing at?

There was only one way to find out. With the policemen standing outside the phone box, I made the call. When he answered, Peter sounded perfectly normal, just as I'd expected. He never got upset or hurt. Only angry.

'What have you done with my son?' I demanded.

'He's here, at home. He's fine. We've had a lovely day.'

'That's not his home!' I shouted. 'His home is here with me.'

'That's where you're wrong, Cathy. So I'm only going to say this once. If you don't come back to me in the next twenty-four hours, you will never see your son again. I promise, we will leave this country and you will never find us.'

That's it, I thought. *He's won. I've got no choice.*

I just wanted to sink down to the bottom of the phone box and sob. Then I remembered the policemen. But what could they do?

When I told them, verbatim, what Peter had threatened, there was a sudden flurry of radio activity. Then they told me I had to call Peter back and tell him I was coming 'home'. I had to agree to whatever he wanted.

At nine the next morning I found myself in front of a solicitor. The radio activity the night before had, among other things, been getting her out of bed and up to speed with my situation. She was like my guardian angel. Just when I needed someone to take control and tell me what to do, there she was, calm and collected and with an answer to everything.

'I've arranged a hearing with a judge to grant you sole custody of your son with immediate effect,' she explained. 'I have also requested an all-ports alert around the country. Your husband will be detained if he tries to leave.'

I couldn't believe how quickly everything was happening, and the scale of it. Out of nowhere, I seemed to have an army on my side. I was whisked in front of the judge and, before I knew it, I had full entitlement to Daniel. From that moment on, Peter was breaking the law every moment he kept my son from me.

After years of being made to feel isolated and alone, it was incredible to have strangers moving so fast to help me. In the past I'd bitten my tongue, worried I wouldn't be believed. But they all took me seriously. All those other battered wives out there who think they're on their own need to understand that they're not. There's help available, whole battalions of it. You just need to be brave enough to ask for it.

So, within minutes of meeting this solicitor, she'd informed me the whole country was on lock-down as far as Peter was concerned. There were only two problems. One, we both knew that there were many, many worse things he could still do to make good his threat of never letting me see Daniel again. And, two, my custody claim only had jurisdiction in England.

The judge was obviously distressed that he couldn't do more. 'Wheels are in motion, but we need to go through the translatory process for it to apply under Scottish law,' he said. 'Then we'll be able to act.'

'How long does that take?'

'About three or four days.'

'But I don't have three or four days! If I don't get there today my son will be killed!'

It was incredibly frustrating. I had the full weight of English law behind me, but we were powerless to act for as long as Peter was in Scotland.

'Of course,' the solicitor suggested, 'if you can get your husband to come across the border, then I can have bailiffs with you in minutes. You'll get your son and Mr Tobin will be told he can't come within a mile of you both.'

'So that's what I have to do then,' I said and I left her office with renewed strength – a mother's strength. I didn't know how I was going to do it, but I would make it work. If I failed, there was a very real chance Daniel could die.

The clock was ticking and I still had to get to Bathgate. That's when other members of my private army stepped in. 'You'll need to fly,' Grandpa said, 'so I've bought you a ticket from Gatwick to Edinburgh. I can come with you, if you want,' he added. 'It's not too late.'

'Thank you, but I have to go alone. If he smells a rat, that's it.'

I phoned Peter to tell him my flight plans. I begged him not to do anything rash, but he sounded almost offended at the idea. There was me at my wit's end with worry and he was acting like I was the one wanting to see him. Not for the first time, I seriously questioned his sanity. There was no emotion in his voice at all, no recognition of the hell he was putting me through.

Well, I thought, *that could work to my advantage.*

I caught the train to Gatwick and boarded an aeroplane for the first time in my life. I was already a mess and everything about the flight seemed to make things worse. I didn't have a clue what I was doing. I didn't know you were allowed to take your seatbelt off and I spent the entire journey gasping for a drink because I was too shy to ask the stewardess whether the contents of her trolley were free or not. I couldn't afford to buy anything. It was such an ordeal, in fact, that it took my mind off the reason why I was flying in the first place. By the time I saw Peter's van, I was calmer than I'd been for a long while. But then I spotted my son in Peter's arms and my emotions exploded.

'Daniel!'

I dropped my holdall and ran as fast as my four-inch heels would carry me towards the van. I didn't say a word to Peter, didn't even look at him. As soon as I was within reaching distance, Daniel flung himself from his dad's arms and into mine.

'Mummy!'

'Oh, my precious boy, Mummy's back,' I said, desperately fighting back the tears. Then, remembering why I was there, I added, 'And this time I'm not going anywhere.'

Peter hadn't said a word. Eventually I looked at him and smiled. 'Thank you for looking after him.'

I truly meant it. Daniel was obviously in fine spirits.

'Don't be daft,' Peter said. 'Of course I'm going to look after him.' He paused. 'That's my job. Just like I'm going to look after you.'

Conversation during the drive back to Bathgate was stilted. While I just wanted to hug Daniel, Peter rabbited on about all sorts of rubbish, like he'd just picked me up from the shops. I replied when I could, but I wasn't really listening. I was too relieved.

I assumed I was on top of my emotions, but the second we pulled up outside the house in Robertson Avenue, I thought I was going to be sick. I'd spent the unhappiest time of my life in that building. It only held bad memories. What the hell was I thinking going back in there? Suddenly the solicitor's plan seemed like the most stupid idea in the world.

Each step up the path brought a fresh memory, each more grotesque than the last. And they all took place in that house. I began to sweat as the task ahead of me rose into my mind. It had taken me months to escape this prison the last time. What made my solicitor think I could pull this off?

Images of what Peter might do to restrain me flooded my mind. Would he board the windows, lock me in one room or tie me to a chair? He had to have something up his sleeve, I knew it. But I had to put that out of my mind now. Peter needed to be convinced that everything was fine, even if my legs felt like lead as I approached the front door.

Entering the place felt so wrong, but once I'd overcome that hurdle I could begin to concentrate on why I was there. I didn't dare rush anything or Peter would get suspicious, so I began by telling him off for kidnapping my son. It would have been unnatural if I hadn't. But then I apologized for running off in the first place. I told him I understood how much he'd been hurt and that's why he'd taken Daniel. No, I didn't believe he would hurt him, of course not.

I basically came out with any old nonsense I thought he wanted to hear. And he swallowed it. He truly believed I was negotiating to come back to him.

Of course, words are one thing. If I really loved him like a wife should, then I would share his bed. That night he subjected me to every sexual act he could think of and I went along with them all. I don't know if Peter suspected my motives or simply got a kick out of his power over me, but he seemed to take pleasure in doing things he knew I would hate. He didn't hurt me this time – perhaps he was saving that – but he came up with something worse. As he pushed me onto my knees and prepared himself to penetrate me from behind, I heard a voice. Daniel had entered the room.

'Stop it, Peter,' I said as calmly as I could. 'Not now.'

But he laughed and kept pushing. That's when I knew that he'd seen Daniel come into the room long before I had. He wanted my son to see me on all fours. That's the only reason we were doing this.

I just closed my eyes and tried to get it over with as quickly as possible. I'd witnessed my own mother subjected to harsher treatment in the same position. However much it hurt, I couldn't afford to show Daniel. He had to believe I was okay. So did Peter. Whatever the provocation, I was not going to rock the boat. If it was a test, I was determined to pass.

On day two I began to seriously work on him. It was no good going in there claiming he was a saint. I had to be semi-truthful, so I said, 'Look, this is why I ran away. I found the relationship very difficult because I was so far away from home. I felt lonely and that made me act the way I did.'

On and on I went, blaming being isolated for the way I'd treated him. Having my phone calls monitored and my friend-ships ended like that had hurt me and I'd responded badly, I said. He lapped up every word – especially when I tried to take the blame.

'I shouldn't have taken your son,' I admitted. 'That was wrong.'

'You've no idea how much that hurt me, Cathy,' he said. 'You shouldn't have done it.'

'I know, I'm sorry. I should have spoken to you.'

'Yes, you should. You can always speak to me, Cathy, you know that.'

What a load of bull. The weird thing is, I honestly couldn't tell if he believed it or not.

For ages we went on, toing and froing. Finally I sensed he'd been softened enough. It was now or never. Time for the killer punch.

'It's this place's fault,' I said. 'Everything would have been all right if we'd stayed down south. I would have been the perfect wife, I know it.'

It was a dangerous game to play. I couldn't just say, 'Let's drive down to Portsmouth and everything will be rosy.' He'd get suspicious at that. But I planted the seed – just as he had done to me so many times.

When we returned to the subject later, I told Peter how happy I was in Portsmouth and how it was a shame we hadn't moved there after Brighton when we'd had the chance of an exchange flat in the area. 'We'd have been happy, I know it.'

Then the miracle happened. Peter said, 'Do you think you'd be happy if we gave it a go in Portsmouth now?'

I really had to hold my excitement back. Could it even be a trick? I wouldn't have put it past him.

'Are you serious? I can't think of anywhere better for us to be a family.'

He grunted, but that night in bed we started planning our new life together like a pair of excited newlyweds. I'd never seen him so enthusiastic about anything. We'd need a bigger place than Middlesex Road, of course, but it was fine to start with. And he wouldn't mind looking after Daniel if I wanted to work. From my side, I promised to keep myself attractive for him and be a better wife. It was sickening really, but it worked. The following morning we loaded his white van and, for the second time in my life, I said goodbye to Bathgate.

As we drove down the M8, Daniel asleep in my arms, I realized I couldn't relax. Was it really happening? Was Peter actually driving us to Portsmouth?

Or is it a trap?

I pictured it all being an elaborate hoax. He'd tricked me into packing up his house and now he was going to dump our bodies and flee the country. Even as we crossed the border into England, I couldn't shake the idea that he was up to something. I was such a terrible liar – I still am. It was inconceivable that the great manipulator hadn't seen through my little act. But the closer we got to Portsmouth, the more I let myself believe he'd fallen for it. I allowed myself a brief flash of pride and a smile at the deception.

I must have learnt something during my life with him.

That smile soon vanished the moment we pulled into Middlesex Road and I realized the hardest part was still to come. Now I had to make the call to the solicitor so she could set the legal wheels in motion. A few days ago it had all sounded so simple. I'd light the flare and the cavalry would come charging in. In the cold light of day, I couldn't see it working any better than when Granny had tried to shift those men from Telscombe Cliffs. Was this solicitor telling me Peter would just be removed from my flat and that would be the end of it? It was all very well these people saying they could do this and stop people doing that, but individuals like Peter live outside the realms of legality.

Their brains work differently. They see laws as things for other people. What they want, they get. Life is all about going from A to B – it doesn't matter how you get there.

I was close to giving up the whole idea. This was the man who'd nearly taken my head off when I'd undercooked his pork chops. He'd killed our son's guinea pigs just for nibbling a bit of wallpaper.

What the hell is he going to do to me when he discovers I've been conning him?

The closer the moment got, the more I was leaning towards not going through with the plan. It was all very well my solicitor throwing him out of the flat tonight. But what about tomorrow night? Where will my protection be then? Or the night after? Or the night after that?

I'd virtually decided to cancel the whole thing, but one look at Peter making himself comfortable in my flat while I lugged a box up the stairs knocked the sense back into me. My future life flashed before me and I did not like what I saw.

'Will you keep an eye on Daniel?' I said. 'I'm just popping out for milk for the tea.'

That was the first test for both of us. For me, I was entrusting my son to the man who had kidnapped him not even a week earlier. For Peter, he was being asked to babysit – something he'd always refused to do. And he had to allow me out of his sight, something else that he hated doing when we were together. He weighed up his answer for a second and then said, 'No problem. Don't be long.'

Even though I had memorized the solicitor's number, my trembling hands meant I had to try it half a dozen times before I got it right. When I heard her voice, I could have cried. She, as ever, was calmness personified.

'Go back to the flat and act like everything is normal. The bailiffs will be there before your kettle has even boiled.'

The realization of what I'd just done hit me like a thunderbolt the second I hung up. In a few minutes Peter was going to discover that I'd tricked him. He was going to learn that it had all been a lie. I didn't love him, I'd reported him to the police and I'd won sole custody of our child.

How on earth is he going to react?

The solicitor was right about the tea not being ready in time. I was shaking so much, I couldn't even do that right. Peter, fortunately, was sprawled out on a sofa after the long drive down. I was so terrified of what was about to happen that I couldn't look at him. When the knock on the door came, I nearly dropped the mugs.

'Who the fuck's that?' Peter called out, but he didn't budge. It was my flat, I could get the door.

I opened it and the daylight vanished. The whole doorway was filled by the largest pair of men I'd ever seen.

One of them growled, 'Peter Tobin?'

I said, 'Yes,' and pointed at the sofa without looking.

I'd played this scene over and over in my mind and usually it ended with Peter grabbing Daniel while the bailiffs backed off. The reality couldn't have been more different. Even as the bailiffs read out their legal order explaining that Peter had no rights to his son and was not allowed within a mile of the pair of us, he didn't move. He didn't resist as they bent down to encourage him up.

I'd expected anger and fury and fists and even weapons. At the very, very least, I'd expected to be called every name under the sun.

But he did none of that. There was no menace in his face, just shock. Utter disbelief that his mousey little wife had dared to do this to him. Total non-comprehension that he had just been beaten at his own game by the woman he had unwittingly trained.

SEVENTEEN

Another Thirty Seconds . . .

You should never threaten a woman's child.

If that thought wasn't going through Peter's mind as he was thrown out of my flat by the thick arms of the law, then it should have been. He needed to know that there was nothing I wouldn't do to protect Daniel. I'd proved that in Bathgate every time I'd turned the other cheek when he'd taken women – they must have been prostitutes, I realized – to our bed, smacked me across the room or put me down in front of strangers. I wasn't scared of him. I'd only subjugated myself to stop him hurting Daniel. And now I'd gone a stage further.

As he was led out of the room, I could see Peter thinking, 'She can't do this. She's not capable of this. I control her. She does whatever I want.'

That's why he hadn't resisted. He'd been literally too confused to fight. He'd misjudged me big time. For someone so adept at manipulation, that must have hurt his professional pride. It was satisfying seeing the tables turned. Just like I'd been blind for so long to his obvious true character, he'd come down to Portsmouth expecting me to be the same malleable wallflower who'd left. He'd ignored my new clothes, my weight loss, my dyed hair – he'd even been with me when builders had wolf-whistled and that hadn't sunk in either. I was a new woman and he never even noticed.

He may not have known me, but I knew him. Which is why, as I locked the door after them and hugged Daniel, sobbing, 'We're safe now. Safe at last,' I didn't truly believe it. I'd just seen the man of my nightmares escorted from my flat, but however it looked now, Peter was not someone who liked to be beaten. He'd walked away this time because it had been the sensible thing to do. But he would be back. There would be repercussions, I was convinced of it. It was just a question of when.

As a consequence, I didn't sleep a wink that night. Every cracking twig beneath the window was Peter shinning up a tree. Every engine was his old van idling to a stop. Every creaking floorboard was him with an axe outside my door. By the time Daniel woke up at six, I was a nervous wreck.

After a week of that, I finally entertained the idea that Peter wasn't coming back. Granny and my new friends assured me that bullies run away when you stand up to them. Peter was the classic bully and I'd well and truly stood up to him.

I've realized that I'm a great believer in drawing a line under events and moving on. I suppose that had started, like everything else, with my mother. We'd flitted from place to place for various reasons, but when she decided to give normal living one last go, we'd moved into Telscombe Cliffs. That address was meant to be a fresh start. Since then, I'd done the same thing with Peter and without him. Now, after the horrors of the kidnapping episode, it was time to draw another line.

Our next home was in Chichester Road, in the north end. On paper, it didn't sound much of an improvement, but it really was, not only because the shared bathroom and kitchen were really clean this time. The building was a normal two-storey house, with three bedrooms. Our two you accessed by turning left at the top of the stairs and the other one by turning right. So even though I had to cross the corridor to reach my other room, there was no one else up that end of the house, so it felt private. As for the rooms themselves, the smaller one was large enough for two single beds, which meant neither of us had to sleep in the living quarters for once. The other room was even better because not only was it large, with an almost floor-to-ceiling window, but it had also previously been used as a bedsit, so it had a work unit with a sink and places for a fridge and microwave. You can tell I didn't have the highest expectations, but it was a palace to us.

We'd been there a few days when I received a letter Peter had sent to Granny's address. He basically apologized and asked to see Daniel again. 'Call me,' the letter said.

No way, I thought, and threw it straight into the bin.

Unfortunately, that was not the end of the story. At some point in the night, my conscience got the better of me. I found myself lying in bed, going over and over how I'd promised my son would know his father. Of course, there were arguments against it – the kidnapping, the threats, the beatings – but these had all been against me. Peter had never actually hurt Daniel. On the contrary, he'd been a good father since we'd separated. And just because I didn't want him in my life, I shouldn't prevent Daniel having that opportunity. He could make up his own mind when he was older, but it was my responsibility to do the right thing for now.

It wasn't an easy decision, but the next morning I retrieved the letter from the bin and called Peter. I could tell he was happy, so I tested him.

'I need a favour,' I said.

'You name it.'

'I want my fridge, tumble dryer and microwave.' I'd paid for all the white goods at Bathgate from my tea shop profits. It was only fair that I had them now.

There was a pause. Then, 'I'll bring them down tomorrow.'

For once, he was as good as his word. There was a moment just before he pulled up when I worried that he'd brought a weapon to get his revenge, but I honestly didn't think so. He was so desperate to get us all back together again, he wouldn't do that. And, I thought, he'd seen the size of the bailiffs at my disposal.

Granny told me I was stupid to let him back into Daniel's life, but I ignored her. When Daniel looked pleased to see his dad, I knew I'd done the right thing.

While Peter lugged my furniture into the room, I happened to mention how nice it would be if there were a door across our corridor.

'Then my two rooms would feel joined, like a flat.'

He thought that was a great idea.

'I'll get the door for you,' he offered. 'I've got the van.'

So off he went and, for the second time in two days, I scratched my head. *Why is he being so nice?*

The surprises continued. When Peter returned, he had a really heavy door and frame.

'That doesn't look cheap,' I said, worried about paying him back.

'It wasn't cheap, but don't worry. It's a fire door. This baby will give you thirty minutes of protection. I can't have my family at risk, can I?'

Half an hour later, he'd got tools from somewhere and was

drilling and banging and sawing to install my new door and its frame. Inspired by his work, I took Daniel out to a DIY shop and then I painted the whole corridor a vivid, rich burgundy – the same colour I still paint everything! It was a really enjoyable day. Daniel scampered around happily, I got to indulge in my love of painting and Peter went hours without once asking me to move back in with him.

By nine o'clock we were all done and I was ready to drop. God knows how Peter felt after a long drive and all that DIY. So I said, 'Look, Peter, it's too late for you to go home now. If you want, you can have the sofa in the lounge and leave in the morning.'

He was like a puppy with two tails at the idea. I didn't feel I was being reckless. The two rooms had their own locks and were separated by a corridor. He couldn't get to us. And in any case, as I told him before I turned the lights out, 'I'm pleased you seem to be over your obsession with us getting back together.'

Despite going to bed so early, being roused by the sound of ferocious banging on your bedroom door at four in the morning is a hell of a rude awakening. It took me ages to come round. Then the banging stopped and there was a crash. And Peter was standing in my room.

'Get out!' I screamed, but I realized he was already shouting.

'Get up, get dressed – there's a fire!'

It still took me a few more seconds to compute. For a while, I was just traumatized by the sight of my dangerous, clearly agitated husband. Only when I saw traces of smoke wafting in from the corridor did it sink in. *Fire*.

Suddenly I was in full self-preservation mode. Seconds later, dressed only in my pyjamas and clutching a still-sleeping Daniel,

I staggered out of the room. The smoke was coming from underneath the fire door.

'Thank God you put that up,' I said to Peter.

'Yeah, well, we can't go that way,' he said.

I agreed. I think we'd seen the same film. You never open a door with fire behind it because the oxygen sends it all up. We'd have an inferno on our hands.

It was late, I was tired and there was a fire in my house, but I wasn't panicking. Not yet. I said, 'We're only on the first floor. We can jump out of our window onto the bay window below and get down to the ground.'

The lounge's window configuration was the same as in every house in the street: one great pane of glass and three louvre panels above it. By the time I reached it, Peter was already there, frying pan in his hand. He looked at me, I think for permission, and I nodded. Then he took an almighty swipe at the glass – and the large metal pan just bounced off it.

'Fucking hell!' he shouted, then threw the frying pan as hard as he could at the window. Still nothing. By now the smoke was seeping under the lounge door fast. It reminded me of one of those *Top of the Pops* stages, where you can't see the performers' feet for all the dry ice.

Okay, I thought, *now it's time to panic.*

I attacked that window with anything I could lay my hands on, but it was the same effect.

'There's no way this is glass!'

'Glass or not,' Peter said, desperation evident in his voice, 'this will do it.'

I watched as he heaved the microwave onto his shoulder. Then he span round quickly and launched this bloody great thing at the window. And yet again it came straight back.

Peter was genuinely scared now. I'd never seen that before. If anything, that just made me calmer.

'We'll have to go out the louvres,' I said and, reaching up to the higher windows, smacked at them with a rolling pin. They smashed first time, glass raining down onto the ledge below. Peter took over and, like a man possessed, knocked every piece out of the frame.

It was getting hard to see out of the window, but I knew my plan to land on the bay window below had just got much harder. Most importantly, how was I going to get Daniel out of there?

'I'll go first,' Peter said. 'You can pass him to me,' and before I could answer he was already hauling himself through the small, rectangular window. That's the moment when I admitted to myself that I could never trust Peter again. Not after the kidnapping. I was completely uncomfortable with the idea of letting Daniel out of my hands, not with his father on the outside and me trapped inside. *But what else can I do? I can't climb out with him.*

That was when the miracle happened.

I nearly didn't include this in my story because it sounds too fantastical. But just as I was agonizing about passing my child over to the man who had abducted and threatened him, I saw a council worker on a cherry-picker fixing a light further up the street. He was wrapped up in a hi-vis coat and helmet, but to me he looked like Superman.

You have never heard a woman scream as loudly as I did. The bloke looked across and took a few moments to process the scene. Then he leapt down and drove his truck over at top speed. Peter was shouting at me to pass Daniel out, but I held on. As long as the smoke was only waist high, I could keep Daniel above my head in the clear air. Then, like an angel from the heavens, the cherry-picker rose before my very eyes and my saviour in day-glo yellow plucked my son to safety.

As soon as Daniel was out of my hands, I screamed at the stranger to get away from the building. 'Go, go, I'll be all right!' I was terrified the house would explode and I didn't want him caught in the crossfire, not with the precious cargo he was carrying. In any case, if Peter could get out of the window, then so could I. I jumped up, swung myself through and, not daring to look down, let myself drop onto the roof of the bay below. The funny thing was, when I opened my eyes, I could see all the thousands of shards of glass near my bare feet, but none of them seemed to have gone in.

A few minutes later I was wrapped in a fireman's blanket on the other side of the road, cuddling Daniel and watching as the brigade extinguished the blaze. It felt surreal to imagine I'd been in there a few moments earlier. If it weren't for the heat pouring out of the building, it would have seemed just like a film.

When it was all under control, a fireman told me how lucky we'd been. 'We estimate another thirty seconds, a minute at most, and the lounge would have been engulfed.'

Thank God Peter woke me up when he did.

I spent the rest of the night at Granny's, still in a fug from our narrow escape. I presumed Peter was sleeping in his van. I hadn't bothered to ask. Gradually I became aware of pain in my feet. When Granny looked, she said, 'Cathy, you're cut to ribbons. Can't you feel it?'

I was just beginning to. I think the adrenalin from the fear had blocked the pain out. I spent the rest of the day at the hospital, having tiny flecks of glass tweezered out. The following morning, I called the fire station and asked if it was safe to return for my clothes. They said the staircase was entirely destroyed, but it was okay to use the fire escape at the back of the house, which the other lodger had escaped from.

It's extremely creepy being in a burnt-out building. A fireman had insisted on accompanying me, but I was still spooked by the charred walls and blackened floors. When I got to my private corridor, I gasped. The fire door was completely gone. And that wasn't all. All my clothes were missing.

They hadn't been burnt because the wardrobe was still intact – someone had taken them! Daniel's had vanished as well. In their place were three men's jackets.

Someone's been sleeping here!

With the fireman at my back, I explored the rest of the flat. Everything in the lounge was just as we'd left it, apart from being smoke-damaged. The frying pan and microwave were still on the floor where they'd landed. In fact, the only thing that appeared to be missing was some Fairy Liquid. Every other cleaning agent was lined up neatly, as usual, by the sink. But there was a gap where the Fairy should have been.

That was such a confusing discovery that I almost forgot my jewellery box. Dashing back into the bedroom, I found it at the bottom of the wardrobe. I didn't have much jewellery myself. In fact, the only three things in that box worth anything were all pieces that had belonged to my mother: a silver ring with a jade stone; a gold ring with a square-cut amethyst which Mum had given to Granny and she had passed on to me when Mum had died; and a marijuana-leaf brooch in silver (there was another clue about Mum that I'd missed at the time). Of them all, the gold ring was the most important because that was the one that linked Mum, Granny and me. But that was the one that was missing.

I could have stood there crying, but that wasn't my way. I

picked up the jewellery box and a couple of bits for Daniel and thought, *There's nothing to be saved from here.* Then I walked back down the fire escape, already thinking, *I'll just start all over again.*

Again.

A lot of things happened after that. The fire brigade told me that they suspected the fire had been started deliberately, which was incredibly chilling to hear. Who would do something like that?

For a second, I entertained the idea that Peter might have been behind it. But that was ridiculous. He'd been in the flat with me. In fact, he had been more terrified than I had. But the idea wouldn't go away. *What if he'd lit the fire so he could play the hero with his big fire door?*

Again, too implausible.

But – my mind was working feverishly now – *what if he'd planned to impress us by smashing the window and lifting us all to safety?* When I thought about it, the shock on his face when that bloody window hadn't broken told its own story. *Surely, though, not even he . . .*

To this day, I don't know, but I still suspect.

I discovered later that the flat window had been made of polycarbonate, not glass – totally illegal in a rented accommodation. Unfortunately, I couldn't afford to pursue a legal claim, so I will always feel the landlord got away with that one.

I didn't really mind though. The only thing I cared about saving, as ever, was Daniel and he'd come through it without a scratch. He hadn't even woken up until he was out in the cold air.

The poor boy had already been through so much before his second birthday. I knew it wasn't my fault, but I really had to think about giving him some stability. I'd had my recovery period and my identity and confidence, hidden for so long, were back. I decided it was time to get a job. *Daniel needs friends. Nursery will be good for him.* Maybe he'd even win a photo on the beach with the mayor, like I'd done all those years ago.

I laughed at the memory. Then, serious face in place, began to devise a plan.

EIGHTEEN

Help Me, Mum

Home after the fire was another flat, but even as I signed the lease, I knew I wouldn't be there long. I'd got a commission-based job in an estate agent's in New Road and, if I played my cards right, the potential earnings were pretty good. Actually, for someone with no experience, they were amazing. But, I figured, I'd bought and sold used cars in a previous life and I'd haggled for the best tea and coffee prices at wholesalers. This was a job I could do, and do well.

The company paid me for every customer I found, every appointment I made, every viewing that came in and, obviously, for every sale. It was a boom time for property because the government was offering people fifteen grand to leave their council flats, so there was no shortage of customers coming through the door with their deposits in their hands. At £50 a time for each meeting, I was soon pulling in an average of £500–£600 a week – not bad for a twenty-one-year-old.

As soon as I had some money, there was only one place I wanted to spend it. I was determined Daniel should have every-thing I never had, so I enrolled him in a lovely private nursery in Purbrook. It cost £110 a week, but I liked its ethical attitudes and the fact that it had wonderful outdoor space. I knew he'd be happy there.

I was happy now as well because after such a long time getting over the ordeal of being with Peter, I had found a new partner. He was an engineer called Steve, about my age, and, for a while, I thought we had a future. Steve was exactly what I needed at the time – mainly because he couldn't have been more different from Peter. Whereas my husband was like a wound coil, ready to unravel without warning, Steve was so laid-back he was almost horizontal. I couldn't have wished for a more easy-going guy.

This wouldn't have counted for anything, however, if he hadn't also been great with Daniel. Only when I was sure my son was comfortable with Steve could we take the next step and move in together. At first I was nervous. After my previous experience, the idea of sharing a home with a man again took a little getting used to. But soon we were all living in a large four-bedroom house in Fareham and I couldn't have been happier. Between my job, my son and my partner, my life was close to being complete. But there was, of course, still another male in my life.

Peter had also been busy, this time once again on the council exchange programme. He'd managed to swap the Bathgate place for a three-bed in Margate, Kent, although I wondered why the council were still giving him all that space. I realized my name was probably still on all the forms, so he was claiming he was still a family. In reality, though, he finally accepted we weren't and were never going to be once I told him about Steve. I'm sure that privately he was furious, but from that day he stopped nagging me to go back to him.

I would even go so far as to say that he had mellowed. To be fair, I hadn't seen anything of his temper since we'd come down from Bathgate. The only recent blot on his copybook had been the fire episode, but, as the months went by, the more ludicrous my idea that he could have been responsible for it sounded. No one was that mad.

Margate was only a couple of hours from us, so at weekends Peter picked up where he'd left off before the abduction and began to spend whole days with Daniel and me. More often than not, he would arrive with some piece of junk he'd found and say, 'I saw this and thought of you.' I never had the heart to tell him I just threw everything away the second he left. For the sake of Daniel and my overriding desire for him to have two parents, I forced myself to search out the positive in as many of Peter's actions as possible. If I'm honest, I was happy with the results. I certainly had no fear that Peter would try to harm his son or run away with him again. That chapter was behind us. So when Peter offered to have Daniel at his place for a sleepover, I agreed.

I don't think I was much company for Steve that night. We were meant to be having a rare evening out and I just sat staring at my dinner, punishing myself with thoughts of Peter abducting Daniel again. It was only when it occurred to me that the all-ports alert was probably still in place that I began to relax. The next morning, though, I was in Margate to collect Daniel an hour early. Everything was fine. I'd worried for nothing.

Peter really seemed to be making an effort. Obviously he was a typical Saturday dad in the way he let Daniel do what he wanted and fed him too much junk food. I lost count of the times I told Peter not to let Daniel watch eighteen-certificate videos, but he never got the point. On the other hand, he really impressed me by building a sandpit in the garden for Daniel to play in. It was out of character, but a nice thing to do. Even so, it was a relief when Peter announced he'd found another exchange closer to ours, a two-bedroom flat in a block in Leigh Park, Havant. I didn't particularly want Peter on my doorstep, but the closer I was to Daniel at weekends, the better.

It all seemed to be going so well. Then, one by one, the plates stopped spinning as they often do. I felt Steve was unfairly suspicious of me sometimes, and at one point even believed I was having a relationship with his mate Andy. So I packed our things and Daniel and I moved into a brand-new home in Campbell Road. I was too much of a pragmatist to be that upset by it. Living with Peter had taught me that life's too short to spend it in the wrong relationship. My main priority was ensuring Daniel wasn't too troubled by another change of scene.

If I'm honest, as an estate agent, I should have recognized that we weren't just downsizing in terms of space – there was a quality drop as well. But I was in too much of a rush to care. Our new home, 32A, was a basement flat that was dark and oddly configured. It didn't even have a proper front door. You had to walk around the side of the semi-detached number 32 to get in. At night it was pretty scary, I admit, although by day the garden was really pretty. I even adopted a lovely fluffy cat who'd been run over. Overall, then, I had to be content. *Money's good at the moment. This is a temporary measure. There are good things round the corner.*

Ever the optimist.

This is the point in a story where you would expect disaster to strike. Right on cue, it did.

Everyone at the estate agent's was doing well; it wasn't just me. But the owner decided he wanted to do better. Over a period of a couple of months, he altered just about every aspect of our pay structure. The ones on wages were okay. But if you were on commission only, like me, your income tumbled. My take-home pay went from £600 to £400 and then dropped even further, until in the end I was lucky to make £250.

At first I thought it would be okay. I'd put some aside; I'd be all right for a while. But when the money kept going down, I began to be really concerned. Daniel's weekly fees were £110, rent was that again and then I had to pay for a car and petrol and everything else we needed to live. My measly £250 wasn't covering it.

I responded to the situation in the only way I knew how. I just worked harder. The problem was, sixty-hour weeks had been my average for months. That's how I'd made the wages in the first place. Now I found myself doing sixty-five, seventy, eighty, just to keep my head above the water. And it was killing me.

The worst thing was, I was farming out Daniel left, right and centre to squeeze in a few more minutes of profit. When I was with him, I was too knackered to enjoy it. It was always bedtime for one of us.

Tiredness was the least of my worries though. Once I'd covered the essentials, there was virtually nothing left for food or power. One by one, the tea, sugar and coffee ran out, not to be replaced. I was buying a loaf of bread and a few tins of beans on a Saturday and praying they'd see us through the week. Just because we had food, though, it didn't mean we could cook it. Our gas and electricity ran off meters and my store of fifty pences gradually diminished – the modern meters weren't fooled by anything as simple as coins made of ice. I'd come home in darkness, put Daniel to bed by candlelight and sit shivering in my own bed, crying at the mess I found myself in. It was barbaric, Victorian. It was just like living with Mum.

That was the point I knew I'd failed my son. After everything I'd done to protect him over the years, all the beatings I'd taken when his safety had been threatened, I'd let him down. I'd sworn on my mother's grave that I would give him a better start than the one I'd had and all I'd done was match it, error for error, darkness for darkness, baked-bean tin for baked-bean tin.

I felt sick. I hated myself. Worst of all, I was still trapped in the cycle of work, work, work. Daniel still went to nursery and I still put on my business suits and smiled at rich customers, but the second I was alone, the tears were never far away. Nothing was going right. The harder I worked, the worse I felt.

I was almost a broken woman when I swallowed my pride and called on Grandpa one Friday lunchtime. He was surprised to see me, even more surprised when I asked him for a loan. Forcing the words out was the hardest thing I'd done in ages. He would never ask for help and, trust me, if there had been someone else I could have gone to . . . I felt a failure for bothering him. But I *was* a failure.

My nerves probably made me sound a bit glib when I finally spat the words out. Grandpa considered it for a while, then shook his head.

'I'm sorry, Cathy, I don't think that will be possible.'

I couldn't blame him. I hadn't revealed anything like the extent of my problems and I suppose, as I was standing there, hair immaculate, in make-up and an expensive suit, he wouldn't have guessed. I should have begged, or at least told the truth about how serious it was, but after all the heartache he'd been through bailing Mum out and then worrying about me, I just didn't have the heart.

Grandpa could never have known, but that was my last throw of the dice. In fact, his rejection just about confirmed my own opinion of myself at that moment. I didn't deserve to be helped. Everything I touched went wrong. My marriage, my son's life, my job, my relationship with Steve, my home. I couldn't get anything right. As I drove back to the office, I was in tears. Over and over I kept asking myself, *What's the point? What's the point of you? You're no good to anyone.* I was twenty-one years old and in the grip of total desperation.

When I picked Daniel up that evening, I took him straight to Peter's. I forget what line I spun – maybe it was the power-cut excuse Mum used to use – but he said he could have Daniel for the weekend. That was the main thing. I kissed my boy and drove away, but I didn't go straight home. First I stopped at a local shop and bought 150 paracetamol tablets. Tonight I would make my problems disappear forever.

Any second thoughts I was having about my plan disappeared the moment I turned the key in the lock at Campbell Road and felt the cold, dark air envelop me. That was what my life had come to. Fumbling around in the dark, I poured a pint of water, then went and sat in the lounge. The street lamp outside gave some valuable light, but I didn't need it for what I was about to do.

I remember being really uncomfortable lying on our two-seater sofa, which is weird when you consider the pain I was planning to inflict on my body any moment. But I've always liked things just so. From smoking Dunhill instead of Rothmans to rushing Daniel into private education when I couldn't even afford to eat, that's how I think. At that moment it seemed important to be comfy.

I'll be honest, I didn't want to go through with it, but in no way was it a cry for help. I wasn't doing it for attention or sympathy, like Peter had with his overdose and slashed wrists. I had no phone, Daniel was away for two nights and hardly anyone knew my address anyway. When you moved as often as I did, friends fell by the wayside. Killing myself was the last thing I wanted to do, but I'd tried everything else. I couldn't see another way out of my situation. I'd worked my fingers to the bone and it hadn't been enough. I didn't deserve to have a beautiful son if I couldn't look after him.

Thinking of Daniel led me to my mother. Where was she when I needed her?

'Help me, Mum,' I heard myself call out. 'Tell me what to do!' I stared at the ceiling, waiting.

And she didn't answer.

I so wanted her to. I really thought she would. Then I thought, *You're no fucking good to me either, are you?* and I started to take the pills.

I didn't tip them in. I just had one, took a sip of water and swallowed. When that was gone, I did it again. But there was no hurry. I wanted to do it right, but I also wanted to give my mother every chance to step in, to make me put them down. If she could just do one thing for me, now was her chance.

I was probably taking one tablet a minute and by now I'd had ten. It was a nice round number, but there were still plenty to go. I'd read that as few as thirty tablets could be lethal. I had five times that in my box and I intended to take every one. I reached once more for the bottle and then I stopped. There was a noise from the back of the house. Someone was knocking.

Wiping the tears from my face, I made my way through the darkness towards the half-light of the door. When I opened it, I could not believe my eyes.

302

'Andy? What are you doing here?'

Steve's old friend laughed. 'It's a long story, Cathy. Can I come in?'

I nearly turned him away, but he looked so happy to see me, I thought, *I can finish this later. I've got all night.*

Then Andy told me his 'long story' and I knew I wouldn't be going back to my pills. Apparently, Steve had only recently told him where I'd moved to. Even then, he'd just said 'Campbell Road', no number. So tonight, of all nights, Andy had decided to start at one end of the street and knock on every door. He'd got to number 32 and nearly walked past, but something made him check round the side. He saw my door and that was that.

I couldn't believe what I was hearing. It was so random. There was only one explanation.

'Thank you, Mum,' I whispered.

I knew she wouldn't let me down. She'd sent a guardian angel. It was as miraculous and unbelievable as the council worker on his cherry-picker. *Maybe he was sent by Mum as well?*

I don't know what was better, seeing a friendly face or having proof that my mother hadn't given up on me. I blurted out the full story to Andy and he just looked at me like I was daft. 'It's only money,' he said. 'It's not worth getting like this for the sake of a few quid.'

He had a couple of coins on him, so he fed the meter and, for the first time in ages, we had light and heating. Then he said, 'Wait here, I'll be back in a minute.' It was closer to ten, but when he returned it was with a bag of groceries – tea, coffee, sugar, milk and wine – and a takeaway.

In the space of half an hour, I'd gone from the lowest I'd ever felt to thinking I could take on all-comers. Nothing had changed; I was still poor. But the fight was back. I wasn't a loser. I would never sink that low again.

With a clear head, I looked again at my options. With the car, which I needed to ferry Daniel around, his nursery and our rent, something had to give. It had to be the nursery, but, with Daniel coming up to school age, that wasn't the end of the world. I hatched a plan – but it needed Peter's help and a lot of trust on my part.

I enrolled Daniel in a school closer to Leigh Park than my own house and Peter and I now split childcare duties. I would take Daniel to school on a Monday, but that night and Tuesday he would stay at Peter's. On Wednesday I would collect him from school and drop him back Thursday morning, then Peter would do the same that night and I would pick him up Friday and have him for the weekend. It was hell at first, but we settled into a rhythm. And it saved me money – because Peter charged less than the school.

I couldn't believe it when he actually asked for payment to look after Daniel. But he knew I was desperate. I was trapped in that cycle of thinking my job was the most important thing in the world and I wanted to keep it. So, obviously, I agreed to his terms. Once a week I'd give him £50 and hate him for it every time.

I didn't have a clue what Peter did with the money, although he clearly wasn't spending it on the crappy gifts he still gave me whenever I visited. They were usually straight out of the car window as soon as I turned out of his road. I say usually because there was one that I didn't throw away – for the simple reason that I'd already lost it once.

I was just about to leave Peter's flat when he leapt up and said, 'I've got something for you.' He disappeared into his bedroom and returned with something small and shiny. It was a ring, but I couldn't understand why he was giving it to me.

'I was walking past a pawnbroker's this morning and it was just there in the window.'

I still couldn't see the relevance until I saw the scratch on the gold.

'It's your mother's ring, Cathy, the one that was stolen!'

I turned it over and over. It really was. But how had it ended up in a pawnshop in Havant? More importantly, as I'd never even worn it and only kept it in the box, how the hell had Peter recognized it as mine?

I knew there was only one answer. He'd stolen it in the first place. *And,* I realized, *those must have been his jackets hanging up.* He was the one living back at the burnt-out flat; he was the one who'd got rid of my clothes. But that still didn't explain the missing Fairy Liquid . . .

I was happy to get my ring back and I didn't honestly lose much sleep over how Peter had acquired it. *He's never going to change.*

For his part, Peter carried on trying to impress me with more ridiculous things, including, once, a membership card to a local casino called Stanleys. He seemed pretty proud of it, although it meant nothing to me. I certainly had never gambled and I wasn't aware he was interested in it either. As long as it didn't affect his ability to look after my son, I didn't really care.

It's funny how quickly things change. One of the first things I'd done to get myself financially straight was take a barmaid's job at the Fox & Hounds in Denmead. That's where I met the next man in my life, also called Steve. If Steve 1 had been the polar opposite of Peter personality-wise, Steve 2 was the physical antithesis. He was six foot tall, broad, blond and about four years older than me – superior to Peter in every way. He also had a Vauxhall Cavalier SRi, which I thought made him stand out.

Steve worked for a small plastic fabrication company based in a couple of farm sheds. In theory, he could make anything out of plastic, but most commonly you would see his work in supermarkets, displaying the apples and magazines and everything in between. I offered to come in to help with selling and proved so effective at it that we decided to go into business together. A wealthy friend of his put up the money, but we would all be equal partners and directors: she did the books, Steve did the estimating and I sold. We were the perfect team and success found us very quickly. With accounts of the calibre of John Lewis and Waitrose soon coming our way, we felt justifiably proud of our efforts.

It wasn't long before I was beginning to earn decent money and I wanted to invest it in a home for my son and me. The first time I viewed the house in Liverpool Road, Fratton, my foot fell through the floor. The state of the rest of the property wasn't much better, but the price reflected the house's condition. I'm sure Granny thought I was mad, but I loved the idea of renovating that dilapidated old shell. I still remember so vividly that feeling of fantastic pride when I stepped through the door as the owner for the first time.

I've done it!

What's more, I'd done it without help from any man. That was important to me. I'd missed out on so much growing up without a father that all my life, I realized, I'd been trying to prove I could cope without one. I'd taken a motor-mechanics course with the Army Cadets, aged fifteen, just so I would never have to rely on a man to help me with my Honda; I'd bought and sold second-hand cars; I'd decorated my Bathgate kitchen single-handedly. They were all attempts at proving I could do it on my own – whether I wanted to or not.

Despite my enthusiasm, work on the house was slow, but I realized I had an eye for interiors and, by the time I'd finished you wouldn't have recognized the place. By then Steve 2 had moved in with us. We were – dare I say – happy. Unfortunately, Peter was always around to keep my feet on the ground.

We'd settled into a nice routine, sharing the childcare, and for a year it worked out just fine. Then, one Thursday night, the phone woke me up. When I saw it was one o'clock in the morning, I panicked. It had to be bad news.

Daniel!

It was Peter on the line, but he assured me Daniel was fine. 'Thank God.'

'But I've called an ambulance. I think I'm having a heart attack. I need you to come and collect the boy.'

He didn't have to ask twice. I threw some clothes on, flew out of the house and reached Havant in record time. Since Daniel had been staying there I'd had a spare set of keys, so I let myself into the building. By the time I reached Peter's door, they were just coming out. Peter had heard me rushing up the stairs.

'Are you all right?' I asked, breathless, as Peter handed me a carrier bag of clothes and toys.

'Probably nothing, but best to be on the safe side,' he said and clutched his chest for emphasis. I was convinced.

'Look, we'll wait till the ambulance gets here.'

'No, no,' he insisted. 'You get that boy home.' Then he kissed Daniel and said, 'I've already kept him up long enough.'

Peter was adamant we should go, so I scooped Daniel up and off we drove into the night. The next morning I rang the hospital and was told it had been a false alarm. Peter had imagined the symptoms. I was actually annoyed. All that worry for nothing. Then I remembered the pathetic attempts at cutting his wrists and the overdose of Amitriptyline.

The man's either a hypochondriac or an attention-seeker – or both!

Over the course of about ten months, Peter called me out three times in the middle of the night on spurious 'heart attack' errands. So when the phone rang in the early hours one Wednesday night, I was almost resigned to the news at the other end.

'It's my heart again. I think this is the big one. Will you come for Daniel?'

By now I didn't even bother getting dressed. I just threw on a gown over my pyjamas, found my car keys and set off. It was only as I pulled up outside Peter's building that I thought, *I've left my keys at home. What if he really is ill this time? I hope he's well enough to buzz me in.*

I shouldn't have worried. As I ran up to the front door, I could see Peter walking Daniel down the stairs. He obviously wasn't at death's door, but as usual I offered to wait until the ambulance arrived.

You never know – this could be the one.

But Peter shooed us away. 'Get that boy home,' he insisted. 'He's had a long day.'

'Okay,' I said, 'if you're sure.'

He nodded and kissed Daniel goodnight – just as he always did on these nights.

As we pulled away from Peter's block, I didn't look back once. I was too tired, too annoyed by the man's medical paranoia to care what he did when he wasn't minding Daniel. If I had looked back, however, I might have seen Peter pretend to return to the building, then stop. I might have seen him wait until we were almost out of sight, then jump into his car and speed off in the opposite direction to us. And I might have wondered: *why?*

NINETEEN

All About Him

Apart from Daniel being more tired than usual, the morning of 5 August 1993 had started out like just another normal Thursday. I was at my desk at half past eight and the phone rang at nine. It was Havant police, asking me to come into the station. At that stage, they wouldn't tell me what it was about. Ominously, though, they said, 'Bring someone you feel comfortable with. A friend or partner.'

That was it. That was all the information I got. As I gabbled down the phone to Steve, I realized the police hadn't told me anything at all.

'You must have done something,' he said.

'I haven't, I swear.'

'Well, is it Daniel?'

'No, that was my first question. He's at school. He's fine.'

So, heads spinning, we got to Havant police station about an hour later. The PC who took me into a back office gave nothing away. Then a more senior officer came in and broke the news.

Peter Tobin, he said, had lured two fourteen-year-old girls

back to his flat in Leigh Park, where he had plied them with cider and vodka and violently raped them. He had then tied them up and left the flat.

What the policeman didn't tell me then, but which I learnt subsequently, was that Peter had sodomized one of the girls with a knife, beaten them black and blue, then turned on the gas and left them to die in the flat. He'd just jumped in his blue Metro and driven away, moments after handing my son over to me. Fortunately, one of the girls had wriggled free and called a neighbour for help.

Later I would spend hours crying about those poor girls, but my initial reaction was utter disbelief. News like that is almost too big for the brain to process. At first my mind just went blank, but then the questions poured out.

'Are you sure?' I heard myself say, but I knew the answer even before it was confirmed.

'Well, when did this happen?' I said.

'Yesterday. Last night.'

I froze in my seat.

'But my son was there!'

And then, I'm afraid to say, all thought of those girls went temporarily out of my head. I just wanted to hug Daniel.

'We don't think he was involved, but we'll know more when the victims are well enough to be interviewed. One of them is in a coma.'

A coma! My God, Peter, what have you done?

Even hearing the outline of the horrific events of that night had me in tears. There would be many, many more to come. But right now the police needed my help.

'Your husband is on the run. Is there anywhere you think he might have gone?'

'I don't know what he does with his time.'

'Please think: any friends, relatives, just tell us everything you can.'

It was hard to concentrate on addresses while still trying to process everything that had happened. Apart from Peter's access to Daniel, I had no interest in his life whatsoever. But I came up with some names and addresses – people like his friend John, his sister and brothers and a couple of pubs and cafés in Brighton and Portsmouth where we'd been a few times. In the end, I just handed over my address book.

'Is there anything else?' the policeman asked. I desperately wanted to help, but the answer was no.

'I'm sorry, I don't know anything about him.'

Realizing that everything you know about someone is a lie takes some processing. When that person is your husband and the father of your child, it defies logic.

I don't know him at all. I never have.

The truth was, however, that I had always known Peter was a man of violence. I knew too that he believed somehow that the world owed him a living and that he was entitled to take whatever he wanted. And I also knew, from my own experiences, that he relished imposing his sadistic will on younger women.

That realization tore me to shreds. The idea that there might have been a chance I could have prevented those girls from being attacked was a heavy burden. But the more I tortured myself over my role in this, the more I realized how he had distorted everything.

When he'd punished me for lazy cleaning or criticized my cooking, I'd always felt that it was my fault, that I'd driven him to it. It wasn't a case of me deserving punishment, but there was a cause and effect in play. My behaviour was the cause. He'd conditioned me to accept the blame for everything. Whether I liked it or not, I was the reason he behaved in the manner he did. Even when he'd brought Lisa and the other girls into our home, that was in some way a result of my actions. I wasn't sleeping with him, so he was forced to go elsewhere. That's how he justified it to us both.

And then there was Daniel. When I'd seen Peter hold my son above the staircase in Robertson Avenue, I truly believed that he was capable of killing. It was only when I'd escaped and had time to analyse events that I realized it was never about hurting Daniel. Daniel was just a weapon, a tool to control me with. Daniel was my weak spot and Peter exploited that. Everything he ever did during that relationship was just because he wanted to own me.

It never, for one moment, occurred to me that Peter was capable of behaving like this to other people. He'd bullied and abused me for so long, I genuinely felt it was all about me. When, in fact, it was all about him.

From the moment the police told me about the events of the previous night, I had only one thought on my mind. *I have to get Daniel.* I was assured he was safe, that if Peter had wanted to harm him, he would have done the night before. But that wasn't the point. I needed to be with him, to wrap my arms around him. I didn't know at that point half the things he'd witnessed, but I did know he would need my help to get over it.

Daniel's school was in Havant, so it was a short journey to pick him up. Even so, I still had plenty of time to curse myself for not noticing anything the night before. Were there clues? Had I missed anything? I'd put Daniel's silence down to tiredness, which was natural, and again that morning. But had there been blood on him? Had he been scared? Had he tried to tell me something? We were in such a rush, I hadn't noticed anything.

When I reached the school Daniel was ready. As soon as I picked him up, I immediately felt him go stiff. He never did that. By the time I got him back to Liverpool Road, I was convinced something was wrong. He was aggressive, shouting things he'd normally say nicely – 'Where's my drink?' 'I need that!' – and the moment he got inside the front door, he hit me. My son had never hit me before in his life.

'Daniel, calm down! What's wrong?'

But I already knew the answer.

When the police were able to interview the girls, the full story emerged. The fourteen-year-olds had knocked on Peter's second-floor door to ask if he knew when their relative – his neighbour – would be back. 'Any minute now,' Peter had said. 'Come in and wait.' He even suggested they could play with Daniel, which, of course, put them completely at ease. And so began sixteen hours of torment and torture that neither girl would ever forget.

As soon as the door was closed, Peter pulled out a sharp breadknife and forced the girls to drink vodka, wine and cider and swallow pills – or else. One of them passed out quickly. The other was sick, then tried to fight. That was when Peter turned nasty. He'd raped the girl, then sodomized her.

The only good thing from my point of view was that Daniel was sent to his room first. Apparently, he'd watched *The Terminator*, which normally I would have hated. On this occasion, it was better than what was going on in the room next door.

But that hadn't been the end of it for him. The girl who'd fought back had managed to twist Peter's arm so the breadknife cut into his calf. That's when he called for my son, my precious son, to fetch ice from the freezer to stem the bleeding. Peter could have gone himself, I know he could. When I'd seen him later that night there was nothing wrong with his leg. But for some reason he wanted my terrified four-year-old to come out, to see what was going on, to be involved. Daniel had to go right over to where the naked girl was writhing and sobbing in agony and watch while his dad shouted at her to be quiet. He had to stand there, shaking, while Peter clumsily packed ice onto his wound. And all the while he couldn't take his eyes off the knife in his dad's hand.

Apparently, the girl begged him for help. But what could Daniel do? He was four years old and traumatized by what he saw. As soon as he could, he ran back into his room and tried to drown out the screams with Arnie Schwarzenegger.

The guilt at not picking up on any signs my son had shown was nothing, though, compared to the anxiety that filled me over what might have been. If Peter was capable of stabbing and torturing strangers, then he was more than capable of doing it to family. What would have happened if the girls hadn't entered Peter's flat? Would the bloodlust have still been there? Would he have found someone else?

Or would he have taken it out on Daniel?

Not knowing is a dangerous place to be. Your brain needs information that you just don't have. So you start to invent things, nightmare scenarios that get worse and worse with every run-through. You start to obsess about the 'what ifs' and then you start looking for the clues that were never there. At a time when I should have been concentrating on my son and the future, my only thought was for the past. It was typical of Peter that, two years after I'd left him, he still had the power to completely screw up my mind.

However, it was Daniel's mind I was most concerned about.

No human being should witness the things he'd endured, much less a child. He was four, so he wouldn't understand rape and alcohol. He saw the girls crying and screaming and he knew they were hurt. But imagine how it looked to him. Every child instinctively believes their parents are right. Look how I'd blindly followed my mother's crazy plans and been completely unaware that how we were living wasn't normal. I'd laid lino, rolled joints, skipped school till I was seven and I didn't have a clue it was wrong. It was the same for Daniel, but far, far worse.

Daniel hated seeing those girls get hurt. It felt wrong hearing their cries, but Daddy wouldn't do anything wrong, would he? That's how we're programmed to think. Daddy was trying to stop them crying. He was angry that they kept screaming. But the girls wouldn't stop.

There are so many things to hate Peter for that it's hard to separate them. Even suggesting to Daniel that what he was doing was okay was unforgiveable, but that was something we could get over in time.

The thing I still to this day can't forgive Peter for is making Daniel feel guilty. Without him, without the bait of playing with him while they waited, those girls might never have gone into that flat. Maybe Peter would have come up with a different temptation, we don't know. But the girls had naturally assumed that a father of a young boy was safe, someone they could trust. They'd taken one look at my son and decided he might be fun to look after – and look where it had got them. Daniel had to live with that. Thirteen years later, however, the tables would be turned.

I had no idea when I'd picked Daniel up from Peter's flat in the dead of night that that would be the last time my son would ever see his father. How I wish I'd made the decision earlier. I still had full legal custody. If I'd wanted to, I could have enforced the court's exclusion zone. But there was always that fire in me to give my son the father I'd never had. It was a mistake and one I will never forgive myself for. I can only say that I did it for the right reasons.

The police were very gentle with Daniel, I have to say, and he began having therapy very soon after we realized what he'd seen. We were introduced to the wonderful Rhona Lucas, the head of the Child Protection counselling division, who promised to work with Daniel for however long it took to purge the experiences from his system. I wasn't allowed into the room, but I could watch through a two-way mirror. Rhona worked wonders. Each session, I saw the anger diminish and more and more of my little boy return. After six weeks, he was back. No shouting, no anger, no hitting. My innocent angel was home.

I don't think Daniel remembers the therapy and we have never spoken about those events. He's put them behind him and I've done my absolute best to protect him from ever being reminded of them – starting with my decision to hide the real reason his father was in prison. The sooner Daniel was able to push the terrible things he'd witnessed in Havant from his mind, the quicker he'd be able to move on. That's why I told him that Peter was in trouble for having drugs. It was nothing to do with knives or rapes or attacks on young girls. When he thought of his father, as I knew he would from time to time, I didn't want his head to automatically be filled with those images of sickening violence.

Back in 1994, though, there were plenty of other people who wanted to obsess about the horrors of that night in Havant and their repercussions. It didn't help that every day the local papers and TV news seemed to talk about nothing else. Every detail of the case was gone over. The main focus, though, was on the whereabouts of the rapist Peter Tobin.

The police were convinced he would contact me. Even though we were separated and I'd moved on with another partner, they felt I was pivotal to their hopes of capturing him. I didn't have a clue how Peter's mind worked, but I'd seen enough films where the criminal wants to get rid of any witnesses. Daniel had seen things. We were both at risk.

I couldn't be too scared though. A panic button was installed by my front door and I was given another one to carry around. One press of that button and the whole of Hampshire's police force would descend on Liverpool Road. On top of that, the police asked if they could tap my phone line. You have to get permission from the Home Secretary for that, I was told. I didn't think Peter would call, but I had no problem with it. On the plus side, it meant there were burly police technicians and officers swarming over the place every hour of the day. I'd probably never felt safer.

Then, about six weeks after the attacks, I finally received word from Havant police station. Two officers had been strolling past a café on St James Street in Brighton, one of the old haunts I had told them we used to drink in. They'd recognized the man nursing a cup of tea without an apparent care in the world as Peter Tobin and arrested him on the spot.

'Thanks to you, Cathy, we've got him.'

I was glad to have been of help, but I couldn't celebrate. I just felt numb.

TWENTY

Turn Round! Turn Round!

I didn't think Peter's story could get any worse. Then I heard he'd been using the name Peter Wilson – my maiden name – when he was captured. *Even in police custody, he can still find new ways to torment me.*

Like everything else, the full story of Peter's forty days at large eventually trickled out. By chance, he'd met a Christian group on a day trip from Warwickshire. Presenting himself as a home-less gent who would work in exchange for shelter, he wangled a trip back with them. When his photo had been shown on an episode of BBC1's *Crimewatch*, not even Peter's hastily grown moustache could hide the obvious likeness. That's when he'd gone back on the run and headed back to Brighton.

Peter was held on remand at Winchester for eight months before his trial. As the date neared, press interest in the case increased. Once the trial began, coverage went into overdrive. There were photos of the flat, of Peter, of the route the girls would have taken. Most distressing for me, though, were the ones of Peter's old blue Metro – because for the last few months it had been sitting on my drive.

I don't know why, but he'd decided I should have it and so one day it had been delivered outside my house and the keys dropped through my letterbox. I had my own, much better car, so I didn't need his old banger. Even if I did, I wouldn't have touched it after I'd discovered what he'd done. As quickly as I could, I sold it to a dealer for £150. I was shocked to later learn he'd shifted it on to a guy who'd paid £900 – just because it belonged to a famous criminal. There are some sick people out there.

None more sick, of course, than Peter himself. I'd always marvelled at the way he was able to detach himself after smacking or insulting me to make me feel guilty. It took chutzpah, especially, to pitch up at Granny's breakfast table that day, knowing she must have been told about the screwdriver launched at my pregnant tummy. But he didn't care. It's like he didn't even know what he'd done wrong. How else can you explain the letter I received from his solicitor asking to see Daniel?

My initial instinct was to rip it up – how dare he put Daniel through that hideous ordeal and now think he could carry on as if nothing had happened? But I couldn't do it, not without getting advice from Rhona Lucas.

'I think you have to ask Daniel if he wants to see his father,' she said. 'And whatever he says, you have to honour.'

That was easier said than done.

'I'd like to visit Dad,' Daniel said.

'Okay, that's fine. I'll sort it out.'

I really wasn't looking forward to driving Daniel out to Winchester. There was no way I could let him go in alone. That meant I would have to come face to face with the bastard as well.

I honestly don't think I can do it.

When it came to the crunch, I wasn't the only one. Daniel

woke up on the morning of our scheduled visit and found me in my room.

'Mum,' he said quietly.

'Yes, my darling? What is it?'

'I don't want to visit Dad anymore.'

'That's okay,' I said calmly – but inside I was jumping for joy.

I'm sure Peter blamed me for Daniel's change of heart, but I didn't care. He couldn't hurt me anymore. When his solicitor wrote back again asking for a picture of Daniel, I took great pleasure in saying no.

'Your client is a paedophile – there's no way he's getting a photograph of my son.'

Part of me was looking forward to the trial because we all knew that Peter was going to be locked away. However, as the last person to see him before he'd fled, I was also going to be called upon as a witness. I know it was silly, but I really wasn't comfortable with going up against Peter so publicly. The idea of his cold eyes boring into me while I gave evidence against him was enough to make me wither before I'd even set foot in the courtroom. But I had no choice. I had to live with it. *As long as they don't involve Daniel . . .*

But then something strange happened. On the first day of the trial, 18 May 1994, Peter pleaded guilty. I think he'd been advised that by not making the victims suffer the ordeal of a trial, he'd be treated more leniently. So he was shocked, I imagine, when the judge sentenced him to fourteen years. *He shouldn't be bothering anyone again until 2008.*

I've said it before, but that definitely should have been the end of the Peter Tobin story, as far as my son and I were concerned. Fate, however, wouldn't be that kind.

*

As soon as I'd discovered what Peter had done to those girls, the efficient part of me had kicked in once again. Daniel was due to start a new school anyway – but he would do so under a new name, Daniel Wilson. I too reverted to my maiden name. One more link to the past destroyed – as long as no one discovered it was the name he'd been using when he was captured.

In contrast to the mess Peter had left, Steve 2 and I were still going strong. After I sold my house for a lovely profit, we decided to rent a four-bed in Emsworth. Daniel was very happy in the private school system and Steve and I both drove nice cars. I had a bright-red Spitfire two-seater which I absolutely loved bombing up and down in. There were probably more expensive cars pulling up at the school gates, but Daniel's mates said we had the coolest.

Relationship-wise, I think I was pretty close to the perfect 'wife'. I know it's old-fashioned, but I'd never had a proper family life. My first chance at domesticity was with Peter and he'd ruined everything. So I really enjoyed serving meals from the Gary Rhodes cook book and looking after Steve's two young girls at weekends. While he was off working, I'd take all three children down to the beach or we'd make our own toys and bake together. It was really idyllic, actually.

Relationships tend to have a natural lifespan though. Ours could have gone on longer, but it was actually our business that got in the way. By taking care of everything to do with home, I left Steve able to concentrate on working every hour under the sun. We both profited as business people, but as lovers it died out. I can't say the break-up was harmonious – some men save their passion for the day you say you're leaving – but I thought I handled it as maturely as I could by moving out and not rising to any provocation. Yet again, ever the practical head when others would be falling apart.

Working together, though, was much more stressful. Steve found it hard to be in the same room as me, but, as fellow directors, I thought it my duty to make it work. Then one day he told me with some relish that I'd never been a director. He and his friend were joint owners. I was basically a well-paid employee.

'Well, in that case, these are the hours I'll be working from now on,' I announced, and suddenly I was able to see a whole lot more of Daniel again.

The things I'd been through with Peter had probably hardened me emotionally when it came to responding to the problems with Steve, but there was another blow around the corner that I hadn't prepared for: Grandpa's death.

By 1996 he'd been ill for a while, needing sticks to hobble around on. It was sad watching a proud man's decline, but I put it down to old age. Then Granny phoned in tears: old Reg was dying of lung cancer – and had been for years.

It was typical of the man that he never told a soul until it couldn't be avoided. Suddenly the Beavises' downsizing move to Southsea made more sense. That was when Grandpa had discovered he had the disease and he wanted to make sure Granny was set up financially before he went.

I had the choice of either telling Daniel or not – and I decided I would. How I wished I'd been told my mother was dying eighteen years earlier. At least he'd get the opportunity to say goodbye – something that had been denied me.

I cried when I saw Grandpa for the last time in hospital. By then the doctors couldn't hide the cancerous growth coming out of his chest. It was revolting. It was no way for such a lovely old bloke, and the closest Daniel and I had to a male role model, to go. No way for Granny to witness the end either.

I was left all his correspondence to do with Mum's death and my childhood, but I didn't want to read any of it, so I put it into a box for another day. I wanted to look forward and, in fact, I didn't open that box until I came to write this book.

Granny was obviously devastated, but regained the family stoicism very quickly. Reg wouldn't have wanted her to spend months feeling sorry for herself, after all. One of her first decisions as a widow was to find something to do with her money. After hearing me moan yet again about my horrible working environment, she said, 'If I lent you £20,000, would that be enough to start up on your own?'

'Easily!' I said. 'I know the plastic fabrication business inside out. I'd love to start doing it for myself. But would you really want to do that?'

'I trust you,' she said. 'And I can't bear to see you working where you're not appreciated and so unhappy.'

So out of the cloud of Grandpa's death had come this amazing silver lining that not only gave me my independence as a boss, but also allowed me to walk away from Steve and co with some pride.

Of course, putting a company together from scratch isn't as easy as it sounds. I found cheap premises in the Paulsgrove part of Portsmouth and then went back to my old company to poach the best staff members. I actually persuaded one older guy, Michael, to come out of retirement for a couple of days a week to help me.

They were exciting times, but I soon realized twenty grand didn't go very far. There are so many costs when you run a business, especially when you employ staff. It didn't matter that we had no orders at the start, the boys still had to be paid. Even as the first meagre bits of business started to trickle in, I could see my money pot trickling away. I was already working every hour I could, but desperation called for innovation.

First, I took an extra job in a bar, then I began delivering evening papers and finally I set up another company catering for the wedding industry and similar events. For a while, I was doing all four. I'd finish work, deliver papers, pick Daniel up, eat and put him to bed and then make cakes to be delivered the following day or do paperwork until the small hours. Then up at six, deliveries, drop Daniel at school, work – and on and on. I was getting three hours' sleep at night – and all to pay my bills and staff. It was hell. The only consolation was that it was *my* hell. If – no, *when* – we turned the corner, I would be the one to benefit.

Right then, though, the workload was suffocating. I was barely seeing my son, but I couldn't stop. Everything I was doing, every hour after midnight I slaved away over the oven, every Saturday I spent on my own in the workshop moulding and drilling plastic while he played with friends, I was doing for him. It had been a lack of money that had driven me to attempt to take my life. More importantly, my poverty had been one of the reasons I'd been so susceptible to the charms of Peter Tobin. It wasn't just him as an unsuspecting father figure I'd fallen for, but the whole package. The promise of a roof over my head and a job had been too tempting.

I swore that I would work and work, so Daniel never had to compromise like I had done.

There were other mistakes I'd made that I didn't want Daniel to copy. When I'd met Peter, I'd considered myself a strong, independent, modern woman. I'd already proven myself as a wheeler and dealer at school. I was obviously going places. But then he'd used brute force against me and I'd crumbled.

As a consequence, Daniel was enrolled in every self-defence class going. Judo, karate, kendo, taekwondo – if there was a martial art course near us, he was doing it. He only took a few belts in any of them, bless him, but he loved going. I couldn't tell him why it was so important to me that he could handle himself. I couldn't shake the knowledge that Peter would be out one day. *We need to be prepared.*

While I didn't really think Peter would ever hurt Daniel, I'd denied him access. He would want to avenge that the first chance he got, I just knew it.

Gradually business picked up and I won some good contracts. My proudest achievement was acquiring the John Lewis Partnership. It meant I was in Bracknell every week for meetings, but I loved that. You couldn't walk into a Waitrose or John Lewis without seeing my handiwork. It was a proud time.

I was able to pay Granny back and, as a surprise, she said, 'I'd like to give you the deposit for a home.' Wow – not a loan this time, *a gift*. It meant so much to me, being able to afford to put down proper roots for my son. In fact, that first moment of opening the door to our two-bed bungalow in Hazlewood Avenue, Bedhampton, as the owner was just as thrilling as walking into Liverpool Road had been. To this day, I still get the same buzz when I buy a new property.

I may have had help purchasing it, but not from a man – and that's how it stayed. After Steve 2, I wasn't in another relationship for several years and I did most of the house renovations myself. With the help of a trusty Collins DIY manual, I single-handedly built a conservatory along the whole width of the back of the bungalow. When that was finished, I honestly don't think I'd ever been prouder of myself. As I poured a glass of fizz to celebrate, I couldn't help thinking of all the potential in me that had been wasted during those years of being subjugated by Peter.

Speaking of him, with everything else ticking along so comfortably, it suddenly occurred to me that I should take care of some unfinished business.

It was 1999 and Peter had been inside for five years. A lot of people don't bother with divorce because it means you have to see your estranged partner again. I didn't have to worry about that. He was locked up. We would only be communicating through solicitors and I was confident it would be pretty straightforward. I was wrong.

'You realize, of course, that your husband is entitled to fifty per cent of your plastic fabrication business and house equity, don't you?' my solicitor said, to which I replied, 'You must be bloody joking!'

I was employing twenty staff and raking in decent money and I owned my own home. Why should that scumbag, who'd contributed nothing to my success, get a penny? The lunacy of the law got worse though.

As far as I was concerned, I already had sole custody of Daniel. For the purposes of a divorce, however, I needed to clarify why this should continue to be the case. I was laughing as I answered the question.

'How about because he's in prison and I'm not!'

It was utterly demeaning, but I had to write out in black and white exactly why I felt I should have sole custody of Daniel. So I mentioned the home, the private education, the swimming lessons twice a week, the martial arts, everything. Peter had given the boy nothing but nightmares. I'd even had to pay him, for God's sake, to look after his own son.

Someone must have been smiling on me, though, because my solicitor advised me to write to Peter asking to be let off his legal claims to my wealth and he agreed. I didn't do it personally, although Peter probably didn't know that. I was grateful though. It was the first selfless thing he'd ever done and to this day I don't know why he did it. He couldn't have been harbouring delusions of winning me back. *Could he?*

Divorce was something worth celebrating and that should have been yet another line in the sand. Somehow, though, I knew it wouldn't be the final cut-off between Peter and me. I just didn't expect him back in my life so soon.

I sold Hazlewood Avenue for another tidy profit, then bought a new place in St Ronan's Road, Southsea. While I was living there, I met the man whom I would be with for the next ten years. His name was Tim and he was lovely. He'd closed his engineering business a year before and was dabbling with the idea of property developing with his spare cash. We decided to move in together, so I sold Southsea, again for a healthy mark-up, and we jointly bought another place in the area for £250,000 – which we did up and sold a year later for £525,000. The day that sale went through I looked at Tim and said, 'I'm in the wrong business.' I followed Tim's lead and wrapped up my own business. Now I was a property developer too.

Suddenly we were enjoying lie-ins, cooked breakfasts and drawn-out lunches together and still finding time to do a few hours' lucrative work each day. It was the perfect career for both of us and life was sweet. And then, in 2001, I received a call from a lady called Susan Blackwell.

'I'm the probation officer for Peter Tobin,' she announced, and at the very mention of his name my heart sank. Steeling myself to get the divorce had been hard enough, but at least I'd had a while to think about it. This call had come out of the blue and her very title gave away the bad news.

'I have a note on Peter's file that you should be kept up to date with his progress.'

'Is he coming out soon?'

'Yes, he's behaved well and he's won parole. He'll be out in a few months.'

Her words were like a slap in the face. I'd built a very comfortable life for me and Daniel. Now, even though there was no way we wanted to see him, Peter could wreck it all.

'Can you tell me where he is now?' I asked.

'Yes, he's on the Isle of Wight.'

'Christ, that's close! I've actually been past there recently.'

He would soon be getting closer.

'Can you stop him coming to Portsmouth?'

Susan was pleased to inform me that: 'Yes, we can.'

'Thank God.'

'Yes,' she continued, 'we're going to base him in Southampton.'

'Oh, that's much safer.' I couldn't hide the sarcasm. This was a man who could take my child for a walk in Portsmouth and end up in West Lothian. A few miles around the coast would provide no obstacle for him.

But I was grateful they'd told me. 'Please keep me informed,' I said, and she agreed.

I tried not to think about it, but by the time Peter was released on parole I was pretty nervous. They'd found him a starter job and a temporary home and he had to sign the sex offenders' register once a week as a condition of his parole. After a tense seven days, I received the call I'd been waiting for.

'Peter has signed the register. All is well.'

Great, I thought. *He's going to keep his nose clean. I can get on with my life.*

The following week, they called again. 'Bad news, Cathy. Peter didn't sign the register today. He's on the run – and we think he's coming to you.'

You cannot imagine the fear that coursed through my veins. I'd had a comfortable few years, put on a pound or two through good living and generally learnt to enjoy the finer things in life now I could afford them. All of that meant nothing now I knew this madman was on the loose.

I swung into action. I told Tim I needed a spy-hole drilled in the front door immediately.

'I think you're overreacting,' he said. He was trying to comfort me, but it just wound me up. He had no clue what I'd already been through – my fault for having kept most of it back.

'Look,' I said, 'that man wants to hurt me. He's still sore that I left him.'

But there was another reason I was scared. As far as Peter was concerned, I had robbed him of his son. I'd done it once when I'd fled from Bathgate. Now, as far as he knew, I'd prevented Daniel from visiting him in prison. I'd even forbidden him from having a photograph!

If there's a chance he could use Daniel to hurt me, I thought, *he'll take it. And I've got to be ready.*

My next stop was Havant police. They were more receptive to my fears than Tim had been. Within the hour, I had a crew round at Southsea, fitting panic buttons. They also arranged for a CID officer to be stationed at Daniel's school. I would still take him and pick him up, but the policeman was there for the rest of the day – on the understanding that Daniel never found out. It was crucial to me that he didn't worry and that his friends didn't discover his past.

Looking back now, the idea of Daniel worrying about anything makes me laugh. He takes laid-backness to new levels. I'd like to take some credit for that, but he's the one who's done it all. He seems to have taken everything that happened before his sixth birthday and just dealt with it. Some kids might have become wallflowers or gone off the rails without a full-time dad around – look how it had affected me. Not Daniel. He was bright and intelligent and was always the first to sign up for new experiences. Junior RAF, the Marines, drums, guitar, camping – you name it, he wanted to try it. When he was sixteen, he would even climb Kilimanjaro with his Uncle Geoff.

But in 2001 this was the last thing on my mind. Back then, I was just desperate that Daniel stayed safe.

Keeping Peter's movements from Daniel was one thing, but I couldn't hide them from his school. It was a tricky phone call, but I had to inform them that their pupil had an escaped convict for a father. He'd savaged two fourteen-year-olds already. The school needed to remain vigilant.

Once again, I was bombarded with questions from the police. They asked where I thought he might have gone. I couldn't help them. In fact, I was annoyed at being bothered. I said, 'You lot have seen him more than me in the last seven years. Look in your records – you've still got my address book from last time.'

Luckily, Peter was picked up shortly afterwards and the police confirmed that he'd been on his way to Portsmouth. For breaking the terms of his parole, he was put back in prison for, I assumed, the rest of his fourteen-year sentence. That turned out not to be the case.

I don't think Daniel was ever aware how close his dad had got yet again. That made it easier to just knuckle down and concentrate on our lives. Tim and I developed well together and fresh housing projects made us a decent income. There wasn't much to grumble about at all. By 2006 we were living in a nice house, had nice cars and, best of all, Daniel had grown into a confident, handsome young man. I had no complaints at all. But then Aunt Anne called and said, 'I think you need to turn on the TV now.'

I couldn't believe what I was seeing and hearing. Peter was being hunted for the murder of a young Polish girl called Angelika Kluk. Just as he'd done when he'd fled Havant in 1993, Peter had been working as a church handyman, this time in Glasgow. And, just like before, he'd changed his name – this time he was calling himself Pat McLaughlin, thank God, and not Wilson. Angelika was a student staying at St Patrick's Church, where Peter worked. She was last seen in his company on 24 September 2006.

As far as the police can tell, Peter had become obsessed with the idea of sleeping with the beautiful twenty-three-year-old the moment he'd first laid eyes on her. His fantasies were fuelled by the fact that he knew she was having a sexual affair with a married businessman. There were even stories that, during her stay at the church the previous year, she had embarked on a physical relationship with the priest at St Patrick's, Father Nugent. But what really appealed to him was the fact that she was so far from home.

With so few friends of her own, Angelika naturally enjoyed

spending time with the charming odd-job man. If she wasn't busy studying, she often helped him out on jobs, so much so that he called her his 'little apprentice'.

One weekend she had been helping 'Pat' build a shed inside the garage attached to the presbytery. That was when he'd struck – literally. Police say Angelika was hit six times on the head by a wooden table leg. The force exposed her skull and sent blood all over the garage. Then Peter had bound her wrists, gagged her mouth and raped her unconscious body. At some point, though, Angelika regained consciousness and found the strength to fight back. That's when Peter produced the knife. He stabbed her sixteen times in the chest, before dragging her body through the church and dumping her in a chamber beneath, of all places, the confessional box.

Then he'd showered, cleaned up the blood from the garage and turned up for work again the next day to finish the shed as though nothing had happened. How many times had I witnessed that detachment, that ability to just carry on as normal after doing the most unspeakable things? For the first time, I began to appreciate how close I must have come to sharing the same fate as this Polish stranger.

Angelika was killed on the Sunday and by Tuesday Pat McLaughlin had disappeared, having already been questioned, along with everyone at the church, by the police. It was days before her body was found and even longer before the police put two and two together and realized they weren't chasing Pat McLaughlin at all but Peter Tobin.

As the horrific news unfolded before my eyes, my heart went out to the poor, distraught family of Angelika Kluk. Then it hit me. How had Peter committed this murder? As far as I knew, he'd be in prison until 2008. Yet the news was saying it had just taken place and they were trying to catch him. I said to Tim, 'I don't understand it. He should be inside.'

But the simple explanation was that he wasn't inside. He hadn't been since 2004. I'd naturally assumed that when Peter had broken his parole, he'd be incarcerated until the end of his original term. But no, he'd served a further three years only. He'd been let out and had immediately fled to Paisley in Scotland, an area he was obviously comfortable with for some reason. The following year a warrant had been issued for his arrest after a knife attack on Cheryl McLachlan, but he'd absconded again. Only now, a year later, had he popped up, this time under the pseudonym Pat McLaughlin. This time as a fully fledged killer.

For years I'd been convinced I was the only one who knew what Peter was capable of. Now the whole world knew – and that just made him all the more terrifying.

'Tim,' I said, 'the police have no idea where he is. But I promise you now: he's heading here.'

Seeing it on the news, Tim finally grasped the magnitude of the shadows of my life.

'I'd better get that spy-hole put in.'

The first time Peter had gone on the run in 1993, the police couldn't have been more supportive. Then, I suppose, it was in their interests to look after me because I might lead them to him. Thirteen years later and they obviously didn't think I warranted so much attention this time. I couldn't understand it, but I didn't let that stop me. When I marched into Havant police station, I noticed there was a copy of the local paper on the desk. Guess whose picture was plastered across the front page?

'Can I help you?' the desk sergeant asked.

'Yes,' I said, pointing at the paper, 'I've come to talk about him.'

Thirteen years earlier that would have been enough to guarantee, at the very least, a cup of tea with the chief constable. Times had changed, the old personnel had moved on. This time I really had to fight for a panic button. I wished I hadn't had to give the last one back, but there were only two or three in any county. Eventually I got one, but I also wanted answers. Why hadn't anyone told me Peter had been released? This was 2006 – he'd been out for two years. Daniel had been walking to school, I'd been working all over the place. We'd been sitting ducks had Peter come this way.

The next twenty-four hours were hideous. I was convinced Peter would be looking to recreate past glories. I didn't dare leave the house once. Even with all my security in place, I still found my greatest ally was the TV. Sky News had updates running like ticker tape across the bottom of the screen and I couldn't drag myself away. Every TV in the house was tuned to a different station, in case I missed some detail. I had the radio on too. I knew nothing would change while I stared at the screen, but I couldn't stop watching. Not until the monster was caught.

Once the media publicity kicked in, Peter – or Pat – was actually picked up very quickly. He'd checked himself into a London hospital, complaining of heart difficulties. I think he must have thought doctors are too busy to read newspapers. Someone recognized him instantly and called the police. He had no heart trouble at all. At last I could turn off the TV. I wouldn't be seeing him ever again.

Or so I thought. The police investigating Angelika Kluk's murder kept me informed throughout. When the case finally went to trial in Edinburgh in 2007, I couldn't help following its progress in the news. It was so macabre, but I couldn't ignore any little detail. To my knowledge, Daniel didn't read a single headline. He just wasn't interested. I'd told him the truth about his father the day we'd seen Peter's image on TV, but a year later Daniel hadn't asked another question. That was his way of dealing with things and I respect that.

I, on the other hand, needed closure. I didn't want to miss a scrap of the evidence that was finally going to see Peter put away for good.

Then, one day in May, a police officer rang.

'Cathy, I thought you would want to know, it's nearly over. The judge gives his verdict tomorrow.'

'Thanks,' I said. 'I'll be up on the next flight. I'm not missing this for the world.'

I didn't know where that spur-of-the-moment decision had come from. Before that conversation, I'd had no desire to ever set eyes on that murdering piece of filth ever again. But the moment I heard D-Day had arrived, I knew I had to be part of it. Unfortunately, Tim and I had broken up in July 2006, after ten happy years. There was no fault on either side; it was just another relationship that had run its natural course. But we were still friendly, so I didn't hesitate to ring him: 'Do you fancy a trip to Edinburgh?'

'Lovely. When?'

'Now. Pack a bag – the flight leaves in an hour.'

I'd received the news at three. By six, Tim and I were on a plane. It was the first time I'd flown to Scotland since I'd been blackmailed into returning to Bathgate. It was the same man responsible this time. The difference was, I wasn't scared. I knew I was going to see him get his comeuppance at last.

The next morning a police car picked us up from the hotel. Two spaces had been reserved in the gallery. We were in the top row. Angelika Kluk's family were at the bottom. I felt so desperately sorry for them, but they were so proud, so impressive. They all held hands, giving each other strength even though they'd had to endure hearing every horrific detail of their beloved Angelika's death and God knows what personal revelations about her life from a defence team struggling to find anything to justify their client's actions.

Standing directly in front of them but facing the opposite way was Peter, the accused, in his protective glass box.

As soon as I saw the back of his head, I started shaking uncontrollably. I'd seen the same couple of grainy pictures of Peter on TV so many times over the last six months, but nothing had seemed real up to now. The headlines and accusations were so far beyond the parameters of normal expectation that I couldn't easily process them and it may as well have been a story about a different person. That's the effect a saturation of TV news has. If I hadn't made the journey to Edinburgh, I'd have felt like I was living in *The Truman Show*. But here we were, in the same room, and the man who'd shared my bed for three years was about to be convicted of murder.

The closer the judge got to his conclusion, the more uncontrollably I shook. Tim clutched my hand, but I was a bundle of nervous energy, rocking in fear that the unthinkable might happen. That was when I noticed the court was packed with armed policemen, all with their eyes trained on the gallery. If there was even the slightest chance Peter would get off, they needed to be able to assert control over a dissenting crowd. And one of them had come to stand right next to me.

At that point, I just wanted to shout out at Peter, 'Turn round! Turn round! I need you to know I'm here.' But I didn't dare, not with the automatic weapon a foot from my head.

Finally the judge gave the verdict. Peter was guilty and was going down for a minimum of twenty-one years. Just as in 1994, I felt numb. I wanted it to mean more, but it didn't. The man in the dock had already stolen so many emotions from me, I didn't have any left to waste on him now.

TWENTY-ONE

The Terrible Truth

It was nice that Tim and I could put aside our differences to fly up to Scotland together. Another relationship, however, had ended permanently. In October 2006, shortly after Peter's arrest, my grandmother had died.

It was hard enough saying goodbye to Grandpa. Granny, however, had been the rock in my life for as long as I could remember. She was the one who'd secretly delivered meals without Grandpa noticing when I was a child. She was the one who'd taken on Mark and friends with no thought to her own safety. She'd lent me money to start a business and had given me the deposit for a house. I couldn't have got by without her. I almost even forgave her that infernal old-fashioned hairstyle that had made me the laughing stock of Longhill School. Almost . . .

Seeing her succumb to Hodgkin's lymphoma – a type of cancer – was heartbreaking, but at least I knew about her diagnosis almost as soon as she did, unlike the way Grandpa preferred to do things. Ever since Granny had been on her own, I'd always popped round once or twice a week and done her shopping. As time went by, she began to rely on me more and more. In her last three months, I was there every day. For the last month, it was a couple of times a day. By the time I managed to persuade the doctors that she needed to be hospitalized, I'd been virtually nursing her. She couldn't stand, she couldn't walk, she could barely eat. I knew the end was close, but until then I needed to be strong for her. Gran had supported me through so much. Now it was my turn to pay her back.

I think she was finally admitted to hospital on a Monday and by Friday it was over. She was cremated on 22 October 2006 and I thought I would never stop crying. Months of worry and grief and trying to show the good old British stiff upper lip that Grandpa and Granny would have expected finally took their toll. A short while later, Anne and I bought a memorial bench and placed it on Lady's Mile on Southsea Common, where Granny used to love to walk with her dogs. A lovely plaque remembers her, Grandpa and my darling mum. After thirty years, I no longer feel the need to visit Mum's crematorium on the anniversary of her death because I can just go and sit on that bench and remember my whole family.

Granny left a lot of interesting things, which Aunt Anne and I enjoyed sifting through. She had an original hairdryer from the 1950s, which I wanted to keep hold of, as well as more documents about my background. One of them made me catch my breath. It was a hand-drawn poem called 'Nil Desperandum'. I had to look it up – it means 'Don't Give Up'. Mum had written it out for Granny during her last days at Telscombe Cliffs. She'd seen it on the wall in St Peter's Church and copied it for her mother as her last act of contrition. I don't know how she held her hand so steady. It was beautiful. I was so glad Granny had kept it and I still have it on my wall now.

While I was taking a tremendous amount of solace from

the words 'Don't Give Up', so were the police. By the time Angelika's trial had concluded, I was already feeling over-whelmed by a relentless questioning process that had begun weeks earlier. Different police officers kept coming to my house and asking the same questions over and over. That was just about bearable – I understood how important this was. Then, a few months later, they started asking me to go to the station at Cosham because, as they explained, they had a tape-recording unit there. I went along, like a dutiful citizen, but I was puzzled.

They've already solved Angelika's murder. What can I possibly tell them?

Then I discovered why they were so keen to keep speaking to me. A psychiatrist who analysed the Angelika case concluded that a murderer who'd disposed of a body so expertly was very unlikely to have started this behaviour in his sixties. This led to the formation of Operation Anagram – a nationwide search for other possible victims of Peter Tobin, based on unsolved missing persons files going back decades. It was hard enough coming to terms with the fact that Peter had done it once. But more? Whatever the experts said, that was impossible, surely?

Unfortunately, not only was it possible that Peter had com-mitted other murders, I would soon discover he had done them while juggling his life with Daniel and me.

Operation Anagram's first move was to search all Peter's previous addresses and within two months it paid off.

In November 2007 police found another body, this time in the garden of Peter's old house in Margate. The discovery of Angelika's body had been bad enough, but this one was worse. It had been dismembered and buried in separate bin bags.

Who could do that to a body?

Faced with crimes of this magnitude, it's very hard to put

yourself in the place of the victim or even their family. The sheer scale of everything, one grotesque revelation after another, is too great for the human brain to process. So you end up focusing on the bits that affect you personally. The body, police said, had been unearthed from under the garden's old sandpit.

Daniel used to play in that!

Suddenly I was overcome by a wave of nausea at the recollection of being impressed by Peter digging the sandpit in the first place. I felt so stupid. He'd only done it to cover his tracks. Yet again, he'd used his son – just as he had in order to claim his victim in the first place.

DNA tests established the body as that of a young girl from Scotland, Vicky Hamilton, who'd gone missing in the Bathgate area of Scotland in February 1991 – a few months after I'd fled with my son. It was so long ago – thinking of her poor family not knowing what had happened for all this time made me so sad. Learning the facts of her death was even worse.

After a weekend with her sister in Livingston, Vicky had been trying to make her way back to Falkirk via the bus network. After asking several strangers for directions to her next linking stop, she'd bought a bag of chips and set off. But when the bus pulled in, Vicky had already accepted a lift from a man in a white van. Perhaps she normally wouldn't have taken the risk with a stranger, but it was snowing and the man's young son in the seat next to him must have given her a good feeling about him.

The police didn't know exactly what had happened to her, but it was obvious Vicky had been horribly hurt and raped before she was killed. When they took apart the house in Robertson Avenue, they found the knife Peter had used to cut her up.

At first I didn't make the connection between the dates. It wasn't unusual for Daniel to have been with his father, after all. Then the penny dropped. By February 1991 we were living in Portsmouth.

If Daniel was in the van, it must have been the weekend Peter had abducted him!

Suddenly my brain was racing at the realization. The police were confident that Daniel didn't see anything happen between Peter and Vicky – maybe he'd been sent to bed – but he must have been in the house with the girl's dead body for a while.

And when I flew up on my SAS rescue mission, so must I!

The police, as you'd hope, reached that conclusion faster than I did. They kept asking the same question:

'When you went back to Bathgate in February 1991 were there any rooms Peter prevented you from going in?'

Unfortunately, I just did not know. I had too much else going on in my mind. All I could think about at the time was luring Peter back into England.

'I don't know if I would even have noticed if one of the bedrooms was out of bounds,' I had to confess.

Again and again, different officers kept coming back to the same question. 'Were there any rooms he wouldn't let you enter?' and the answer was always 'No, not that I recall.' But I could have been wrong. It was later reported at the trial that the Margate family with whom Peter had swapped Robertson Avenue had been denied access to the upstairs when they'd travelled up to view the house. Vicky's body, police think, was up there awaiting disposal.

It gives you an insight into the mind of a serial killer, I think, that he could apparently invite people to view his house, forgetting he had a dead body stored upstairs. It was clearly as mundane, in his mind, as misplacing his house keys. He just didn't see it as wrong.

The more the police investigated, the more they would come to me with fresh information about my time with Peter. Sometimes I could help them, but most of their questions opened up completely new areas to me. In fact, if I hadn't known they were talking about me and Peter, I never would have guessed.

For example, one day they told me that Vicky's body contained traces of the anti-depressant Amitriptyline.

'Peter used to take that,' I said, trying as usual to be helpful.

'We know,' the officer said. 'And so did you.'

An outrageous claim!

'No I didn't! I never had a problem with depression. Nor did Peter, if you ask me. I don't know why he was always on so much medication.'

'No one's accusing you of having depression,' the officer said. But Amitriptyline, he explained, is a powerful sedative.

'Were there any times when you woke up and couldn't remember falling asleep? Or were awake but not completely in control of your senses?'

I thought about it. All those nights when I'd curled up next to Daniel, just praying for Peter not to make an advance had usually ended up with me sound asleep. Was it possible he'd drugged me? Is that why I'd slept through so deeply until morning in that really cramped, tiny bed?

The police were convinced. Peter, apparently, was renowned in Brighton and then Bathgate for his drug-dealing. I tried to say that wasn't true, but they batted me away.

'We believe it's correct. There are too many people saying it.'

Who were these people? I was his wife and I hadn't noticed anything.

But then, I realized with a chill, I hadn't noticed anything with my mother either. Had those early days conditioned me never to notice drugs or their effects again?

As for why they thought I was drugged regularly, they knew for a fact that several times a week Peter was out of the house at night, frequenting casinos and tormenting prostitutes. He'd built up a reputation as a trouble-maker in both areas. In fact, it was a few of the prostitutes who'd initially told the police I'd been drugged. They'd been to my house. They'd seen Peter do it or heard him talk about it.

I admit, my instinct was to dismiss it as just another preposterous claim. *What sort of wife – or mother – wouldn't notice if their husband was out so often at night?* But I did remember women like Lisa coming to the house. And I did remember sometimes being very, very groggy when I watched them with Peter. All those times my head felt cloudy – was that the effect of Amitriptyline or Rohypnol or a similar narcotic kicking in?

Yes, I had to conclude. There was no other explanation. I didn't know when he was slipping me the pills or in what sort of quantities or how often. But staring across the interrogation table at Cosham police station, I was forced to admit, 'He drugged me. That must have been what happened.'

I couldn't believe it. Yet another parallel to life with my mother . . .

When the police in Margate had originally dug up Peter's sandpit, it wasn't actually Vicky Hamilton they'd been expecting to find. By trawling through the missing persons lists and re-examining evidence in dozens of old cases, they'd concluded that the man who had picked up a young hitchhiker, Dinah McNicol, on the A3 out of Hampshire in August 1991 had to have been Peter. It was her body they were expecting when they discovered Vicky.

A week later, however, the dismembered remains of Dinah were dug up as well.

The way the police had narrowed in on Peter as the likely suspect took a convoluted path. Initially they thought he'd been living in Bathgate when the girl disappeared on Monday 5 August, so they'd dismissed him. Then they learned he'd actually moved to Margate by then, but even so, the A3 wasn't exactly local to his new home. And then they discovered he used to spend weekends with us in Portsmouth, Hampshire, and the pieces fell into place.

After two excellent days attending the Torpedo Tour music festival in Liphook, Hampshire, Dinah and her new friend David had decided to hitch home. They didn't have to wait long at the service station on the A3 before a green car pulled over.

'Where are you going?' the driver asked in a thick Scottish accent.

David lived in Redhill, Surrey, so not far around the M25. Dinah, on the other hand, faced a long journey to Tillingham in Essex.

'You're in luck,' the man said. 'I can drop you both off.'

Like all hitchhikers, David and Dinah would never have got into the car if they'd been at all suspicious. But the child's booster seat in the back of the car pushed any fears out of their minds.

By the time David was dropped off at Junction 8 on the M25, however, he seemed really keen for Dinah to get out with him. But the eighteen-year-old wouldn't think of it. It wasn't every day a stranger offered to give you a lift almost to your door. And so she stayed in the car and was never seen again until her body was disinterred sixteen years later.

It made me sick to hear of the small role Daniel and I had played in this poor girl's unpleasant death. Daniel and I were the reason Peter had been on the A3 that day.

'If he hadn't come to see us, Dinah McNicol would still be alive.'

The policeman across the table shook his head. 'He might not have got Dinah, but he would have found someone. I'm sure of it.'

Discovering that my ex-husband was a vicious, sadistic 'serial killer', as the police were calling him, affected me every single day. I could be washing up, having a shower or driving to view a house and suddenly the realization would hit me and the familiar wave of nausea would wash over me again.

But coming to terms with the dark side of Peter's personality was actually easier than coming to terms with some of his other secrets.

Each time I was interviewed at Cosham, the police produced new revelations. At first I just refused to believe them, like, for example, when I was told the truth about Peter's illustrious war record.

'Your ex-husband was never in the military, Cathy – and he certainly didn't see service in Aden.'

'What are you talking about? Everyone knows he did. He's got the shrapnel to prove it.'

'Has he really, Cathy? Have you actually seen any evidence of it?'

Of course, I hadn't. The only time Peter's war wounds came out was when he used them as an excuse not to do something.

'He never worked on oil rigs,' the copper continued. 'He never ran supermarkets or hotels. In fact, as far as we can establish, he has never held down a proper job in his entire life.'

That wasn't all. While Peter had admitted to being married once before when I'd asked, in actual fact he had two ex-wives. I prayed that he'd treated them better than he'd treated me, but, as my contact with the police increased, I learnt they'd suffered as well. Both Margaret Mackintosh and Sylvia Jefferies had also known the fury of his fists and the tyranny of his controlling personality, especially in the bedroom. One vile rape using a knife left Margaret close to death and unable to have children. I wonder sometimes if we should form our own support group, but really we all just want to get on with our own lives. Peter's claimed enough of our time.

The new versions of Peter's life came so thick and fast that, after a while, they ceased to shock and I became resigned to the fact that everything I ever knew was almost certainly wrong.

Gradually, though, as 2007 progressed, I realized the police were telling me less and asking the same questions again and again. I kept saying, 'I've told you this. Can't you check your notes?' But then I'd turn up again the following week and a new officer would try again. The sessions went on all day – they started as soon as the patrol car arrived to pick me up and didn't finish until I was dropped off again ten or twelve hours later.

It was so taxing, but I think I could have coped if I'd felt we were getting somewhere. In fact, so many of their questions seemed totally pointless. Once a deputation from Scotland flew down to my house just to show me a purse.

'Do you recognize this?'

'I can't say. I'm thirty-nine; I've had plenty of purses. It could be one of mine.'

That was the wrong thing to say.

'Well, is it or isn't it?'

'I don't know. I've lost loads over the years. I can't remember them all.'

I thought that would be the end of it, but the policeman in charge had another idea.

'Where's your son?'

'He's at college.'

'Can you get him back?'

'What, now?'

'Yes, now. If it's not too much trouble.'

Daniel was only at Portsmouth Uni, but he still had to leave a lecture halfway through.

'Is everything all right, Mum?' he asked as soon as he stepped into the room.

Before I could answer, one of the coppers showed him the purse.

'Do you recognize this?'

It was ridiculous. The poor boy hadn't even had a chance to take his coat off. Like me, he had zero recollection of it. Sensing the futility of their errand, the lead policeman said, 'What if I told you we found it at your father's house in Margate?'

Daniel shrugged. 'I was three when he lived there. What do you remember from when you were three?'

On another occasion, a couple of detectives arrived clutching a photo album. When they opened it up, I couldn't believe it. Each page just had pictures of black sacks.

'This has got to be a joke,' I said.

'It's no joke, Cathy. We need to know if you recognize any of these sacks.'

I managed to keep a straight face long enough to get through it. Then Daniel was summoned yet again.

'Do you recognize this?' they asked, pointing to a particular photo.

'It's a black sack.'

'Have you ever seen it before?'

'I've no idea – it's a black sack.'

'Where do you think you would find one of these?'

I think they wanted him to say something like 'In Dad's shed in Margate.' But Daniel answered how he saw it.

'Where would I find one? Underneath the sink probably.'

I had to laugh. It was all so preposterous, I had no choice.

By 2008 I seemed to be always either playing host to a houseful of plods from various stations all over the country or being chauffeured down to Cosham twice a week.

I'm sure if I'd had a proper 9–5 job I'd have put a stop to it earlier, but because I was self-employed, I could always make time, even though it was really taking its toll. I'd always gone out of my way to downplay my links to Peter Tobin, but eventually I'd had enough. I was out with a group of girlfriends one night and I just flipped and told them everything. It was such a relief to get it off my chest and we shared a lot of tears that night. At the end of it, though, one of my friends remembered what had triggered my meltdown.

'You need to see a solicitor about the number of these interviews,' she advised. 'I bet it's not right.'

I took her advice, and I'm so glad I did. 'You don't have to put up with this,' the solicitor said right at the start.

'But they're the police – you can't not answer their questions.'

'That's absolutely true. But you're under no obligation to keep answering them.'

Not answering had never even occurred to me. It must have been my grandparents' respect for authority rubbing off.

'From now on,' the solicitor said, 'if they ask you any question more than twice, I want you to say this: "I've answered that question already. If you ask me again, I will consider it harassment and I'll take appropriate action."'

'What appropriate action?'

He laughed. 'Hopefully it won't come to that.'

So, beginning the very next day, that's what I did. It wasn't easy and I shook like a nervous child delivering her only line in the Christmas play. But I got my point across and that made me happy. I wasn't going to be a pushover anymore.

I thought that would be the end of my involvement with the police, or at least the start of them winding down their interest in me. But it didn't work like that. As soon as I revealed I'd been speaking to a solicitor, their attitude towards me changed. Without anyone telling me, I was upgraded from special witness. To suspect.

'You've admitted you were a battered wife,' one policeman explained. 'You've admitted there were threats made against your child.'

'Only once – and that was just to control me.'

'So you're saying you would do anything to protect your child?'

'Yes, of course. But not that. I'd never hurt anyone.'

'Not even if it meant saving your son?'

'Stop it! You're twisting my words!'

I couldn't believe what I was hearing. *They think I'm another Rose West.*

Honestly, the things they were intimating were evil. Aiding and abetting a murderer, abusing prostitutes with my husband, taking part in the violence against those girls, grooming Peter's victims, luring them into his clutches.

After everything I'd been through, this was a real low, low point. And the worst thing was, I couldn't see how it could end.

At some point, however, I must have convinced the police that I was innocent. More than innocent, in fact: a victim. But if I thought there would be an apology, I was mistaken. In fact, they found an even worse way to torment me.

'We're going to need you to testify at the trial of Vicky Hamilton.'

'She was killed in 1991,' I said, taken aback. 'What on earth can I contribute to that?'

He consulted his notes. 'We'll need you to talk about being in Bathgate while her body was in the house.'

'But I didn't see anything, I told you that about twenty times.'

They wouldn't have it though.

'What if I don't come?'

'Then we'll subpoena you. One way or another, you'll be going to Dundee with the rest of us.'

I began to cry, but not at the thought of standing up in court. 'I don't want to see him,' I said. 'Do you have any idea what he put me through? What he still puts me through?'

I think they'd expected me to say that.

'Don't worry, we can erect a screen. He'll be able to hear you, but he won't get a glimpse.'

'Okay,' I said. 'Then I'll do it.'

That really should have been the end of the matter, but as the police team were packing up, one of them said casually, 'Of course, we'll be needing Daniel to testify as well.'

That was it – the gloves were off.

'You bloody won't!' I shouted. 'He's got enough shit in his life without that. He was three years old, for God's sake. What the fuck do you think he can remember from then? Tell me

352

what you can remember from when you were three? Go on, try it!'

The guy wouldn't be drawn and my anger disappeared as quickly as it had arrived. In its place was pure fear.

'Please, I'm begging you,' I cried. 'Don't make him do this. He's twenty, he's at the start of his life. Don't ruin it for him before he even gets going.'

But would the bastards listen? No. The only consolation was that he too would be shielded by the screen. I insisted on that.

'That paedophile has not set eyes on my son since 1993. I do not want Peter to know a single thing about him.'

That night I called Daniel over and broke the news to him. He took it better than I had, but he was just as perplexed.

'Is it about that purse?' he asked.

'Yes.'

'But I can't even remember it. What use is that going to be?'

'I don't know, darling, I really don't.'

All I knew for sure was that the horrors I'd managed to protect him from for so many years were about to be picked over in the minutest detail – and there was nothing I could do.

Vicky's trial began on 3 November 2008. A year earlier hundreds had attended her funeral – sixteen years after her death. As Daniel and I entered the court building in Dundee, you could feel the whole town wanted justice. I was so proud of my boy. He looked a million dollars in his suit and no jury would ever doubt a word he said. Unfortunately, we both knew he had nothing to say.

At some point, I think the prosecution must have realized that as well. We'd been there a day when a note was passed along saying we wouldn't have to testify after all.

'Thank God for that!' I said. 'Come on, let's get out of here.'

It was only when we saw the news coverage later that I realized Daniel had actually played a starring role – or rather his DNA had. That old purse neither of us could remember had actually belonged to Vicky. After Peter had killed her, he planted it miles away in Edinburgh, to throw the police off his scent. But by then he had already given it to Daniel to play with. DNA evidence now placed Peter and Vicky irrefutably in the same house and car. As soon as the jury heard that, Peter was going down.

We never discussed it, but fourteen years after Peter had saddled Daniel with the guilt of being used as bait to nearly kill two innocent young girls, as well as to lure both Vicky and Dinah into trusting Peter, the son had got his own back. How fitting for a boy whose name means 'God is my judge'.

After the wasted trip to Dundee, I wasn't at all fazed six months later to receive word that I'd be needed as a witness at Peter's trial for the murder of Dinah McNicol.

They probably won't even call me, I thought. *It's not worth getting stressed about.*

Daniel wasn't needed this time, but, along with my partner Stuart, he offered to come along for moral support.

'We're all in this together, Mum,' he said.

I loved him so much for saying that, but I wished it hadn't been the case. I'd have given anything for him to still be blissfully ignorant.

The longer the investigation into Peter went on, the more the claims against him stacked up. Although they couldn't prove it at the time – and still haven't been able to – I was told the police suspected Peter to have been behind the 'Bible John' murders which had terrorized Glasgow during the late 1960s. Peter had been living in the area, after all, and the deaths of the three young female victims bore the same hallmarks as his other crimes.

From my point of view, if Peter was capable of killing one girl, he was capable of killing more. Although he has always denied each murder, when newspapers reported that he had gloated to a prison psychiatrist, 'I've killed forty-eight people' – and then challenged the police to 'prove it' – I believed it. Even his most outlandish lies were often founded on truth.

December 2009 arrived and I found myself in the waiting room at Chelmsford Crown Court, Daniel and Stuart by my side, about to face my worst nightmare. Even screened off, just knowing Peter was in that room would be enough to make me feel sick. Just knowing he was already in the same building had already got me trembling. When I saw a court official coming over, I prayed and prayed that he was going to tell me I could go home. But he didn't.

'You'll be called in about an hour.'

I crumbled.

Sixty minutes later, I was ready. My official escort and a lovely policeman called Bernie were by my side and we were just waiting for our cue to enter the chamber. The silence was deafening. I swear I could hear my knees knocking – I thought they only did that in cartoons. When the green light came, I struggled to put left foot in front of right.

Bernie had barely started to open the door to the court when I froze. There, right in front of me, was Peter Tobin.

'Where's the screen?' I said, suddenly panicking. 'There was meant to be a screen!'

Bernie let go of the door and looked at the official, who hurriedly consulted his notes.

'No,' he said, 'there was never a screen for this case.'

I was getting hysterical. 'But I was promised a screen. They said I wouldn't have to look at him.'

'Look,' Bernie said, 'I've been watching this guy every day for three weeks. He never, ever looks up from the floor. You've got absolutely nothing to worry about.'

It was kind of him to say that.

'Okay,' I said, wiping my face. 'I'm ready.'

I was in there for twenty-five minutes. The prosecutor asked me every single question he could think of about Peter's old cars – their colours, their child seats, their condition – and then the defence lawyer did the same. I couldn't look at either of them, though, because directly behind them was my ex-husband.

When the judge said I could go, I nearly ran out. Panting, I collapsed into a chair. Stuart and Daniel rushed over, but Bernie the copper beat them both.

'Now there's a thing,' he said. 'For three weeks that man does nothing but stare at the floor. Then you take the stand and he didn't stop looking at you for one second. Not one single second.' He laughed. 'I think you've got him spooked.'

I wasn't sure if that was good or bad. The only thing I knew for certain was that I had seen Peter Britton Tobin for the very last time.

EPILOGUE

This is Where it Begins

2010 started well. The Dinah jury had taken just a couple of hours to convict Peter. On top of all his other sentences, he wouldn't be a free man again if he lived to be a hundred.

I also made progress with my bête noir, the team driving Operation Anagram, when a new officer took over the project and promised me it would end very soon. He was as good as his word. From two meetings a week in 2007 to two a month in 2008 and one every two months in 2009, I was now free of their questions, bar the odd phone call. They finally accepted I'd had nothing to do with any of Peter's crimes. They also admitted I'd been pursued in rather too enthusiastic a manner.

I was grateful for the new man's candour, but in a sense it had come too late. The stress of the constant interrogations and, in particular, intimating that I was Peter's accomplice had driven me to find a therapist. After years of pretending the name Tobin meant nothing to me, I needed to tell someone everything. I have to say, it's going well. The final piece in my recuperation, in fact, is this book. Not one person in the world knows the story you've just read. Some have known bits, but no one, until now, has had the full version.

One person who definitely will not be reading this book is Daniel. He had his closure with his father many years ago. Ironically, it was my obsession with giving my son the family I'd been denied that nearly ruined it for both of us. But we survived.

And how! In July 2010 I climbed into my finest stilettos, pulled on my fanciest frock and cheered loudly as Daniel was handed his degree in Business Entrepreneurship from the chancellor of Portsmouth University, the actress Sheila Hancock. Looking around at the hundreds of other jubilant families in the great hall, I wondered if any of them had secrets as chilling as ours. But as I glanced at the proud family gathering of Anne, Geoff and Stuart, all showering praise on my wonderful son, I thought, *I don't care.* All that was in the past.

The future – mine, Daniel's, everyone's – starts right here. This is where it begins.

POSTSCRIPT

Fifteen Years On

It seems a lifetime ago that I was too scared to leave my front door, had spy-holes fitted and carried a panic alarm. I lived in fear. But that was the past. It's been eleven years since I finished *Escape from Evil*. Finally rid of Peter Tobin's oppression, not a day has passed where I have allowed myself to waste a single, precious second of freedom from his tyranny.

My new-found independence has allowed my confidence to grow and my horizons to expand, which has ignited a passion for travelling the world. Now when I get on a plane it is not to rescue Daniel from Peter's kidnap attempt or to fly to a court hearing. It is for adventure. In 2010, I hired a camper van and drove around South Africa. Exhilarated by the freedom that afforded me, I bought myself a little van to travel around Europe and the UK. Since then, Daniel and I have travelled off the tourist track in places as diverse as Japan, Cuba and Canada. Best of all, I've discovered a new closeness between Daniel and myself. After many years of living in the shadow of Peter and his crimes, I think we are both starting to breathe again.

Having discovered my love of travel, I decided to open my home to international language students and fulfil the role of host mother. Some would arrive knowing just a handful of English words and by the time they went home, they were able to have basic conversations. That was incredibly fulfilling. It was a very happy time; some students extended their stays to several years while others left kind words and photos. At one point, I had a young man from Germany and a young lady from Brazil. They kept in contact as pen pals after they went home and a few years later emailed to tell me they were getting married.

Working with young people has been infinitely rewarding, so much so that I am training to be a volunteer child mentor with the local council where I work one-to-one with a young person who has had difficulties at home. The next stage will be to train as an independent volunteer; I will be teamed up with a young person in the foster-care system and will support them through to adulthood. My hope is to provide stability and care. Every child deserves that.

I am also writing a children's picture book inspired by the stories I would tell to help Daniel fall asleep when he was a young boy. *Tangles' Tales* centres around a friendly hedgehog called Tangles and explores his daily adventures as well as introducing the other creatures he meets.

My property refurbishment business is also developing nicely. I get to be my own boss, which is a lovely place to be in life. I particularly enjoy taking a run-down house that no one would want to live in and, with hard work and a positive mindset, turning it into a home that someone will enjoy for many years to come. Beauty can come from the most unexpected places.

*

Peter continues to be in my life.

I have an almost obsessive need to search for him online and find myself compelled to check for news. There is always something being reported, no matter how inconsequential or mundane. His notoriety keeps his name in the papers.

I imagine Peter would enjoy this constant stream of news. It's been reported that he likes to watch documentaries about his crimes. I don't know what kind of access he may or may not have in prison, but I can picture him in his cell, reliving his life in colour, so many years after he was incarcerated.

Some of the stories that are reported are difficult to make sense of. According to the media, his health is rapidly deteriorating: he had a heart attack in 2012, a stroke in 2016 and was diagnosed with cancer in 2019. He apparently weighs just five stone. Inevitably, this prompts discussions with my loved ones as we simply cannot understand how that can be.

As Peter's health worsens, there have been reports of further confessions. According to the news, he bragged to a fellow inmate that he has killed ten women in total, including one from Brighton who the police have never found. I was particularly sickened by this news. Brighton is where we spent time together.

I wonder if he will ever dig deep and find compassion – compassion to allow the families of his other victims to finally be able to put their loved ones to rest. I fear that sadly he will not and, rather, that he will take the truth to his grave.

But I won't let his presence affect Daniel or myself as we move on. Not any more. Over the years, we have built a new life, filled with wonderful memories, surrounded by the greatest of friends who know and love us as Cathy and Daniel Wilson.

In August 2021, I had great delight and huge pride in handing Daniel a bottle of champagne. He was taking his first steps over the threshold of his first property refurbishment.

We will keep growing; the future is ours . . .

ACKNOWLEDGEMENTS

I would like to thank Jeff Hudson for his ability to put my memories and emotions into words. Thank you also to my editor, Ingrid Connell, Karina Maduro and all the staff at Macmillan who convinced me that I had a story to tell.

Above all, thanks to all my friends and family who have loved and supported me through these difficult fifteen years. In particular, thank you to Hayling Andy, Gunwharf John, Bamber, Phil, Irish Peter, Tina, Sarah, Clare and Ray. And, as always, special thanks to my son, lovely Daniel, who through his own life has given me the strength and courage to continue with mine.

ACKNOWLEDGEMENTS